G000161077

Children at War
1914–1918

Dedication

This book, whose writing spanned the first year of her life, is for my grandchildren Cecelia Earl and Tess Connell-Smith. Their great-grandmother and great-grandfather experienced 'War in the Nursery'. Their great-great-grandfather staged his own 'Teenage Rebellion' by serving at Gallipoli. Tess C-S's great-great-grandfather is named on the Thiépval Memorial; Cecelia, daughter of an infantry officer, is herself an 'Army Child'. My fervent hope is that, unlike the children you are about to meet and millions of others before and since, they will *never* experience 'War from the Inside'.

Children at War
1914–1918

Dr Vivien Newman

PEN & SWORD
HISTORY
AN IMPRINT OF PEN & SWORD BOOKS LTD.
YORKSHIRE – PHILADELPHIA

First published in Great Britain in 2019 by
Pen & Sword History
An imprint of
Pen & Sword Books Ltd
Yorkshire - Philadelphia

Copyright © Vivien Newman, 2019

ISBN 978 1 47382 107 1

The right of Vivien Newman to be identified as Author of this work
has been asserted by her in accordance with the Copyright, Designs
and Patents Act 1988.

A CIP catalogue record for this book is available from the British Library.

All rights reserved. No part of this book may be reproduced or transmitted
in any form or by any means, electronic or mechanical including
photocopying, recording or by any information storage and retrieval
system, without permission from the Publisher in writing.

Printed and bound in England
By TJ International Ltd.

Pen & Sword Books Ltd incorporates the Imprints of Pen & Sword Books
Archaeology, Atlas, Aviation, Battleground, Discovery, Family History,
History, Maritime, Military, Naval, Politics, Railways, Select, Transport,
True Crime, Fiction, Frontline Books, Leo Cooper, Praetorian Press,
Seaforth Publishing, Wharncliffe and White Owl.

For a complete list of Pen & Sword titles please contact

PEN & SWORD BOOKS LIMITED
47 Church Street, Barnsley, South Yorkshire, S70 2AS, England
E-mail: enquiries@pen-and-sword.co.uk
Website: www.pen-and-sword.co.uk

or

PEN AND SWORD BOOKS
1950 Lawrence Rd, Havertown, PA 19083, USA
E-mail: uspen-and-sword@casematepublishers.com
Website: www.penandswordbooks.com

Contents

Acknowledgements

My thanks

First and foremost, to my husband, Ivan, for his unflappability, his willingness to listen to multiple drafts, make apposite comments *and* sort out errant computers, not to mention upscaling images to the necessary size and resolution for publication.

Lubomyr Luciuk, Andrea Malysh and Don McNair pointed me towards documents relating to the Canadian internment programmes and generously shared their own knowledge.

Jon Giullian (University of Kansas) provided information about the hitherto unknown to me Sofja Nowosielska.

My editor Karyn Burnham, the more I learn about the writing process, the more I appreciate her skills.

Foreword

Children at War 1914–1918 is not the book that I had anticipated writing. The original intention had been to focus primarily on British children during the First World War. However, glancing along my bookshelves, I noticed two – then barely opened – French books. One showcased an archive of recently discovered Parisian children's wartime drawings, the other the children from German-occupied France who had been 'repatriated' to Free France. The sources these books led me to revealed a depth and complexity of (at times deeply disturbing, sometimes amusing) information largely unknown to English-speaking readers. So, while there is still plenty about British children, the text is both wider and more 'intimate' than planned. Wherever possible, children from across the combatant nations speak to you in their own voices.

One 'problem' for all childhood historians/researchers is when does childhood end? I decided to include youngsters aged under 18, the official age at which a man could enlist and a woman work in the 'Danger Sheds'. While this excluded the 18-year-old/ten-day married French war widow who, in 1918, was prohibited from returning to her Girls' School in Lyon (and instead offered a place at a Boys' School!), it included the youngest VC in George V's army.

The next dilemma was organising the material. I rejected the chronology of either war year or children's ages. Instead, opening in the pre-war nursery, the book edges increasingly close to the Front, exploring how children became ever more direct participants, either willingly or unwillingly, in a war that, as they were constantly reminded, was being fought to make the world a safer, better place for them.

CHAPTER ONE

War in the Nursery,
War in the Schoolroom

In his Foreword to Nina Macdonald's jingoistic, anti-German *Wartime Nursery Rhymes*, reviewer George Sims noted, 'the tragic note of war has been brought into the nurseries and playrooms of the rising generation'. A cursory glance through toy seller, manufacturers' and children's books catalogues, both immediately before and during the war, demonstrates his comments' veracity. With increasing pre-war affluence, at least among the middle-classes, leading to more disposable income, toys had become big business. By the 1910s, all but the poorest children would have possessed a few, including a board game such as snakes and ladders. Girls might have owned a rag doll, its china face often made in Germany, while most boys had some painted tin soldiers, initially of German origin until the end of the nineteenth century when a British manufacturer began to dominate the home market.[1] Model soldier expert Henry Harris received his first box when his regular officer father returned from France in 1916. Two years later Henry owned over 400 figures, subsequently losing a number in a war game in 1918.[2]

German children were equally enthusiastic collectors. Young Piete Kuhr's soldiers suffered a more dramatic end than Henry's. In March 1915, schoolchildren were instructed to bring in tin, lead, zinc, brass and old iron for the war effort. 'Out of this are to be made gun-barrels, cannons, cartridge-cases and so forth. There is keen competition between the classes.' Having zealously ransacked her home, her grandmother, with whom she lived, 'cried "better give your lead soldiers than take the last of my possessions!" So my little army with which Willi [her brother] and I had so often played had to meet their deaths. To avoid all the soldiers being sacrificed, I drew lots for the candidates for death ... I placed the unlucky ones two by two in a large metal spoon and held it over the gas flame. The heroes in their lovely blue uniforms melted to death for the Fatherland.'[3]

CHILDREN AT WAR 1914-1918

Miniature soldiers not only adorned toy cupboards, they appeared in wartime picture books destined for the youngest children. Swiss-born author and illustrator Charlotte Schaller-Mouillot's *L'histoire d'un brave petit soldat* [*The story of a brave little soldier*] opens in a toy cupboard. Immediately war is declared, the nameless brave little solider, thereby representing all brave French soldiers, rushes to enlist, cheered on by all the other toys, depicting Allied nations but not Central Powers. Armed with his fellow toys' gifts – such as chestnuts he will deploy against the Boche – the soldier heroically defends France, shoots down planes and holds back the enemy. Decorated for bravery, imprisoned (he cunningly escapes), is seriously wounded, is miraculously brought back to life by six Red Cross nurse dolls – a suitably gendered girls' wartime gift, he is conveniently fit enough to join in the toy cupboard's victory celebrations, even though, when the book was published, the war had another three years to run.

Schaller-Mouillot's 1914 *En Guerre!* [*At War!*], equally rife with political and didactic imagery, appeared in English in 1917. The French National Library website Gallica's English-language copy is dedicated by 'Mr and Mrs Davidson' to 'our little French boy Abel Joss'.[4] With war declared, the book's hero Bobby, 'astride his fine [rocking-]horse', inspects his toy soldiers, convinced that they, aided by France's brave Allies, including the legendary Highlanders in kilts who intrigued many French in the early days, will strike fear in France's enemies' hearts. To underline his brutality, the Boche is graphically illustrated with an enormous black boot stamping on 'Gallant Little Belgium'. Chapter titles include one anticipating the longed-for, but in 1914 still distant, liberation of Alsace-Lorraine, the Miracle of the Marne and, to ensure that girls are included, Nursing the Wounded. Along with stereotypical images: 'Boche gluttony', 'the brave and heroic Belgian Army', the book includes activities familiar to all children: writing letters to Daddy – who is 'fighting so bravely to protect them', and, for Bobby, winding the wool 'with which his mother and his little sisters knit gloves, mufflers, jerseys and caps'.[5] Like children in all belligerent nations, loyal Bobby empties his money-box to buy comforts for the troops.[6]

English children who empathised with these juvenile protagonists included David, Jean and James Thirsk. Despite only being born in June 1914, James nostalgically recalled this 'treasure ... I knew this book before I was able to read the text and Jean would have told me the story.' James assumed that his father, who had enlisted in 1914 and was eventually commissioned, must have purchased the book on his way home on leave. James noted the extent to which the three children, deprived of a father for the duration of the war, empathised with the little French protagonists. James' understanding of the war was hazy, to the extent that he believed that he had 'two daddies', one in 'the France', and one who periodically appeared in England bearing such gifts.[7]

Bellicose picture-books with fictional children demonstrating patriotic behaviour were not restricted to French authors. Tapping into a well-established pre-war tradition, many 'ABC' books were available for the very young. The garishly illustrated 1914 *The Child's ABC of the War*, dedicated to 'Little Robin not yet four years old', reminded pre-readers, 'E that's for England/true to her trust/Peaceful but ready to fight/When she must', while a group of children to whom 'N' asks, 'Are we downhearted?' reply with a resounding 'NO!'[8] Although in 1914 'Z' stumped author Geoffrey Whitworth and illustrator Stanley North, in *Our Soldiers – An ABC for Little Britons* (1916), 'A' might be for the 'Great British Army whom everyone fears', Z was, unsurprisingly, for the Zeppelin, 'floating on high, laden with bombs to drop from the sky. Are you afraid of it? No, not I!' Naturally, the Senior Service featured, *The Royal Navy – An ABC for Little Britons*, reminded readers that 'B is Britannia the land of the free/And thanks to our battleships/Queen of the Sea'. Although the child dressed in sailor uniform on the last page is only 'seven', he intends to 'sail on the iron Duke with Jellicoe' where 'I'll do my best to fire the guns and sink the warships of the Huns'. Whether fought by toy soldiers or 7-year-olds, the war was graphically present on pre-readers' bookshelves.

German-speaking children were equally well catered for. Ernst Kunster's 1914 *Hurra! Ein Kriegs-bilderbuch*, [*Hurra! A War Picturebook*] illustrated by Swiss national Herbert Rikli, features small, cherubic-looking Willi who, dressed in his Christmas gift uniform and Pickelhaube, is intent on destroying all the Fatherland's enemies. As in most children's books, the enemies are mocked: the French ride on frogs, the English on magpies and the Russians on mice whom Willi gleefully shoots, 'Piff paff the Russian lives no more'. Joined by his Austrian friend Franzl, the boys heroically see these enemies off and revel in their advanced technology: Zeppelins, torpedoes and submarines. Finally, the distressed Willi, with sword clutched in his hand, discovers that he has been dreaming – the Fatherland's enemies still need defeating.

CHILDREN AT WAR 1914-1918

In Arpad Schmidhammer's *Lieb Vaterland magst ruhig sein* [*Dear Fatherland Don't Worry*], a small band of German and Austrian boys play peacefully in their garden until Serbia, his big brother Russia, aided by French, Belgian, English and Japanese boys, cruelly attack them. Battle is joined but the little gardeners are victorious. Having imprisoned their enemies, they peacefully continue gardening. Such books' popularity eventually waned but, in the early years, however fictionalised its portrayal, children who were too young to read for themselves could still be reminded of a war in which many of their fathers and older kin were fighting, female relatives nursing and which was, apparently, being fought to make the world safe for them.

That the books depict children in military uniform is unsurprising as children were encouraged to hero-worship the fighting man and the nursing woman. Although Christmas might mark the birth of the Prince of Peace, many wartime Christmas gifts underlined the dominance of the gods of war. What could be more exciting for a young child to receive than their very own uniform? All belligerents' Christmas 1914 toy catalogues offered multiple outfits to those who could afford them (in France these could cost around £70 today). In Canada, uniforms were available to fit children aged between 3 and 10 years. Although his may have been too big, 2-year-old Eric Hamilton, 'the most snap-shotted baby in town', was dressed 'in his military uniform for the purpose of collecting funds for the Red Cross.' According to *Young Soldier* (24 July 1915), little Eric sold flags and gravely saluted every purchaser.[9] Tsar Nicholas II even dressed his son in a private's uniform and allowed him to accompany him everywhere.[10]

Although there was significant uniform choice for boys, girls had to be content with being Red Cross nurses. Just as there seem to have been a plethora of Red Cross dolls but no munitionettes, there is no evidence of munitions outfits adorning girls' dressing-up boxes. The class system remained entrenched in the nation's toy cupboards as nurses and nursing auxiliaries, including member of the Voluntary Aid Detachment (VAD), were drawn from the middle or upper classes and munitions workers predominantly from the working-class. While poorer parents tried to ensure that their child received a Christmas gift, a dressing-up outfit, be it a soldier or a nurse, would have been an unimagined luxury for children who rarely possessed more than one set of clothes. Eight-year-old Edith Hall remembers how on 'Empire Day 1916, we ran round the playground in our worn-out clothing, waving our new Union Jacks; some of the girls could have done with some new undies judging by the rags they revealed.'[11]

As well as child-sized uniforms and jingoistic books, war toys abounded.[12] Parents wanting to keep their sons fit (for the army) invested in the popular *Punch the Kaiser Dummy*. This, *Toy and Fancy Goods Trader* September 1914 claimed, would keep boys 'strong and muscular'. During Christmas 1914, British families could sink German submarines while playing 'Kill Kiel' inspired by the Dreadnought. The most adventurous could find their 'Way to Constantinople' while others could 'Dash to Berlin'. Priced at 1 shilling trade (around £5.50 today), this 'new and breathless game for winter evenings' promised 'all the excitement with none of the danger'.[13] Players representing Great Britain, France, Belgium and Russia rolled the dice to move along the grid, the winner being the first one to reach square 90, Berlin. In 'Recruiting for Kitchener's Army', players rose from private to field-marshal depending on the number of recruits they enlisted. Appeal may have waned by Christmas 1915 with conscription but weeks away. Those still eager for war-themed board games in 1916 could have indulged in the 'new game of *Jutland*', according to the producer: 'a fascinating game of naval strategy'; those interested in aerial warfare, and there is significant evidence that children were fascinated as well as frightened by Zeppelins, could indulge in 'Bombarding the Zeppelins', while the traditional Snakes and Ladders lent itself easily to Central Power snakes and Allied ladders. 'Peace with Honour', with its goal of reaching a sensible détente, and conscientious objector dolls were rare exceptions to the jingoistic theme.[14]

Not all games were board games; 1915's most gruesome offering was 'The Exploding Trench'. A 30cm-long wood and cardboard, muddy green-coloured, 'trench' contained half a dozen miniature soldiers. When the Union flag was struck, the [German] soldiers were catapulted into the air 'in all directions' as if by an explosion. Despite the box claiming that the game was 'Very Interesting' with 'No Danger!', it was deemed to have crossed the line dividing acceptable and non-acceptable toys and its life was short-lived – so much so that a rare example was snapped up at auction for US$7,200 (2013).[15]

In France, the ever popular 'Jeu de l'Oie', a board game dating back to the sixteenth century in which players land on lucky or unlucky squares, had long lent itself to topical variations. As 'oie' means 'goose', versions punned on the idea of the German goosestep – mocked by children in Free France and feared and loathed in equal measure by those in the Occupied Zones. The 'unlucky' squares contain horrific pictures of the anti-hero, his character, his actions, and even his industries. However, not all French families were eager for war-themed games; Lucie, a young French peasant woman, wrote to her poilu husband Gustave expressing relief that the children's Christmas 1917 gifts were not war toys and their new Jeu de l'Oie was a traditional farmyard one.[16] By now, Lucie may not have been in the minority – advertisements for war games noticeably decreased after 1916, indicating that the public was wearying of them – although war continued to dominate children's games in playgrounds and the street.

Germany, the pre-war 'Mecca' of the toy industry, was equally quick to offer similar board games with pedagogic benefits. Parents were advised that because a wrong move could give the enemy an advantage, young players would learn to think through their tactics. 'Hunt for the *Emden*' and the submarine adventure 'U-1000' proved popular Christmas gifts in 1915. In *Viktoria Kriegspiel*, the wrong move carried fatal consequences for one's own troops. Manufacturers stressed their product's authenticity, 'The method of play is worked out according to a tactical military point of view and is as close to reality as possible'.[17] German games also used real events and heroes to provide layers of verisimilitude; despite the appetite for war-themed toys diminishing over time, board games remained popular, finally falling victim to acute shortages of raw materials, including paper.

Although demand seems to have waned after the death of Emperor Franz-Joseph, Austrian parents were initially keen to purchase war-related board games and militaristic toys. Viennese youngsters had the added bonus of being able to visit the 'Schützengraben' [Trench] in the Wurstelprater [Amusement Park]. By 1916, the mock-up trenches covered some 160,00m^2 (approximately twenty-two football pitches). Schoolchildren were taken on 'virtual reality' tours to experience soldiers' life in the trenches. The visit was enhanced by the landscape with shattered farmsteads, abandoned positions and barbed wire, behind which the enemy lurked, while a colossal painting helped create the illusion of being in the line of fire; a naval battle was also reconstructed nearby.[18] Either children imbibed the lessons or at least were thought to have done so as postcards, 'Our Children in Great Time', were subsequently sold for the Austrian Red Cross. These show children playing war games using their sofa as a trench claiming, 'In the trenches we are well covered,/Only the rifle barrel is stretched out./Begin! Give fire! Those with red trousers,/

They are now tumbling down there, that's the French!' In another series, young children adapt everyday equipment for their bellicose games, thus a sewing machine is transformed into a machine gun firing at miniscule enemy soldiers.

In Britain, Lord Roberts' Workshops for Disabled Soldiers began to manufacture toys. Now customers could rest assured that their gifts were 'authentic' – while their purchase contributed to a worthwhile cause. That there was a business opportunity for the workshops stemmed in part from the fact that, before the war, toys had crossed national boundaries with Germany the dominant manufacturer. Some British children were heartbroken when told that a favourite toy was now an 'enemy'. Elizabeth Owen remembered the day war was declared,

> I was seven and I was playing in the garden when I was asked to go and speak to my grandmother. She said "Now children, I have got something very serious to tell you. The Germans are fighting the British, there is a war on and all sorts of people will be killed by these wicked Germans. And therefore there must be no playing, no singing and no running about.'"

Elizabeth accepted the prohibitions but was deeply distressed when her favourite toy, a German-made camel, 'of which I was very fond', was confiscated.[19] Teddy bears of German origin faced a similar fate while Ivy Keen, seemingly more patriotic than Elizabeth, rejected her 'lovely china-faced doll' when learning from her brother of its German origins. Ivy 'promptly divested it of all its clothes and hung it upside down in the gooseberry bush'. Despite her siblings, Jack, Percy and Molly trying to dissuade her, she refused to retrieve the doll.

With enemy toys discarded, children revelled at playing at war. In August 1914, 6-year-old Simone de Beauvoir who 'rapidly adopted the cause of righteousness', invented games 'appropriate to the circumstances. I was Poincaré, my cousin George V, my sister the Tsar.' We held conferences and we set about the Prussians.'[20] Aspiring to less exalted ranks, one French boy explained that they were 'playing soldiers in order to become officers when they go to war'.[21] At the seaside in August 1916, 7-year-old Françoise Marette and her friends built a trench, complete with barbed wire. They fashioned both a periscope and a machine gun and delighted in bombarding the opposite side. Reflecting her junior status in the family, she was simply a 'solider', while her older brothers were officers.[22] In Germany, in December 1914, 12-year-old Piete and friends refused to be beaten by the weather, 'It is so cold that we can hardly play "soldiers" in the yard. I had however arranged to have a drill session to harden us; after all our troops at the Front suffer much greater cold.'[23] Children in the Occupied Zones faced greater difficulties when acting out war games: in occupied Sedan, Yves Congar was outraged when, on 10 June 1915, 'Now it's even forbidden for children to play at soldiers and nurses in the streets and even in their own homes. It is outrageous 'cos we were all doing it.'[24]

In Yorkshire, Leonard Smith and schoolfriends turned a heap of rubble in the school grounds into Hill 60 and opposing groups of boys fought for 'supremacy on the top of that heap of rubble.'[25] As Hill 60 is in Belgium, the 'group of Belgian refugee children' provided additional authenticity. German children took their war games straight onto the street. As many as 150 youngsters would engage in epic battles. Girls wearing Red Cross uniforms bandaged wounds and administered cherry juice for medicine and 'massive graves' were dug for the dead. Occasionally the wounds were genuine as the games descended into gang warfare.[26] However much children enjoyed these games, adults began to complain; some were understandably unimpressed by whole streets being taken over by bands of unsupervised children, others felt that the levity and the seemingly chaotic war games 'mocked the seriousness of the times'.[27]

Playing war games occurred across all combatant nations. Russian pedagogues voiced concerns about children's bloodthirsty games, 'little beasts are awakening inside kids and there are no words to describe the hatred that they violently express against the Germans'.[28] With games increasingly bloody and few children willing to play Germans, cats and dogs were 'recruited' and the violence perpetrated on them 'unsettled everyone'.[29] By 1917, some were arguing that the omnipresence of war through tabloid newspapers, cheap illustrations and posters, was a psychological and moral 'catastrophe for millions of children who never got close to the actual zone of combat.'[30] When countless children found ways to enlist, front-line soldiers felt that, 'after the war they will be the cutthroats, criminals, God knows what kind.'[31]

In Turkey, with the stated aim of raising orphan boys in 'the most profitable way possible both intellectually and physically', 300 rifles were sent to Kadıköy (Istanbul) Orphanage. These proved so successful in instilling 'order and nationalist feeling', that the War Ministry despatched a further 1,000 across Turkey. Turkish flags as well as 'enemy flags, uniforms and military equipment captured at Gallipoli' further enhanced orphan boys' nationalistic pride. It was decreed that, using these genuine items from the Front, the boys should play war in the orphanage yards thereby 'instil[ing] nationalistic and militaristic feelings with reference to both their fathers' martyrdom and their fatherland's victory.'[32]

It could be argued that war toys, dressing up as soldiers and nurses, and acting-out war as a game with replica (or, in Turkey, real) guns, swords and adapted paraphernalia helped children address fears they could not always articulate. Manufacturers were more concerned about sales: 'Toy rifles, air guns and similar model weapons are proving good selling lines throughout the country and in conjunction with uniforms and helmets enable boys to make up in a very soldier like style'.[33] Some of these replicas were so realistic that, in Britain, a permit was needed to sell them or risk a £5 (£545 today) fine. There is no evidence of similar actions being taken in Germany where an enterprising Leipzig dealer manufactured toy hand grenades, not to mention the ever popular 'stink bombs'.

Acting out what they saw around them allowed some children to empathise with those in distress as much as with soldiers. In Schneidemühl, (East Germany) Piete records how her younger friend Gretel was distraught at the sight of refugee babies fleeing from the advancing Russians. 'The little ones' behinds are bloody because the mothers haven't enough nappies to lay them out to dry'. Gretel subsequently painted her doll's bottom red.[34] The two girls developed an increasingly elaborate war game which adapted to changing war conditions, thus when in August 1915, the soldiers stationed at Schneidemühl departed for the Eastern Front and fighter pilots arrived, the girls simply used an elaborate construction of garden benches and a steering wheel made from a dolls' pram to mimic aerial combat.[35] The game palled when, as with the refugees, reality intruded, 'Every week some airman crashes near us; they are then taken, accompanied by a military band, either to the war cemetery or to the goods station, where their coffins are sent off to their relatives. I can't bear to hear funeral marches anymore.'[36]

For many children the best props were those that serving relatives brought home from the Front. No doubt Piete's Uncle Bruno believed that the gift of his old army boots and an 'enemy' soldier's steel helmet on 15 October 1916 would simply enhance her war games. The reality proved different,

> When I looked more closely inside the helmet I saw that on the edge of the neck there was a name scratched with a sharp object. The name read van Glabeke César. This man is no longer alive. I am holding his helmet in my hand. A German girl, one of those who killed him. I pictured his mother. I immediately resolved to write to her … I addressed the letter to the French Red Cross in Paris,
> "La guerre est un
> désastre; Dieu ne la veut,
> ma famille
> Désire la paix."
> [War is a disaster, God does not want it, my family wants peace]

Piete longed to tell Madame van Glabeke that 'I cry over her César every night.'[37] By January 1917, the helmet and boots have become increasingly significant to this sensitive German adolescent,

> Why has fortune sent me the soldier Glabeke's helmet and Uncle Bruno's army boots? There must be some meaning in it. I have actually told Uncle Bruno that one day I would invent a dance that portrays a soldier rising from a mass grave or something like that. I don't know yet how exactly I shall do it.

On 8 November 1918, Piete's brother arrived home from the war in his torn uniform, This would complete the dance costume:

> Steel helmet, army boots, battle dress. I would paint 'blood' on my forehead and nose … also on my hands. I had to have it at all costs before he surrendered it to some idiotic quartermaster [They fought over it until Piete wins] … I held the uniform pressed against me with both arms, sobbing bitterly – the poor, poor German field uniform.[38]

With her war games relegated to her former existence, 16-year-old committed pacifist Piete choreographed 'Spectre of War', a dance which she subsequently performed professionally on stage and which would eventually lead her to staring death in the face when the Nazis gained power.

War in the Schoolroom

If war had dominated play, although sometimes with unexpected consequences, it also invaded schoolrooms. In the late nineteenth century, elementary education had become increasingly compulsory for all children up to about the age of 13 across the Western world. On 8 August 1914, the [British] Board of Education circulated *Emergency Measures with regard to Elementary Schools* (855). The Board considered, 'The unrest to which the present crisis in the affairs of the nation naturally gives rise, should [not result in] any avoidable interruption or dislocation of the public educational services of the Country'. For millions of children across all combatant lands, this proved a vain hope.

Despite attendance being compulsory in Great Britain, loopholes existed allowing for the early removal of children from school, either temporarily or permanently. One increasingly exploited loophole was the pre-war agricultural by-law which allowed children over 11 who had passed the Fourth (of Six) Standard(s) to be employed fulltime on farms for part of the year.[39] Teachers considered this a ruse, giving farmers access to cheap workers; the *Times Educational Supplement* (March 1915) agreed. Factory owners also clamoured for boy labour and *TES* noted a significant spike in the numbers of school-age children engaged in paid work and not attending school. Teachers struggled to prevent this as farmers and factory owners were often members of the Education Boards which granted or refused work requests. When local newspapers began praising youngsters for 'doing what they can for the country', teachers were fighting a losing battle with both the Board and with many parents to retain pupils.[40] With separation allowances being inadequate and payments slow to arrive, hard-pressed mothers welcomed their child's wage. While girls were less likely to be recruited to work on farms (other than at milking), exemptions for 'home duties' could be requested for girls whose mothers were agricultural labourers or factory hands. To make exemptions more palatable, it was argued that, 'The work will have a high moral value, [it is of] national service of the first moment [and it] will be organised as to be of direct educational value'.[41] By 1917, H.A.L. Fisher, President of the Board of Education, estimated that '600,000 [British] children had been put prematurely to work', not counting those employed in total violation of the law during the first three years of the war.[42]

For those attending school, it was not 'Business As Usual'. Every aspect of elementary education became subordinated to the war effort. Civilian life was subservient to the war machine, buildings were requisitioned heedless of the consequences.'[43] Six-year-old Elsie Dutton attended Tootal Road School, Salford, 'before long [it] was taken over for a Red Cross Hospital.' The children were moved to another school and 'they had to split the times so that two lots of children could be accommodated in one school.'[44] By November 1914 some 705 English Elementary Schools had been occupied wholly or partly by troops and 178 remained occupied in April 1915.[45] While some heads accepted the 'shift system' as their school's contribution to the war effort, others remained unimpressed.[46] With hundreds of thousands of children having been deprived of an education or been adversely affected by school closures and shortened hours, the 1918 Education Act raised the school leaving age to 14 and removed exemptions.

Requisitioned school buildings were not confined to Britain. In the few weeks before Belgium was occupied, classes were suspended and troops stationed in school buildings.[47] With most of Belgium overrun, teachers who had not fled, endeavoured to continue educating the young but with the occupier scrutinising lesson content, unlike in other belligerent countries where the war dominated nearly every lesson, teachers mainly focused on the core subjects – albeit with 'a good dose of patriotism'; they strove, not always successfully, to give children living in extraordinary situations a sense of normality.[48] Schoolteacher Mme Boquet placed a carefully folded national flag on a chair during a group photograph, mentioned the Belgian king's courage in dictations, and discussed the bravery of those at the Front, subsequently noting in her diary, 'the Germans have conveyed an order for the removal of all patriotic indications from my classroom.' Teachers assured bereaved children that their relative had died for the homeland. Schools could also be invaded by the occupier, on 13 February 1917, Mme Boquet found twenty-five soldiers in her classroom. The following day, school was suspended.[49]

As conditions in Belgium deteriorated, many children were living barely above starvation level, without the American feeding programmes (which also functioned in Occupied France) thousands would have starved to death. Teachers noted increasingly poor levels of concentration, exacerbated in winter by unheated school buildings. Schools as well as homes were raided for all non-precious metals (including wool from mattresses) that could support Germany's war effort.[50] That conditions were equally harsh in Germany would have been no consolation to Belgians. In the bitter winter of 1916–17, shortages of clothing, fuel and food made near starving children increasingly susceptible to disease. Unsurprisingly, schoolwork suffered.

Although children in unoccupied countries were not forced to live with the enemy nor see their homes and classrooms raided, when the bell rang for the start of morning lessons, pupils did not temporarily leave the war behind. Many arrived 'frequently distracted, sometimes distraught and occasionally delinquent' because of wartime conditions at home, fear of news from abroad and 'the sights and sounds of military operations around them', not to mention being subjected to air raids.[51] Some of these, like the June 1917 raid that killed eighteen children at London's Upper North Street School, occurred when school was in session. Despite being advised to the contrary, worried parents frequently collected their children from school once the sirens sounded. When raids happened at night, children arrived at school exhausted from sheltering in cellars, tunnels and, far from this being a Second World War phenomenon, in London tube stations – where on at least one occasion, panic led to a stampede and to a number of child deaths.[52]

Air raids, soon part of the fabric of many children's lives, provided an excellent topic for developing their composition skills. Following the 12 October 1915 'Theatreland Raid', boys at London County Council's Holborn Princeton Street School, Bedford Row, were tasked with recounting their experiences.[53] The compositions give a group of 11- and 12-year-old working-class boys' varied responses to this early raid. T. Allen was both excited and appalled when his brother Charlie said excitedly,

> "They're here again!" In my excitement I forgot any possible danger and ran out into the street ... I went to Chancery Lane and there saw a sight that fill[ed] me with horror. In the Strand and Aldwych, a large amount of damage was done and people say that large amounts of flesh were found sticking to the walls and posts.

Another boy, J. McHenry,

> was astonished to see crowds of women and children going into the tube in Holborn. They looked like Belgian refugees and then I guessed what it was for they were expecting an air raid, so they were sending the women and children down there for safety. I then ran as fast as I could to tell my mother but she did not take any notice.

J. Haynes, simply 'walked up the Kingsway. On the corner was a pool of blood about one yard diameter. There was pieces of flesh almost as big as my flick fist. A driver of a motor-bus was killed ... I then went home to bed.' Richard Sandell was more bothered by his mother having 'lost nine pence farthing' than by the raid. J. Littenstein concluded that 'the bomb insurance office was very busy paying out claims.' R. Beasley, whose father worked at the Lyceum Theatre and to whom he had to deliver a parcel, gives the most detailed account. Just about to enter the theatre, he

> heard a tremendous bang ... saw a blue light which lights up the place like daylight and the power of the light knocks you down ... I went inside the theatre when the man that was next to me had his left arm blown off and I thought I was going to be hit ... When the second bomb was dropped, I saw a man fall in the road with his head blown off.

To his horror, he hears that his badly injured father had been 'taken to Charing Cross Hospital. I then started crying because I thought he was dying.' Thankfully, Mr Beasley survived. If 13-year-old Florence Gower, who witnessed the 12 August 1917 raid on Southend (in which nine children were killed) is typical, many of these boys would have forever retained their memories of the gruesome sights. As an elderly woman, Florence could still recall 'bread baskets being brought out from Garons' bakery for the collection of body parts'.[54]

There is no indication of whether Holborn schoolmaster A. Field felt that it would be therapeutic for the boys to write about the event, or whether the raid was simply a composition exercise. Fortuitously, he and headmaster J. Bate considered the boys' efforts worth preserving. However, if writing about air raids was acceptable, there were fears that children might divulge information useful to the enemy when writing about military activities they had observed. It is hard to know to what exactly *Teacher's World* was referring when it stated, 'British boys and girls have all unknowingly given Germany help of a kind that she could have got in no other way. Without knowing, it we have been traitors to our country.'[55]

Even without air raids, many pupils arrived at school exhausted. In schools near military camps or factories, teachers acknowledged that tiredness could be exacerbated by already small homes having soldiers or factory hands billeted upon them. Edith Hall from Hayes in Middlesex, shared a bedroom with the munitions girls whom her impoverished mother accommodated, 'When they were not too tired, I lay and listened to them recalling the day's highlights, how some had been searched for matches and metal objects, and that some of their workmates had heard that their husbands or 'blokes' had been killed or wounded.'[56] Such conversation constantly reminded Edith of the dangers her own father faced. Decades later, she recalled the anguish when her 'dark-haired upright daddy' [was] posted as 'Missing'. It was months before news was received of his whereabouts. 'I still have the formal letter in which we were informed that he was missing; then a card telling us he was a prisoner'.[57]

Millions of children shared Edith's worries. Elsie Dutton, whose mother had died in 1911 and whose father was in the Navy, went seven months without hearing from her father serving in the Dardanelles. For thousands of children, the daily walk to school carried its own constant reminder of their fathers' danger, 'Sometimes when we were going to school or on an errand we would see the messenger boy from the GPO and that meant a telegram for somebody. We would wait to see which house he would go to. They were coming very frequently.'[58] Boarded with a hard-hearted, if not downright cruel aunt, Elsie had little room in her young mind for her school lessons – although she was a precocious reader, 'Auntie decided to buy a 2d book each week called *The War Illustrated* and if I could manage to get hold of it, I would try to find out what was going on.'[59]

Elsie's war may have been assimilated via *The War Illustrated*, some children longed for glimpses of the latest technology; airplanes proved a compelling sight. According to its school's logbook, when a plane descended in Gilston (Hertfordshire), 25/30 pupils went missing.[60] With aeronautics in its infancy, watching airplanes could have fatal consequences, the *Hemel Hempstead Gazette* reported two occasions in 1915 when an airplane killed a watching child. It was not only airplanes that proved irresistible. To teachers' annoyance, children who lived near military camps frequently truanted to watch soldiers, and pupils in some schools were eventually accorded half-day holidays to allow them to watch military parades. Older pupils often sought out soldiers' company. Irrespective of nationality, for some adolescent girls, this had inevitable consequences. Troops were garrisoned in Schneidemühl and to Piete's dismay,

A few days ago a thirteen-year-old baker's daughter was expelled from our school because she is going to have a child by a First

Lieutenant ... The whole school was in turmoil. The head went to each class and gave us a talk about morals ... We thought it was quite unnecessary to make a schoolmate the occasion for a talk on morals.[61]

Even better than watching military parades was when real soldiers were brought into the classroom. In still conscription-free Britain and in Australia, soldiers' visits served as examples to which boys should aspire and all pupils should encourage older male kin to emulate.[62] Soldier old-boys visited their former schools; Birmingham's Bloomsbury Road School logbook reported,

Two gentlemen, Messrs Watson and Jephcott, visited the school. They being newly enlisted in Lord Kitchener's army were introduced to the First Class as examples of what their brothers should do. [18 September 1914]

'Messrs Watson and Jephcott' would not yet have seen service overseas. Things would soon change; headmasters proudly recorded visits by ex-pupils who had been in the trenches. Like Public Schools, elementary schools began Rolls of Honour of those serving and in due course killed. These supposedly served 'as an inspiration to boys and girls, and a permanent reminder that they too are called upon to play what part they can in the great struggle.'[63] School logs often recorded the names of pupils' and teachers' relatives serving in the armed or nursing services, noting when these became casualties.

Teachers across all combatant nations had to confront bereaved children – some managed to do so sensitively, others failed dismally. The Australian *School Paper* from which many teachers took their cue, instructed children that by keeping their emotions private they were being as brave as those who had sacrificed all.[64] British schoolgirl Edith Hall was more attuned to her schoolmates' distress, 'One day when we were singing "God Save the King", I asked Miss Gilbert if we could also sing "God save the Phillipses" because out of ten children, five of their boys had already been killed in the war.'[65] Perhaps themselves neurasthenic, some schoolmasters found it hard to acknowledge pupils' anguish. French boy Jean-Louis Barrault's father had perished three weeks before the Armistice. When on 11 November, Jean-Louis' teacher, an ex-soldier invalided out, found the child weeping in a corner for his father rather than cheering the victorious French Army, he beat the little boy until his cane broke'.[66]

Some schoolmasters felt children quickly shook off grief. One French teacher believed that 'most children are unaware of the terrible situation. Certainly, they are concerned by the wounding or death of their father but only a few days afterwards they seem to have forgotten and pick up their own lives seemingly unbothered.'[67] In England, Freddie Harker, whose mother had already died, also lost his father, a regular correspondent from the Front, in 1915. Following the father's death, 13-year-old Freddie's aunt told a friend, 'It is a merciful thing that Freddie does not realise things'.[68] As a public schoolboy, Freddie's teachers could have encouraged him to demonstrate a 'stiff upper lip'. Alternatively, some children, used to their father's long absences, might only realise that 'the dead were dead forever' when the war finally ended.[69]

Teachers who volunteered were also seen as bringing credit on both their school and themselves – although their departure would frequently create additional staffing problems. If an old boy or teacher were wounded or captured, current pupils were encouraged to support them with gifts, while writing letters to them formed part of the day's lessons. Those without their 'own' school soldier could, like Garden Field School for Girls (Herts), 'adopt' one,

Dear Soldier, We are sorry you are cold at night so we are sending you a blanket. We mean to send one every week if we can because we love you so, for being so brave and taking care of us and our dear country. We all send our love and pray God to end the war soon and bring you back safe.

Your loving little friends.

In true patriotic spirit, these little girls, like millions of children across combatant countries, were 'not going buy any sweets 'till the war is over but save our money for blankets and tobacco.'[70] Such activities were far from the preserve of elementary school pupils. Having heeded the words of Henry Hibbert, chairman of the Lancashire Education Committee in which he reminded pupils 'every one of you can help, whatever position you occupy in your school', Lancaster Girls Grammar School pupils were heavily involved in charity work, frequently but not exclusively undertaken for 'their' POW Private Frank Cooper, who had been captured in Salonika in December 1915 and to whom they regularly wrote.[71]

French children could adopt a 'godson' soldier with whom they corresponded. Some of the letters were joint class efforts with every pupil adding some lines. The contribution from a boy who had lived in occupied Lille before being repatriated to France via Switzerland, may have warmed the teacher's heart with his overt patriotism, hatred of the Boche, and love/admiration of France's defenders, 'Without knowing you I love you and admire you as I do all French soldiers'. He adds that having had German soldiers billeted upon them, he had personally witnessed the invaders' cruelty. 'When we arrived in Switzerland and we saw French soldiers we hugged them and they were so nice to us ... When Victory is achieved, we will be able to tell our soldiers how proud we are of them.'[72] Irrespective of country, the 'godson' would visit the class when on leave giving pupils the opportunity to display their pride and admiration.

'Godsons' did not compensate for absent, missing or dead (frequently disciplinarian) fathers. In Britain, juvenile indictable offences rose from 14,325 in 1913 to 24,407 in 1917.[73] In a letter of 30 March 1917, the Earl of Lytton, Chair of the State Children's Association which was 'deeply interested in juvenile delinquency', pleaded with H.A.L. Fisher, Minister of Education, for a 'greater understanding' of the problems facing children in wartime which needed to be 'handled with spiritual courage and insight'. Partly blaming the military's requisitioning of schools which left children unoccupied for half of the day, Lytton added,

> In thousands of homes, the father is absent; in many, the mother is employed outside her home; school hours have been curtailed and there is a serious lack of men teachers in the boys' departments. The darkened streets, the lessened number of police and the absence of social workers from boys' clubs ... all have their widespread effect.[74]

The cinema was also blamed for crimes ranging from prostitution to murder, at least one case of the latter involved a juvenile.[75] The *Daily Mail* of 19 February 1917 was not alone in reporting how 40-year-old Louisa Walker, after shopping in Leigh-on-Sea, was approached from behind and shot with a revolver; 15-year-old agricultural labourer Frederick

Livingstone was arrested, found guilty and sentenced to death. Supporting a plea for leniency owing to Frederick's youth and believing this was a copycat action, the judge blamed films at the Picture Palace for portraying 'horrible things'.

Absent fathers and the paucity of male teachers – about 80 per cent of whom were serving in the army, were blamed for the significant increase in crimes among German and Austrian youth. Exacerbating the difficulties, mothers of all social classes increasingly left their children unsupervised at home while they stood in line, sometimes for ten hours a day, to buy scarce clothing, food and coal.[76] Mock wars fought on the streets became ever more violent as secondary school boys, often revered as soldiers of the future, acquired guns and makeshift hand grenades, sometimes stealing money to buy these. Writing to Austria's Minister for Education, Franziszka Pollabrek's desperation is palpable,

> My boys will become nothing but thieves, liars, and murderers if you, dear Sirs, don't intervene soon ... The fathers are in the military, the male teachers are mobilized, and I work in the factory. You want to do nothing, so where should I begin? Since you have taken away their father, why don't you take the children as well, let the boys be locked up or shot, so that I don't have to see them anymore.[77]

Frustratingly, whether the authorities reacted to her plea, or what became of her sons is unknown.

Irrespective of nationality, most children committed themselves wholeheartedly to the war effort. Not only did those lucky enough to receive any bring in their pocket money to buy wool which they would knit into comforts (those unable to knit soon received instruction), they served as unofficial fundraisers who put pressure on family members to donate to war causes. War charities soon recognised public susceptibility to youngsters selling flags and begging for comforts for the wounded. Simone de Beauvoir, looking back on her wartime self, concluded,

> It doesn't take much to turn a child into a performing monkey. I wholeheartedly threw myself into the role of mini patriot. Wearing my blue greatcoat, I collected money on the main boulevards for 'little Belgian refugees'. Money rained down on me and the smiles of the passers-by confirmed in my mind that I really was an adorable

little patriot. Nevertheless, I was dumbfounded when a woman swathed in black asked, 'Why Belgian refugees, why not French ones?' I was disconcerted the Belgians were our brave allies ... I felt my patriotism was being put under the spotlight.[78]

Pupils across combatant nations were instructed to collect acorns, fruit stones, blackberries, dandelion and white bryony roots and horse chestnuts. Although this was to be kept secret, the latter were used for the distillation of acetone, a solvent used in the manufacture of cordite – as German children also collected these, their usefulness was undoubtedly common knowledge.[79] Thrift and lessons in using every scrap of food entered the girls' curriculum. Whether time-impoverished British mothers, adept at feeding growing families on tiny budgets, welcomed the invitation to attend their daughters' lessons is open to question.

As early as 7 August 1914, pupils could request an exemption from their parents to go and help with the harvest. However, Piete's offer was cruelly rejected, 'Go back home you naughty, horrid-looking child! Girls like you are no use to the Fatherland.'[80] Such exemptions were granted to German children throughout the war, 'even in 1917 and 1918 when a good many had no shoes.'[81] German pupils were often accorded whole or half-day holidays to celebrate victories (including the bombing of Scarborough) when patriotic children could 'voluntarily' go foraging; with eighteen Victory holidays in the first year of the war, foraging kept pupils suitably occupied.[82] Although all school children were involved in some form of voluntary activities, be these knitting, foraging or writing letters to soldiers, German children 'volunteered their labour more expansively and consistently than those in the other belligerents'.[83] Perhaps this was not totally voluntary for the 'Prussian education minister was singularly committed: the vast majority of his orders during the war had to do not with the curriculum but with the productive use of [pupils'] labour. About 50% of the 13 million German boys and girls aged 6 to 18 ... did voluntary activity regularly.'[84]

Although in the earlier years of the war, children had been encouraged to help with the harvest, in Germany from 1916, the *Landaufenthalt fur Stadtkinder*, the most successful welfare programme of the war, was an imaginative way to try to counter the havoc starvation wrought upon young lives. Urban children were sent to strangers' farms where, in return for some help, they were fed and housed. Children mustered in their schoolyard, marched to the station and then entrained for a still undisclosed destination. Parents were forbidden from accompanying children to the station, or of knowing their whereabouts to prevent them from visiting and perhaps inveigling food. While some youngsters were traumatised by the separation and many were doubtless sick with worry about kin at the Front, most children settled well into their new lives and, temporarily at least, escaped the spectre of starvation stalking the cities.[85]

Despite being less acute than in Europe, food shortages existed in Britain's Dominions. Canadian boys could become 'Soldiers of the Soil' and help increase food supplies. By 1917, around 25,000 urban Canadian boys aged between 13 and 15 disrupted their education and went to work on farms. Apparently appeals were even sent to them from the trenches, 'Because you are too young to get in at this end of the fight, do your bit by working on a farm'.[86] Urban gardens were used to grow crops to sell, so successfully that by June 1917, Ontario children had earned enough from their potato crop to buy an ambulance for the Red Cross.

The war soon permeated every belligerent schoolroom. Red Cross representatives 'descended on school managers to incorporate teachers and children into the nationwide efforts to maintain a constant supply of warm clothing and bandages created out of recycled wool and linen.'[87] Schoolgirls converted thousands of pairs of disused woollen stockings into mittens; boys' woodwork classes in both England and Australia became mini factories for manufacturing splints and crutches for the Red Cross and even hand-grenade boxes for the Ministry of Munitions, while older girls sewed heavy hessian into sandbags. Just as girls would enclose letters to recipients of their garments, boys did the same with their handiwork – on one occasion, the crutch made by a boy was, to their mutual surprise, given to a relative. With the line between patriotic endeavour and child exploitation being a fine one, pupils found themselves manufacturing iron beds, repairing old stretchers (some still blood-stained) as well as school furniture, toys for private companies and, as church shrines to the local wounded began to dominate the landscape, even the shrines.[88] The *Herts Advertiser* of 1 April 1916 complacently claimed that such activities brought 'children into closer touch with conditions that are prevailing in the country now'.

If the Red Cross visited English schools to harness pupils' enthusiasm, Piete notes on 28 January 1915 how, at her school, each class was ordered to visit a military hospital in a barracks a long way outside the town – parents had to pay for the trip. 'It was an awful hospital!' As many of the patients were only covered with newspapers and this was the start of National Wool Week, in which everyone was expected to 'hand over to the authorities old jackets, trousers, blankets, shirts, coats and woollens of all kinds', this appears an unsubtle way of harnessing children's commitment. Piete's grandmother was unimpressed.

In Canada, J.S. Gordon, Inspector of Schools for Vancouver, proudly noted how, 'The spirit of self-sacrifice, self-denial and service shone out in the public schools of the land in all its full-orbed radiance.'[89] Early in the war, *School: A Magazine Devoted to Elementary and Secondary Education* reminded teachers of the moral and patriotic imperative to teach the war and, conveniently, supplied them with information enabling them to do so. Although *School* was not initially jingoistic, by March 1915, the tone had changed, pupils were to be reminded, 'It is the Empire's war. It is Canada's war; Canadians must believe in it, pay for it and help to win it'! By the amount of fundraising undertaken, Canada's schoolchildren certainly appear to have helped pay for the war as well as learn about the British Empire's rights and her enemies' wrongs in every lesson. The *Canada War Book*, designed as a teaching tool with chapters entitled 'Why Canada entered the war', 'What Germany stands for,' emphasised Canadian soldiers' achievements; works of art recommended for study included those overtly linking fallen soldiers with the crucified Christ.[90]

In Australia, the monthly *The School Paper* (cost 1*d*) was prescribed reading for teachers, children (who were quizzed on it during lessons), and their parents. Harnessing war and schoolwork, young Australian knitters were encouraged to compose letters, frequently supervised in class to ensure accurate spelling and grammar, to soldiers for whom they had knitted socks. One teacher was particularly imaginative in their knitting/ fundraising/patriotic activities. The whole school began knitting a pair of socks for Australian hero, General Birdwood, each pupil had to pay for the privilege of knitting a row, their name being added to the accompanying decorative leaflet. One can imagine the pupils' delight when the great man replied, 'I think it is really wonderful that your school with only 10 pupils has been able to build up a fund of £50 [£5,500 today]'.[91] If any finished garments were considered too small for Australian 'Diggers', they were sent to Belgian children. If Australian pupils did not knit the Empire to

Victory, they knitted their way to an additional week's holiday, awarded in 1917 and only reclaimed seven decades later.[92]

Like peers in Australia, Canada, England, Germany and Austria, French children were encouraged to make personal sacrifices through knitting and making articles for soldiers. Françoise Marette was, by her own admission, 'very talented' with her hands. So talented that aged 6, she was set to work knitting scarves which,

> had to be 1 metre 20 long. That's a lot of work. So much so that at night I used safety or hair pins and fastened them to the backs of chairs and wet them so that they stretched out to 1m 20. But when they dried they shrank back down to size and…in the mornings… the scarves were all hard. I got very fed up with it all as I had to spend all my time knitting and the adults got cross with me saying that the soldiers were waiting for their scarves and would die of cold if I didn't buck up and finish them. And I didn't see that people were actually making fun of me. Nor did they realise what a chore it was. They just looked at me and I didn't even have time to speak just to knit.[93]

An acute, precocious observer of the disintegrating world, Françoise was frequently in trouble for misunderstanding wartime euphemisms. When a distraught neighbour said that she had 'lost her husband', Françoise suggested that if he was lost then his wife 'should go and look for him properly. Then I was told I was stupid and was punished because "lost" now meant dead.'[94] Françoise practised her reading by,

> reading communiqués to my mother … These would just say things like 'All quiet on the Western Front'. I learnt to read all the words like Dardanelles and Argonne. I only found them on the map later. I really thought it was strange that people were fighting on the Chemin des Dames [Ladies' Road] – that didn't sound the right sort of place for canon fire.

Sadly, it *was* the 'right sort of place for cannon fire', Francoise's beloved Uncle Pierre perished there.[95] French childhood historian Manon Pignot argues that all 'French children [were] subjected to a much more all-pervasive mobilisation than their European counterparts. There was

23

almost a normalisation of war and its violence for children.'[96] As Jeanne Lavabre, headmistress of Ecole de la Rue Alouette (Paris) noted, 'The curriculum has been adapted to the questions raised by the war, handiwork, history, citizenship, reading, writing, songs and poetry.'[97] Exercise-book covers depicted the war and almost every lesson was constructed around it. German pupils were similarly exposed: arithmetic in both countries related to munitions of war, soldiers and artillery; composition involved writing to soldiers or describing a return from the Front, while art lessons inevitably had a war theme. By drawing the sinking of the battle-ships *Aboukir, Hogue, Cressy* (September 1914), Piete gained a rare moment of praise as she listened attentively when the master explained 'the characteristics of battleships'.[98] Two months later, however, hinting at her future pacifism after another lesson on battleships, Piete muses, 'When the *Titanic* hit an iceberg and all the people were drowned, the whole world cried in horror. Now ships go down every day and no one asks afterwards what happened to the sailors.'[99]

The words of a teacher in Nantes (France) stand for all official attitudes: 'We used all school exercises in such a way that the patriotic effort was also a pedagogic one' – this pedagogy included instilling hatred for the enemy in every pupil's breast.[100] Mr Judic, head of another Nantes school, appears more concerned about the disruption to his pupils' education than lessons of patriotism. Far from the Front, he was unimpressed by the way his 'school's life was totally disturbed. During the holidays we had territorials billeted on us, children in the nurseries, French and Belgian refugees accommodated in the classrooms'.[101] Worrying about the effect of these war-themed lessons on already nervous, even traumatised children, not all teachers were enthusiastic. Their concerns went unheeded.[102]

Art lessons gave pupils an ideal opportunity to depict their war-maddened world and, according to modern child psychiatrist Roland Beller, drawing gave children, particularly those who had experienced and escaped from the German invasion, a medium through which to exorcise their demons. If propaganda tried to present a somewhat sanitised view of the struggle between 'Might' and 'Right', many of the drawings are disturbingly realistic. A series from a working-class school in Montmartre (Paris), whose pupils included Belgian and French refugees, depict some of the atrocities they had witnessed, 'particularly those perpetrated on children from le Nord who even drew concentration camps.'[103] Although there is nothing to suggest that children's hands were cut off or babies bayoneted, the enemies' sadism is apparent; the pictures confirm much of the oral testimony Manon Pignot gathered in the 2000s. There are drawings of young children in the Occupied Zone being forced to work for the enemy and others depicting the courage of children who refused to be cowed. One shows a summary execution of civilians while several portray homes being put to the torch.

Some young artists depicted the war as recounted by relatives home on leave. Children drew rats in the trenches, bursting shells, soldiers losing eyes, limbs, while young 'Jolivet' drew one soldier with his head blown off and another with blood spurting. In another, he shows crows feasting on a body, commenting that although people might have meatless days, crows don't.[104] Beller was convinced that young Jolivet had witnessed several terrifying events and if he himself were not in the burning house drawn in one picture, he was probably just outside, maybe with loved ones inside. Although some might argue that children frequently draw gratuitous violence, the psychiatrist is convinced that these pictures were by deeply disturbed children – of which there were many due to the Occupation. There is ample evidence, both from these drawings and from diaries (discussed in Chapter Two), that for French children the war was not 'Over There', but right here.

The pictures show children deeply involved in day-to-day wartime life. Food shortages, queuing for food and coal became part of all children's daily life, much mentioned in their diaries and oral testimony and by teachers who reported pupils being exhausted from queuing, from hunger and shelling by 'Big Bertha' (the gun which threatened Paris and named for gun manufacturer Krupps' eldest daughter). A detailed series of drawings of air raid shelters, some depicting scenes of casual promiscuity, may not have found appeal with the teachers. The excitement some youngsters felt during raids also features.

One particularly moving drawing depicts a boy who, to his classmates' envy, is being met at school by his father who is unexpectedly home on leave. Not all were so fortunate, a rough estimate is the 1.3 million French dead left 600,000 widows and around 1.1 million orphans, not to mention those living with hideously wounded fathers. As the war continued, the blind, the disfigured, the crippled, and the shell-shocked are portrayed; 'little refugee Debièvre' poignantly pushes his legless father in a perambulator. Unsurprisingly, grief and bereavement feature: hearses, funeral processions, the tricolore, and children with their widowed mother praying for their father.

While some of the pictures appear spontaneous, others may have been conforming to teachers' instructions. Children draw themselves selling flags and collecting money for the plethora of charitable causes ranging from tubercular patients to war orphans, to Serbia, as well as giving money and encouraging donations to War Savings schemes. One that doubtless met with approval is of a young boy emptying his money box on his teacher's desk, the little 'poilus of the rear' are supporting the brave ones at the Front. All belligerents considered schoolchildren easy targets for drumming up financial support. By 19 September 1914, pupils in Piete's school were being exhorted to, 'Enlist the Support of your parents, relatives and friends for the War Loan'. Her 50 marks 'contribution secured 'a prize in the school in the form of a cardboard brooch.'[105] So persuasive was Piete, at least initially, that at one point her grandmother, with whom she lived, believed that her grandchildren would bankrupt her.[106]

Food economy was ever more widely promoted. Older French children were encouraged to submit posters to promote both war-savings and food economy schemes. Among the work of ten youngsters aged under 17 used by the Comité de Prevoyance et d'Economies (War Thrift and Savings Committee)[107] were 14-year-old Louisette Jaeger's 'Cultivons Notre Potager' (Cultivate our Kitchen Garden) and Yvonne Vernet's 'Economisons le Pain en Mangeant des Pommes de Terre' (Save Bread, Eat Potatoes); 15-year-old Yvonne Colas' 'Partageons le Sucre', with a sword halving a bag of sugar to ensure that everyone has a little; and young Andrée Menard's advice to those at home to save tobacco so there was plenty for those at the Front, not to mention her admonition to 'Lend your bank notes to France'.

While her compatriots were being 'taught' about the war, young French girl Anaïs Nin, living in America but anxiously following French war reports, was deeply frustrated by her teacher's biased views:

Sister Gertrude was talking about the war and said, 'Of course Germany is going to win, because God will punish France and England by counteracting all their efforts. France made the Catholics suffer ... And England became Protestant ... so the hand of God will punish them both and lift up Germany which has been faithful to Him and respectful of His church.' As she talked my hands clenched into fists, my blood boiled in my head and my lips trembled. From beneath the ruins I seemed to see the cathedral at Reims and all the other churches that the Boches have burned.[108]

An emotional child, once America entered the war, Anaïs felt sympathy for her German schoolmates who were 'looked on with suspicion and all the games are at their expense.'[109]

For children living in occupied areas, attending school became increasingly precarious. In Sedan, Yves Congar noted how after the 1915 summer break, school resumed without a full complement of teachers or classes.[110] In Ham (Picardy) Henriette Thiesset's mother engaged a private tutor to ensure that Henriette's education continued – this had to be abandoned when citizens needed German-issued permits even to move around the village. Unlike those in free countries who were lauded when they enlisted, school teachers in occupied areas were sometimes taken as hostages or deported to Germany, thus placing even greater pressure on the school system.

Those of the Jewish faith can be accused of conflicted loyalties in wartime. Many children attending the London Jewish Synagogue Saturday School knew where their loyalties lay. Leslie Israel states emphatically, 'Kaiser Bill is very silly', Alice Englebert's 'Judgement Day' portrays the 'Kaiser Crowned by Sin'; Sybil Izbiki's weeping girl examines the poster calling for '100,000 men', wondering 'Why wasn't I born a man?' However, Nina Goldstein sees the universality of suffering, conditions on the Eastern Front are, 'as terrible ... as in Belgium'.[111]

Some serving teachers strove to remind children of this universality. Writing about entering a captured dug-out, rather than recounting tales of derring-do, one teacher brought home to former pupils (and to those reading his words today) how, irrespective of their nationality, children's experiences, their hopes and fears for their soldiers and fathers, were identical,

> In a corner an officer's cap was thrown on a heap of cake boxes. These boxes were of cardboard and sewn in with calico just as the parcels come to us from [home]. The addresses were in a child's handwriting as were one or two letters. In another corner, a coat was rolled up. I opened it and found it stained with blood ... I could not help thinking sadly of the little girl or boy who had sent him the cakes.[112]

Caroline van Westerborg's June 1915 simple prayer would undoubtedly have struck a chord, 'O God of Love, O King of Peace/Make wars throughout the world to cease.'[113]

On 1 August 1914, the tocsin had sounded in France calling men to their units; within twelve days of the declaration of war, the German army had expanded 'from 808,280 to 3,502,700 soldiers'; in Britain, on 7 August, Lord Kitchener appealed to civilians to 'Enlist Today!' Few of the men who responded to these and subsequent summonses between 1914 and 1918 could have imagined the extent to which the sons and daughters they were leaving behind would become swept up, in the nursery, in the playground and in the schoolroom, in this Great War for Civilisation.[114]

CHAPTER TWO

A Guiding Hand: Girl Guides, Diarists and Letter Writers

GIRL GUIDES: *'The idea of doing proper was work was really thrilling ... perhaps it was because the whole world was in uniform then.'*[1]

If delinquency were blamed, at least in part, on the lack of youth leaders, one youth group that lacked neither leaders nor recruits were the Girl Guides. Overshadowed post-war by the frequently told wartime story of the Boy Scouts, Girl Guides' contribution to their nations' cause is a proud one.

Between 1907 and 1909, Boer War General Sir Robert Baden-Powell, the so-called 'hero of Mafeking', responding to what was seen during the South Africa wars as the 'effete' state of the nation, founded an organisation for boys which would promote health, discipline, patriotism and manliness. In 1909, a Boy Scout rally was held at London's Crystal Palace. A serial in the popular magazine *Girls' Reader*, having constructed Scouting as a 'wholly fresh phase of woman's activity [for] healthy open-air adventure-loving young women who go about their work of tracking, spying, signalling and what not with a zeal and intelligence that may well set an example to their male confreres,' some 6,000 girls had formed their own troops with little adult input.[2] A number of girls attended the 1909 Boy Scout rally clamouring to become officially recognised as Girl Scouts. Unimpressed by the concept of women in uniform, Baden-Powell passed the issue over to his sister Agnes, and in 1910 the Girl Guides movement was formally founded. The 1912 *Girl Guides' Handbook* subtitled 'How Girls can help build the Empire', may have included suitably feminine sections on 'Tending the Injured' (First Aid, hospital duties), and 'Home Life', but significant space was allotted to 'Woodcraft', open-air pursuits included 'Tracking' and 'Frontier Life', where Guides could heroically use weapons – if only in self-defence.

Although today the language jars, *Headquarters Gazette* recognised that while, 'You do not want to make tomboys of refined girls, yet you want to attract and raise the slum-girl from the gutter.' The embryonic organisation successfully appealed to all classes; by 1914 there were around 300,000 Guides.[3] The cover image of *Girl Guide Gazette* (January 1914, price 2*d*) tapped into the national mood of patriotism and service: two uniformed Guides salute a laurel-wreathed Britannia proclaiming, 'For God, Our King and Empire'. Although sometimes mocked, pre-war, for either being an off-shoot of the suffrage campaign or pseudo army cadets, by August 1914, Girl Guides were becoming established in both the adult and juvenile consciousness. Four years later, rallies graced by royal personages had been held. To East Ender Dorothy Chegwidden's envy, her sisters were inspected by 'a princess (almost certainly Mary) in the local park', while Cicely Stewart-Smith from Kensington remembered being called upon to demonstrate 'proficiency in front of Queen Alexandra in June 1918'.[4] This proficiency included showcasing fire-fighting skills with Guides carrying each other out of first floor windows and down ladders – a firefighter's badge was an early proficiency badge.[5] By 1919, Girl Guides were recognised as having made a significant contribution to the war effort.

Young Dorothy listened avidly to stories told by her elder sisters, 'Amy [who] had badges from her wrist to her shoulders, and Winnie [who] was a lieutenant', and longed for the day when she too could join.[6] In the West End, Cicely practised Morse code while crossing Kensington Gardens to school, 'A long-legged tense faced schoolgirl of twelve in blue coat and scarlet tam o'shanter is seen walking towards the Bayswater Road. Suddenly she yells "PIP", jumps, gives 2 strides and jumps, calling the while dot-dash-dash-dot.'[7] Cicely was working for her Telegraphist badge which required Guides to be able to construct their own wireless receiver and send messages in Morse at a speed of thirty letters per minute.[8]

Amy and Cicely's interest in badges is unsurprising. In August 1914, Agnes Baden Powell had immediately encouraged Girl Guides to do their bit for the war effort not only by using all their 'strength to help others to be resolute and hopeful, confident that good will come', but also gaining badges useful in wartime, these reflect Guides' multiple endeavours: in 1917, Air Mechanic, Bee Farmer, Dairy Maid, Motorist and Telegraphist were added to the extant First Aid, Cooking, Nursing, Knitting, Florist/Gardener.[9] The most dedicated could (like Boy Scouts) earn the coveted annual War Service badges, which necessitated twenty-one days of recognised voluntary war service, 100 hours of agricultural or hospital work, the making of fifteen specified garments including a pair of pyjamas, four pairs of socks and two shirts. Although proficiency badges were sewn on the right sleeve, the War Service badge held the 'spot of honour' above the right breast pocket while Ambulance, Child Nurse and Sick Nurse badges were prominently displayed on the left side. In the Dominions, Tasmanian Guides' possible War Service duties included undertaking 'rifle practice by shooting rabbits' which they skinned, cooked over their campfire and, thrift being close to Guiding's heart, 'made rabbit-skin jackets for soldiers'.[10]

In 1916, Boy Scouts gained a fillip. Before enlisting as a Boy Sailor, 16-year-old Jack Cornwell VC had belonged to the St Mary's Mission Group Manor Park, London troop. Previously, the highest award to which a Scout could aspire was King's Scout – for which a wartime board game was available to enable a lad to hone his skills. Now, a Jack Cornwell Scout badge (still in existence) was awarded to exceptional Scouts 'in respect of pre-eminently high character and devotion to duty, together with great courage and endurance.[11] Not to be outdone, Girl Guides could aspire to the Edith Cavell badge for exceptional conduct, 'pluck in saving life, self-sacrifice in work for others, endurance and suffering or calmness in danger.'[12] Recipients have not been traced, but as Guides were known to step up to the mark following air raid disasters and Guides worked in munitions factories, these badges may have been awarded following explosions and other calamities. Girl Guiding's link with Edith Cavell was reinforced when Guides lined the route of her post-war funeral procession.

As their impressive record for reliability increased, some munitions factories specifically recruited Girl Guides aged 14 and above. 'During their lunch hour they would assemble in the factory yard and remove their working overall and caps to reveal their uniforms and their long hair in single plaits. Their captain wore a long skirt, navy blouse and white kid gloves to go with her felt hat and lanyard. They practised first aid on each other and learned new skills towards more badges. When the factory whistle went, they would put their overalls and caps back on and return to making armaments.'[13] In some poorer areas, Girl Guides' companies raised the leaving age beyond 16 hoping that this would enable munition workers to spend leisure time productively. Keen to have Guides, some employers paid for their uniforms.

In 1914, Agnes Baden Powell had advised Guides, 'Many of us will not be called into the fighting line but let us put forth all our strength to help others to be resolute and helpful.'[14] One way in which Guides followed this advice was during air raids. They rescued people from damaged buildings, sometimes at personal risk, and entertained and cared for people using rest shelters, sometimes staging concerts to offer distractions from the aerial warfare being fought above shelterers' heads.[15] When an air raid occurred in Folkestone with calamitous consequences, Girl Guides were visible on the streets helping the wounded. The honour of the most dramatic care of civilian wounded goes to Canadian Guides. On 6 December 1917, the then largest ever manmade explosion occurred in Nova Scotia. French munitions vessel *Mont Blanc* carrying 2.9 kilotons of explosives, collided with the Norwegian-flagged relief ship, *Imo,* in Halifax harbour. Just under 2,000 people were killed, 9,000 injured and thousands more rendered homeless.[16] Guides rushed to assist and for over a month used their First Aid skills at the Emergency Hospital and worked in children's wards with young disaster victims.[17]

Not short of imagination when it came to novel ideas, Girl Guides proved adept fundraisers. At one event hosted for wounded soldiers, men had to brush and plait Guides' long hair and then pin it up neatly and quickly. The Guides even raised enough money with Sales of Work to buy a large motor ambulance built by Clement Talbot of Wormwood Scrubs.[18] In 1916, responding to the (far more numerous) Boy Scouts having already provided a Rest Hut in France for soldiers' use, Guides set about raising the necessary £500 (£48,700 today) to fund their own hut. Their endeavours were so successful that the £2,348 (£228,695) raised enabled the hut to offer not only a canteen where the cost-price tea, coffee, cocoa and sandwiches were a taste of Blighty, but games and letter-writing rooms. Countless soldiers and nurses record the solace these huts offered and the joy of writing a letter/diary sitting at a table rather than scrawling on a knee. The Baden-Powells were rightly proud of the Scout and Guide-funded huts; Olave, Sir Robert's wife, left her two infants at home to run the Guides' hut for several months.[19]

Somewhat surprisingly, Girl Guiding was born in Belgium during the Occupation. Although Boy Scouts had been founded in 1910, little had been done for girls. Following the invasion, despite Scouts endeavouring to offer what civil assistance they could, the movement was frowned upon. Sometime before April 1915, Roman Catholic priest and head chaplain to the Belgian Boy Scouts, Melchior Verpoorten, and a wealthy Belgian woman, Berthe d'Huart, had become increasingly worried about the plight of (frequently orphan) girls living in Brussels' tough Marolles area. Impressed by what Guiding had brought to British girls, they hoped that a similar organisation in Brussels could 'provide a moral foundation for "girls of the street"' and give them sight of another world 'beyond their neighbourhood'.[20] Having gained financial support from the Archbishop of Mechelen (the anti-German outspoken Cardinal Mercier), and Olave Baden-Powell's approval, companies soon sprang up. With increasing numbers of Belgian men deported, and with the country essentially dependent upon women-power, girls suddenly became a valuable asset. Although the outspoken Verpoorten was arrested and imprisoned in June 1917, one of his recruits assumed responsibility for the still fledgling organisation. While Girl Guides and Boy Scouts offered young people in free countries an opportunity to add their youthful weight to the country's war effort, Guiding gave Belgian girls a brief respite from life under a brutal occupation.

British Guides' greatest contribution to Victory remains little known. On 29 October 1914, Boy Scouts were engaged to work for MI5. By 4 September 1915, the experiment was considered a failure. The boys were 'found to be very troublesome ... The considerable periods of inactivity which fell to their share usually resulted in them getting into mischief.'[21] When the Admiralty began to employ Scouts as coast watchers, the powers-that-be at MI5 breathed a sigh of relief. Might girls prove more malleable or at least less boisterous? A secret document, 'Duties of H Branch', specifically covers the role of the Girl Guides who worked for MI5 in ever increasing numbers offering fascinating insight into this overlooked part of Guiding History. Section H6 stipulated that the Guides were to be 'of good standing, quick, cheerful and willing.' Engaged initially on three months' probation, they earned ten shillings a week (£55 today) 'with dinner and tea included', and an extra four shillings a month for those who also worked in the kitchen. Higher rates of pay subsequently became available for particularly reliable Guides with supplementary duties.[22] Although initially the intelligence messages were written, and a girl pledged on her Guide's Honour not to look at these, the Guides were eventually considered so trustworthy that they delivered counter-espionage reports and 'Top Secret' messages verbally. Most of the ninety Girl Guides, who had to have written parental permission as well as that of their Guide Captains to apply, worked at Waterloo House, although some were posted to two other London locations. 'Each is allotted to a floor and the patrol leader is responsible for the work, discipline and good behaviour of her patrol.' Few, if any, were found wanting. Ever higher standards of efficiency were achieved through marks being allocated to each patrol. The girls worked an eight-hour day and alternate Sundays with a weekly half-day holiday. Illness lasting longer than forty-eight hours had to be accounted for by a doctor's certificate.[23] To prevent potential angst, Guides had to observe a strict dress code. Their blue skirts could be no more than 8in off the ground; their belts and distinctive hats had to be worn at all times. With uniform-frenzy sweeping the land, this was probably no hardship.

Soon Guides' duties extended far beyond delivering messages. Perhaps exploiting their desperation to serve the war effort, they were to be,

> responsible for dusting all rooms on their floors between 9 am and 10 am, cleaning and filling the ink pots and disinfecting the telephones, as well as answering any bells which may ring between those hours. After 10 am their work consists chiefly of collections for the despatch room, for the posts, and for running messages, sorting cards, collecting files, collecting waste paper and rolling it up ready for burning.[24]

Repairing as well as cleaning typewriters soon also fell to their lot. Again replacing 'boisterous' boys, guides worked in postal censorship offices. At times, the level of responsibility placed on these young shoulders is striking.

By 1917, there was even a special MI5 Guide Company: 'every Monday they paraded across the roof to Waterloo House for inspection'. Occasionally at least, their enthusiasm for their roles was too much for MI5 employees. After working with Girl Guides for several days, Miss M.S. Aslin of MI5 reported,

> She speeds from floor to floor bearing messages of good will, and no obstacle is too great for her to fall over in her devotion to this happy task. Released for the moment, she retires to her attractive little sitting-room where she reads and converses quietly[?] on high topics with her friends.[25]

Guides even featured in *The Nameless Magazine*, MI5's in-house 'journal' edited by female staff. A cartoon depicted four Guides sitting in their uniforms in a corridor captioned, 'The Electric Bells having broken, the GGs (*not* the Grenadier Guards) sit outside Maj. D's door in case he wants them.'[26]

By 1918, the experiment was deemed a complete success, the girls were 'more amenable and their methods of getting into mischief … less distressing … than were those of the boys'. Guiding's greatest accolade came in 1919: seen as utterly reliable, a contingent accompanied the British delegation to France. They ran errands for the Paris Peace Conference delegates at the Palace of Versailles and a group of Senior Guides (aged over 16) were invited to witness the signing of the Peace Treaty.[27]

War By Children's Hands

State education pioneers of the late nineteenth century could not have anticipated that children's writings would provide one of the richest sources of record for cultural/social historians of the First World War. While behind some of these writings, one senses (or is told about) an adult's guiding hand, others are undoubtedly spontaneous. These frequently overlooked writings tell a great deal about what it was like to be young during the First World War.

Painful Partings

Like British ones, French schools were on holiday when the first rumblings of war were heard. Robert Mouton, aged 13, was staying with his grandmother in Epagny, 16km from Soissons. He noted in his redacted diary that although there was a sense of fear and 'damp eyes', with people interrogating those who had lived through 1870–1, in the days immediately before mobilisation, people remained hopeful until the tocsin sounded at 4 pm on 1 August.[28] Robert is far from alone in writing about walking to the station to watch the men entrain. Having embraced their sobbing wives and children, Robert wonders whether, rather than this being an indication of high spirits, the departing men are singing to give themselves courage and fool themselves into anticipating a quick victory. Henriette Thiesset, 12, lived in soon-to-be-occupied Ham with her station master grandfather. With a ringside view of the station, Henriette witnessed many departures. Contrary to Robert, she was struck by the troop's 'ardour' when, 'buoyed up with courage', 'laughing and singing' they left the station for possible death.[29] On 2 August, 13-year-old Parisian Marcelle Lerouge watched the spectacle of departing men surrounded by their families commenting in the matter-of-fact style which is her hallmark, 'It wasn't very gay.'

In Lorraine, a German possession since 1871, 10-year-old Marie-Louise Binet empathised with the departing German soldiers, 'Such heart-breaking farewells. Here a mother, here a wife, here a group of children, a thousand sobs as they kiss and kiss their loved one'.[30] Marie-Louise's compassion for these families is unusual as the prevalent French attitude in Alsace-Lorraine was that the sooner the Germans were removed the better. Although 12-year-old Piete Kuhr's descriptions of 'our' 149th Regiment's 4 August 1914 departure from Schneidemühl station are initially upbeat, 'the crowds shouted, "Hip, Hip Hurray"', a different tone develops, 'An old lady wailed loudly: "Paul! Where is my darling Paul?"'. Seeing her 'little red eyes, probably inflamed with crying[, Piete] made a quick prayer, "Dear God, protect this Paul! Give him back to her"'.[31]

Children who were personally affected by a father or relative's departure retained the memory of this moment of rupture into old age. Not quite 4 years old, Georges Creux considered 13 August 1914, the day his father left, marked the day 'his' war started. Their agonising separation was his first childhood memory.[32] The colours of the Metro stops as they journeyed to the train station and the two tears sliding down her mother's cheeks made an indelible impression upon 6-year-old Simone de Beauvoir; she was however, she realised later, too young to connect her father's October 1914 departure with his possible death. She simply believed that God would protect him – which He, or at least a medical condition, did.[33] Louise Weill, aged 14, seemed almost surprised to find herself 'choking with emotion' when, on 2 August, she bade her brother-in-law good-bye.[34]

Most British children experienced their father's departure later in the war. James Thirsk, too young to fully comprehend what was happening, wrote how his father's departures became almost ritualised. Awaiting the cab for the station, Lieutenant Thirsk always entertained his children by solemnly putting on his puttees, 'to us this was a hilarious ritual', all the while James' mother was 'holding back the tears that would upset Dad.'[35] Then aged 10, Lucy Neale clearly remembered the last time she said goodbye to her father, 31-year-old Sergeant Harry. Her mother Alice was too distraught to accompany her husband to the station and eight decades later, Lucy could still recall how tightly she held Harry's hand. When he gently extricated it, he told her it was time to go back home. Turning round, 'He was still waving when I went and that was the last time I ever saw him.'[36] Like Simone, their mothers' grief struck all these children. Teenage Cecil Hewitt noted his father (a London Chief Inspector of Police)'s loss of composure when Cecil's brother Harold left for the first time, 'The occasion of his departure for France remains in my memory indelibly distressing to this day ... My father knew only too well that anyone going up the line at that time [late 1916] stood a poor chance of surviving and when Harold said good-bye, I was severely shaken to see my father embrace him in tears.'[37]

Although for many children a soldier's departure, be it that of a relative or part of a collective exodus, was striking, some children were themselves removed from home as a consequence of the war. Robert 'M', aged 3, was evacuated from Amiens in autumn 1914 and remembered how, travelling alone, he was 'picked up and plonked into a train through the Assistance Publique' which was removing children living close to the Front Line.

> First I rocked up at Denfert-Rochereau [Paris]. I was held there for eight days and then hop, into another train. Then I was dumped at Moulins and taken by horse and wagon to Bourbon-l'Archambault where someone came to collect me. I was deposited in the middle of the night at a huge farm and I was so cold after 33kms in that wagon that they put me in front of a fire to try to warm me up and I started to sob, crying as I have never since cried.[38]

Only seeing his mother once a year throughout the war, Robert soon barely recognised her.

When the Bichon-Freys took their three children from Mulhouse to their grandmother in Switzerland in 1914, neither side anticipated the length of their separation. Having settled their children, the parents returned, supposedly briefly, to Mulhouse, only to find that when they wished to join their children, the border was sealed. Born in 1912, Eliane always remembered her distress at barely recognising her parents following their 1918 reunion. Even communication between parents and children was impossible as all (heavily censored) correspondence had to be conducted in gothic German script. The heartbroken parents poured all their love and anguish into making toys in anticipation of their children's longed-for return. Eliane described in minute detail the lead soldiers and fort meticulously prepared for her brother, her lovingly constructed dolls' house, its furniture a replica of the family's own, not to mention a complex, fully functioning model railway – she realised that all her parents' energies had been devoted to their absent children with whom they had no contact for over four years.[39] Some arrangements were voluntary, other evacuations were part of an official Franco-German agreement.

Tales of Belgian refugees in Great Britain are well-known. Few British readers are aware that 499,137 French people (including approximately 150,000 children) from the ten wholly or partially Occupied French Départments (counties) were either forced or permitted to leave their homes. Known as 'Rapatriés (Repatriates) they were circuitously transported via Germany and Switzerland before being deposited once again in France, primarily in Evian on Lake Geneva. While many mothers accompanied their children, sometimes also taking responsibility for children whose mothers were refused permission to leave, some travelled with grandparents, others with neighbours, including 'a 3-year-old girl surnamed Sauvage [who] had been picked up in a cellar' during the first bombardment of Lens. Her mother was far from alone in having 'gone mad'. Jenny Huart, aged 14, was among several teenagers who arrived in sole charge of, in Jenny's case, six tubercular siblings.[40] Medical authorities were aghast at children's traumatised state, some had seen their parents killed or deported, but also at their 'deplorable' health; dire living conditions endured for years, malnutrition, and, finally, long overcrowded journeys all took immense toll. To many repatriates' embarrassment, a stringent disinfecting policy led to all clothes being immediately boiled in a steriliser for fifteen minutes.[41] Although understandable, such treatment must have increased many repatriates' sense of dislocation – and feature in memoirs.

Sadly, we are now all too familiar with images of starving children living in war zones, sights which were distressingly common in wartime Evian. Occasionally whole convoys consisted of malnourished children aged between 2 and 12; on average, children from the Occupied Zone weighed 7 per cent less at age 4 and 18 per cent less at age 15 than peers in Free France, graphically described as 'frog-like' with 'small, skinny chests with deep holes dug out between their ribs, protruding backbones

... poor emaciated skeletons the like of which you have neither seen nor known'. Moved by 'the distress of children who do not laugh, children who cry silently, whose tears flow soundlessly down their small hollow cheeks', few adults could understand the psychological damage inflicted upon these youthful victims of man's inhumanity to man.[42]

Although there is photographic evidence of repatriated children's arrival in Evian, only one written testimony has been traced, that of Germaine Paruit (b.1900), daughter of bourgeois shopkeepers from Sedan (occupied throughout the war). Sensitive and well-educated Germaine's diary provides valuable insights not only into living cheek-by-jowl with the occupier, but also her December 1917 journey to Evian.[43] After three years of brutal occupation and multiple privations, despite being 1m 70cm tall, she weighed only 45kg; her worried parents requested the occupiers' permission for Germaine and her sister Suzanne to leave Sedan.

Having accepted the considerable (and hidden) costs of the journey and the restrictions which included not a scrap of paper nor even a writing instrument, the sisters were allocated places on a departure anticipated in approximately late November 1917.

> A sad day as this is the day [12 December] we leave. Those who are staying envy those who are leaving and those who are leaving would now rather be staying. Already we can see people going with their bundles. It's time to say goodbye. Everyone around is looking sad but we must go. A policeman is waiting outside the door; he pins a number on us, I am 93, Suzanne 94.

Marched to an old factory transformed,

> into a barracks ... I put all my packages on a desk; they are gone through item by item while I am being strip-searched, even the inside of my mouth and my hair is checked. When I come out of the cubicle, all our stuff is scattered over the table and some of our food has been stolen and my coffee cup broken.

To Germaine's disgust, 'some children had had the boxes of powdered milk supplied by the Americans for the journey stolen. Everyone was so outraged by the barbaric behaviour of the Germans, strip-searching, checking in women's hair, the soles of their feet to ensure that nothing was written on them.' After hours of hanging around and what passed as a sparse meal grudgingly provided, despite having been paid for in advance,

> Eventually we were piled into the train – the coach was freezing. Thank goodness we had paid for second class as the seats have a little padding. We left Sedan at 2.15 am. The train was unheated and there was no light either, so we could not even see where we were until it was daylight.

For thirty-six hours, the train meandered through Occupied France and part of Germany, 'We were given one cup of coffee and one portion of noodles; there was a baby of a year old in our carriage and even she didn't get anything to eat – even though it was promised.' Finally, at the German-Swiss border, to Germaine's outrage they were forced to hand over the small amount of French money they had been allowed to take in exchange for 'billets de ville'; 'the swine, they told us we could take 27 francs but only to steal it from us. Our last impression of the Boche was as bad as all the other ones.' [44]

Germaine's first impression of the Swiss city of Basel and its welcoming population were as positive for this teenager who had endured years of deprivation as the last one of the Boche was negative, 'The station was decorated with French flags and banners proclaiming, "You are most welcome", "Safe journey back to France". There were nurses to tend the sick and help with the young children.' Germaine was overwhelmed, by the

> delicious [meat] not sausage, snow white bread, a large apple each and as much coffee and hot milk as we could drink. It was such a wonderful feast and then the children were given a cake, sweets and chocolates. We were all so touched by the warmth of the welcome.

Living up to their nation's reputation for compassion in wartime, Swiss children took young repatriates' plight to heart. Teachers in francophone Switzerland encouraged pupils to send toys and gifts and knit for children now living just across the border who had suffered so much. In January 1915, a shipment of toys was sent from Les Brenêts (Neuchatel) to Evian. The teacher's letter explained, 'In one box, you will find a tiny purse inside a saucepan that contains the savings of a very small boy'.[45]

Having left Basel, the Swiss authorities now assumed responsibility for the repatriates. Deeply impressed, Germaine reported how army medics and nurses patrolled the train 'to check that everyone is all right and see if we need anything. There is electricity and the carriages are warm. Every station we go through there are crowds cheering us…people shout, "Vive la France"…Every time we pull up at a station, there is coffee and hot soup waiting for us…Such a welcome – we who are so used to abuse can hardly believe what is happening.' After a long stop in welcoming Lausanne for more refreshments and a 'briefing', the repatriates glimpsed Free France just across Lake Geneva.

Once in Evian, 'We are almost mad with happiness. Chasseurs alpins come to meet us at the station, the bells are rung, so many people have turned out to greet us and banners proclaiming, "Welcome home" "Long live France" are everywhere.' Although it was now 10 pm, the exhausted travellers were 'marched with drums to the Casino [where] the orchestra plays the Marseillaise and we sing and cry … The mayor of Evian welcomes us then it is time for the formalities.' Perhaps with more eagerness to gather information than sensitivity to travellers' exhaustion and emotional fragility, 'we are taken to another office where we are asked to tell everything we know about what is happening militarily at Sedan, munitions, railway traffic, food, troop morale etc. I am so exhausted I can barely stand. It is after 2 am.' As the teenagers had been traveling continuously since leaving their home and parents four days' earlier and with their final destination still unknown, such an interrogation may have been better postponed.

Initially resilient, Germaine appreciated the beauty and hospitality of the small spa town, bought a notebook in order to resume her diary-keeping as well as postcards as souvenirs. But, as the temperature plummeted to minus 18C, surrounded by well-meaning but nevertheless strangers, fearful for her parents in Sedan and uncertain about the future, she expressed relief that their mother could not see her lonely daughters in their donated second-hand clothes. 'What a sad Christmas Eve – one we will remember.'

An intimate view of the war: Children's diaries.

Germaine's diary is a rare, vital resource. Nevertheless, any historian using children's diaries and writings as source material has to be aware of a potential guiding adult hand. Of this section's main diarists, Lucie

Congar suggested that her two younger children, Yves (b.1904) and Marie-Louise (b.1902), should keep war diaries; however, Yves' spelling, grammar, and child-like voice – at times one can almost hear him giggling, at others the sense of juvenile outrage is striking (he matures noticeably during the four years), would indicate that she 'interfered' relatively little in what was being written. Their contemporary Piete Kuhr's 'mother has advised me to write a diary about the war; she thinks it will be of interest to me when I am older'. However, as early as 16 September 1914, Piete's mother is critical of the diary which should be more 'heroic'. [46] Exactly two years later, Piete's mother is still more disdainful. Her daughter ripostes, 'actually you have not for a long time wanted me to go on with it' – but 'go on with it' she does, until the bitter end. Elisabeth Sczuka (b.1904)'s schoolmaster father encouraged her to keep a diary during their long internment in Siberia. On the other hand, neither Germaine Paruit (b.1900) nor Henriette Thiesset (b.1902) mentions parental encouragement.

Irrespective of any adult guidance, children's diaries provide a unique, intimate view of *their* war. The French translation for a personal diary is 'intimate journal'; aware of its value to her and fearful, at times of heightened tension between occupier and occupied, of its loss, Henriette sewed hers into her underwear, subconsciously stressing its intimacy while the Congar children buried theirs in their garden when Sedan was bombed in late 1918.[47] Although some diaries consist of little more than copied facts with no audible child's voice, the best make frequently disturbing, occasionally entertaining reading. They provide insight into what it was like to experience war as a child.

In 1914, the very name Sedan, home to Marie-Louise and Yves Congar and Germaine Paruit, aroused deep passions in both France and Germany; for the French, Sedan reminded them of the humiliating capture of Napoleon III and the rout of the French Army; for Germany, it was the site of their greatest victory in the 1870–71 Franco-Prussian war, some French historians arguing that it was here that the seeds of the First World War were sown. Sedan Day, 2 September, was a German national holiday never more enthusiastically celebrated than in 1914 as news had just broken of the great German victory over the Russian Army at Tannenburg. At the (compulsory for schoolchildren) Sedan Day church service, Piete felt the pastor conflated both victories claiming, 'God had stood by our gallant soldiers and blessed their weapons'.[48]

Although 10-year-old Yves' diary opens on 27 July 1914 with a summary of events following 'Archduke Ferdinand's assassination and rumblings about war', he gets into his stride on 25 August: this diary will tell 'a dark and tragic story' of life under the heel of a 'cruel' occupier.[49] Inevitably the perspective is juvenile; his amazement when his mother wakes him, telling him, 'put your [lead] soldiers away, the Germans aren't far away.' Yves was outraged by the advancing Boche (the name used by all young diarists in the Occupied Zone) armies' destruction of Sedan's churches and its shooting of dogs 'to make sure that they didn't bark and warn the French that the "Alleboches" were coming.' It is impossible to know whether humour was intentional, 'At lunchtime we weren't very hungry – nor was the dog.' Throughout the war, Yves was outraged by the continual destruction visited upon Sedan which rapidly became a vast logistics camp comprising hospitals, ammunition dumps, cinemas and brothels; French citizens had soldiers billeted on them and, as shortages increased in Germany, they were continuously stripped of possessions. The brutal treatment of Sedan and its citizens with constant hostage taking and deportations, including of Yves' father and brothers, are integral to the Congar/Paruit diaries.

Situated 67km from Verdun, the sounds of this and other battles were frequently audible but, to their frustration, neither Germaine nor the Congars – nor indeed Henriette who lived 20km from the Somme front line – had any idea which way any particular battle was going. Almost immediately, all Occupied Zone diarists relate of being starved of reliable news. On 20 October 1914, Germaine wrote that the ever-lengthening list of interdictions imposed upon civilians included possessing/reading French, English or Belgian newspapers. Although the occupiers published *La Gazette des Ardennes* (1 November 1914 to 8 November 1918), this was never seen as being anything other than a propaganda tool; 'the lying paper is out again' (Henriette, 26 November 1914); children were as thirsty for news from 'their side' as their elders.[50] On 2 April 1915, Yves was 'still without news and this diary must be unpleasant to read but it tells of life in the Occupied Zone and life in the Occupied Zone is unpleasant.'[51] On one occasion, 14 January 1916, the Congars glimpsed a genuine French newspaper as a French aeroplane dropped a rapidly confiscated batch. After years of 'it is reported that...' followed by news of French disasters, Marie-Louise automatically distrusted information circulated by the occupier, doubting reports of the Russian Revolution (19 March 1917) and also what is now called Operation Michael, 'shame on those who swallow their lies' (25 March 1918).[52] As is frequently the case, it is Piete who sees her way most clearly through the fog of war reporting; following two articles concerning the sinking of the *Lusitania*, she noted with, 'Two opinions, one saying this, the other saying that *I* [to her mother's displeasure] preferred to write nothing.' (1 July 1915)

As early as September 1914, the lack of newspapers made Henriette in Ham, 'more aware of our isolation. Without letters, without newspapers, we feel ever more remote from our family and compatriots whom we cannot even visit'.[53] The need to seek permission and *laissez-passer*, more often withheld than granted, to visit relatives in adjacent occupied areas, was a frequent irritation to those in Occupied France. Communicating with Free France was hazardous. On 25 December 1914, Sedanais had been warned, 'all the carrier pigeons are to be killed under pain of imprisonment or fines', (Yves). On 14 July 1916, Yves reported, 'Mr Busson, director of the gas factory has been shot for communicating with his wife via carrier pigeon. His sublime courage is an example to us, he died shouting "Vive la France"', then in a voice that hints at juvenile war-weariness, 'There is nothing more to be said about it, I've said it all.' The next day, 'the cemetery is out of bounds for 5 days for fear of patriotic demonstrations but as soon as it re-opens we will all be there with flowers for murdered Mr Busson.'

While Yves constantly prayed for and anticipated French victories, the pragmatic Germaine is unsure what to hope for, noting presciently on 2 February 1916, 'if the Germans are forced to retreat they will turn their rage on [the] civilian population.' Volunteering at the local hospital, Piete neatly sums up the victory dilemma, 'On how many nations exactly is God to bestow victory. I would be only too glad if He would make these severely wounded men whole again.' (20 July 1915)

Yves' comment that 'Life in the Occupied Zone is unpleasant' was not an exaggeration. Children in these areas had intimate contact with an enemy frequently billeted upon them. On 3 September 1914, a 'Captain Caspari demanded we [the Congars] would billet men'. Two days later, an 'officer called Captain Nemnick [is] billeted on us. He takes tea and invites 8 others to have it with him. He also takes wine and made us cook 4 chickens. In the morning the batman ate a whole one.' Yves is disdainful, Nemnick 'was so scared that he made his batman and a lieutenant sleep with him.' Yves also worried about the burden such billeting placed upon his beloved grandparents. In another area of Sedan, Germaine's family were also coping with the misery of sharing their home with the occupier. While Yves listed the food that the soldiers were consuming, 'They eat our salad and our potatoes' (10 September 1914), Germaine described in detail the damage inflicted upon families' possessions. Aghast that her and her sister's communion dresses had been stolen and their games damaged, she described how soldiers had relieved themselves on their possessions. (February 1918).

Henriette understood that the lascivious officer billeted upon them was seeking to frighten her with stories of French girls being 'harnessed to the plough' and others being forced to work in the fields until they 'dropped from exhaustion' (26 April 1915), a point made by Marie-Louise (27 December 1917). Pre-pubescent Piete also had to learn to protect herself, 8 August 1915, 'I'm just furious with the [billeted] orderly [who tried to fondle her]. It is the first time a man has looked on me as a girl.'

In spring 1915, Piete's grandmother was ill, forcing the 13-year-old to assume all household duties. 20 March 1915, 'To my horror, during this time we had soldiers billeted on us. A captain and his batman … I made breakfast for the captain and his batman. Sometimes I really groaned because I had to do everything before school.' With Grandmother recovered, Piete was less bothered when on 2 August 1915, 'Every family in the town with a spare room [now] has billetees. The field-greys go from house to house with billeting notices in their hands. They came to us too.' With these being her countrymen, Piete sometimes enjoyed their presence, but, with the compassion that is a hallmark of her diary she concluded, 'We listen to their stories from the Front … In a few days' time the soldiers will probably be killed.' Increasingly outspoken in her anti-war attitude, on 14 July 1917, she told the major billeted on them that 'the soldiers now all looked wretched and dirty and had tatty uniforms and only one wish, to be able to go home.' Aware of what her jingoistic mother would think about the increasingly pacifist diary, she adds, 'I can't possibly show her what I am writing.'

As food shortages increased, food became an obsession. All six diarists understandably bewail and record its lack, almost as though this will negate their hunger. As early as 26 September 1914 with bread, so essential to the French diet, diminishing, Yves bewailed, 'These accursed

Boches are changing our diet'. On 4 November 1914, 'They are leaving us to die of hunger. Never mind - after all we are French and if we have to die, we will have died and France will be victorious.' No month goes by without some mention of food or lack thereof, and, for Yves, increasing anxiety about whether the few crops they were able to grow in their allotment would thrive. With elation he wrote on 4 February 1915,

> the USA are going to send us flour and the Spaniards dried vegetables ... Kind people. A Boche started to protest but a notice was put up on the door of the mill saying 'The German authorities are forbidden from entering this mill under pain of diplomatic complications with America.'

The 'amazing' news that America was coming into the war was considered a mixed blessing, 'we will now sacrifice the rations we were sent', (14 April 1917). Generally dismissive of Sedan's mayor whom he sees as supine, he was impressed by his attempts to redistribute land so that everyone might grow a few crops, 'Now we see even the very richest people ... dragging a wheelbarrow. It's a bit sad but there is a delicious irony.' While food does not feature quite as extensively in Germaine's diary as in the younger Yves and Henriette's, she too mentions constantly queuing for ever-diminishing rations, American generosity, and records her own and her families' weight loss.

Food shortages, largely caused by the British blockade, were a key topic in Piete's diary. The grandmother's constant, increasingly helpless, attempts to feed her grandchildren distressed Piete almost as much as her own hunger,

> Something really shook me, I saw an old woman sitting on the coal box crying ... Her thin white hair was gathered into a meagre bun and she looked so hopeless, so terribly sad ... I didn't recognise the woman on the coal-box. Suddenly I realised it was Grandma. I was paralysed with shock ... I shall never forget how Grandma sat on the coal-box crying [because there was nothing for the children to eat.]' (20 August 1917).

Piete was not alone in sometimes stealing food, on one occasion a 'sugar snail' from a cakeshop, 'Perhaps I shall regret it later' (2 September 1917).

In Occupied France, children stole food especially if soldiers were on manoeuvres, accepting that they were thereby taking significant risks. Children did not see these actions against the occupiers as transgressions, rather that the food growing in French fields was rightly theirs. Pierre Bach from Neuville-Saint-Rémy wrote almost proudly in his school exercise book for 1917 that he could have been severely punished by the Boche but he 'did not regret it at all'.[54]

The occupiers frequently put youngsters to work, their personal rebellion was to work as slowly as possible; 12-year-old René Henrion (Meuse) proudly wrote (7 June 1916), 'As we knew that the harvest was for them, we worked as badly as possible. Pointless to toil for the King Of Prussia.' The fury of the 'Commandanture' and the announcement *Nothing has been done*' increased these totally disempowered children's satisfaction.[55] While those in unoccupied lands could contribute to the war effort by being Soldiers of the Soil or earning proficiency badges, those in the Occupied Zones were forced to labour free of charge for the hated Boche.

French, Belgian, (although no Belgian child's diary has yet been traced) and German civilians, faced continuous requisitioning, 'I have already coaxed out of Grandma a great 20 liter copper boiler … Now cartridges are being made out of it' (Piete 21 September 1914). Children's diaries are frequently a litany of what has been taken from them: on 16 February 1915, '4000 palliasses, 8000 tea towels, 4000 washbowls', to which were added animals, balls of wool, shallots, garlic, even wool from citizens' mattresses for which, according to Germaine (13 November 1917), they were eventually given kelp in return. Semi-precious metals were in high demand; 'Now they want the church bells and organs' (2 August 1917 Yves). To Sedanais' horror, church bells, some dating back to the seventeenth century, began being systematically destroyed in October 1917. Despite his impressively increasing vocabulary, Yves struggled for words to describe this latest outrage, 'infamy, ignominy' seemed inadequate. Along with losing what would now be termed Sedan's cultural heritage, there were constant demands for money which, to Yves' fury, Sedan's mayor generally paid. 10 July 1915, 'Sedan rolls over and asks its businesses to pay up. Shame on you French who ask other French to pay to kill fellow Frenchmen.'[56] The boy may not have understood that the mayor could have been hoping to avoid further reprisals as the sums demanded were frequently to 'atone' for acts of civil disobedience. Hostages were regularly taken to cow the civilian population – both

Congars and Germaine talk about these hostages including their own fathers; thus, the mayor's decision may have owed more to pragmatism than Yves with his black-and-white vision of the world could understand. Four years older, Germaine sees the dilemma more clearly, 'whether to give the Germans what [goods] they demand or refuse and risk terrible fines which would give them the money they need to buy from neutral countries' (12 September 1917).

In one respect Yves was prescient beyond his years. In a long entry composed between 4 and 7 January 1917, he correctly anticipates how those in Free France will turn on those from the Occupied Zones seeing them as 'Boches du Nord', who worked for and supplied the enemy. He pleads with his compatriots, 'Oh, Frenchmen do not come and accuse us after the war saying, 'shame on you demi-Boche who worked for them' as we will reply, 'why did you abandon this earth which you had vowed to defend to the death?'

All children delight in small acts of rebellion and Yves was no exception:

Yesterday I was going with Robert [elder brother] to Grandmother and as is my custom to annoy the Boches when I saw one I decided to decorate him with a campaign medal and so I spat at him and it landed on the right-hand side of his chest. As he was just an enlisted man, he didn't say anything to me. (12 March 1915)

Marie-Louise proudly drew Yves' actions in her diary. Spitting, pilfering and hiding food which the Congar children and their father did by 'making a cache for our potatoes so that the Boches can't take them' (26 October 1914), gave subjugated children some sense of empowerment.

Dogs proved an ongoing area of conflict between Occupier and Occupied as well as a money-raising ruse. Germaine, Yves and Henriette mention that taxes (60 francs in Sedan, 20 in Ham) are being levied on dogs; pets of those who could not, or would not, pay are shot, the bourgeois Congars may have been among the refusers. The first hint of pending disaster came on 18 April 1915, 'Poor Kiki might have to be killed.' The whole entry for 15 May 1915 is devoted to Kiki: 'they killed my dog'. Two poems are composed in honour of Kiki, 'martyred' for her country. Perhaps as a form of grief work, he writes in some detail of the euthanasia for which the family paid, thereby guaranteeing Kiki a peaceful end; it is hard not to be moved when the child writes, 'we buried her when she was 'still warm'. Yves' nephew remembered his uncle still talking tenderly about Kiki eighty years after her demise.

The 'execution' of pets was not restricted to Sedan and figure in numerous children's writings, most chillingly of all in Henriette's. She describes the 'bloody executions' in disturbing detail (7 April 1916). Owners had to take their pets to the Sébastopol Distillery where those who could serve as rat-catchers in the trenches were requisitioned; the others were simply bludgeoned to death. Dogs in nearby St Sulpice had been 'chucked into the Seine with a rock around their necks'. The outraged child picked up on the suggestion that the Germans kept the best dogs to make 'into sausages'. All children who wrote about the killing of dogs saw the animals as 'war heroes' and their brutal deaths numbered among the atrocities so many of them regularly witnessed.

It would have been no consolation to French children to know that, in Germany, dogs were requisitioned to 'serve' in the army as rat-catchers and as First Aid dogs, a fate that befell Piete's friend Dora's dog, Prince. On 3 February 1916, a tearful Dora told her that Prince was to be trained as a Red Cross dog, 'I loved this slim Dobermann and no one else. When I left, I laid my forehead against Prince's head and kissed him … It is funny that you can suffer as much over a dog as over a human being.' Luckier than the French dogs, Prince nevertheless suffered for his 'war service'. Returned on 22 July 1917, probably because he had outlived his usefulness, 'You wouldn't recognise him, he is very shy and if anyone cracks a whip, his whole body trembles. He really thinks it is a shot.'

Dogs were not the only cause of juvenile anguish. The hostage taking and deportation of men and youths (their own or friends' fathers and brothers) to act as slave labour in Germany was a constant source of terror. Having deported local men, the occupier used POW labour in and around Sedan and the levels of malnutrition and the brutality inflicted upon POWs traumatised the youthful diarists. On 2 January 1917, both Yves and Germaine give detailed accounts of the arrival of Romanian prisoners. Yves, 'today these living corpses that were once soldiers arrived at Sedan'. In images that still shock, both children graphically describe the starving, bleeding Romanians stumbling under the blows rained down on them by their captors. As the horrified Sedanais watched this parade of pitiful humanity, they endeavoured to give what little food they had – which led to a stampede with the prisoners 'turning on each other for a crumb of bread' (Germaine). Yves highlights German brutality, with one soldier using the 'butt of his rifle as though he were a logger felling a tree'. When guards chuck empty cigarette boxes to the desperate prisoners who are fooled into believing these might contain a fag, Yves is distraught that the Germans see this as funny; Germaine notes the animal-like sounds emitting from the prisoners' throats. She understands how the incident has shaken women whose husbands/sons/loved-ones are held as POWs. Might they be being treated in similar fashion? Both children are proud of Sedanais who tried to share what little food they had with the prisoners, 'We will be hungry tonight' wrote Germaine while Yves detailed the fines imposed on those who were caught throwing food, not to mention the baker, who the next day refused to sell bread to the Germans. Her bread was 'reserved for Romanians and French'. Sedan was fined 50,000 marks for its humanitarian actions. The episode marks both diarists' loss of their last vestiges of innocence.[57]

My Enemy My Friend

Although not subjected to witnessing such acts of brutality, Piete was deeply distressed when, in October 1914, she discovered a camp holding predominantly Russian POWs on the outskirts of Schneidemühl. She and Gretel visit 'the little Russian [POW] cemetery to rake it and clear the graves of weeds'. Having completed their task, the girls stand to attention and Piete prayed, 'Dear God, Take these dead enemies into your care. For ever and ever. Amen.' On numerous occasions, sometimes accompanied by Gretel, Piete visited both the camp and the cemetery. On 19 March 1917, suffering herself from severe malnutrition,

> Just what do the 45,000 prisoners in the Russian camps eat, that's what I'd like to know. Gretel and I still go past the camp and put a few eatables through the fence when the guards are looking the other way. I think they look the other way on purpose.

In France, Marcelle Lerouge discovered that German soldiers were as human as French ones. Shown a cache of letters removed from dead Germans (these were scrutinised for possible military intelligence), there are hints that she realises that much of the negative propaganda fed to the French public about their enemies was simply that, although many in the Occupied Zone would have disagreed. The soldiers 'display no enmity towards us and do not speak of victory but of peace which they await eagerly.' One soldier's seemingly mundane letter particularly distressed her, 'His poor mother will never know that he died suffering from a head cold'. She sees the irony of letters destined for loved ones in Germany remaining in France and wonders if the reverse happens to letters from dead/captured French soldiers (2 June 1915).

Although there was nothing positive about the Congars' and Germaine's experiences, children in less strategically crucial areas than Sedan experienced the Occupation differently. In time, both sides shook down together. As early as May 1915, Henriette wrote quite affectionately about the German (Landsturm) billeted on them recognising that,

> He's not evil and even tries to help us a bit. He will buy things from the German grocer for us. He tries not to inconvenience us but comes and chats a bit in the evening to try to learn French and teach me a few words of German. I've bought a small dictionary and he makes me read, write and pronounce a few important words properly. He's quite old … and he is longing for the war to be over.

Aware where to place the blame, she goes on, 'the really guilty ones in Germany are the government and their protégés the officers who make the soldiers' lives hell and see them as objects.'[58]

To schoolteachers' horror, children could develop friendships with 'their' billeted (enlisted) soldier, who was often missing his children as much as the French ones were missing their father. When 12-year-old Pierre Jodion made a little speech thanking the Germans for the Christmas party and gifts organised for the children in Avioth (Meuse), his schoolmaster declared himself deeply saddened – but consoled himself that the errant Pierre came from a different village![59] Other teachers blamed 'fraternisation' either on the children's very young age or on mothers who were too friendly with the billeted Boche. No doubt René Lhermite's 3 January 1915 remarks would have found greater favour. Despite 'their' Germans having given the youngsters cakes and Christmas gifts, René thought about his 'own dear papa' who should have been at home with them while, whatever their short-term generosity, the Germans were our 'masters and our enemies'.[60]

Children in Free France became used to the sight of German POWs. Although she was only 5, Simone Pissis from Saint-Victor never forgot her first sight of them; previously terrified by tales of German bogeymen with their Pickelhaube and ogre-like bellies, she could not believe her eyes when a prisoner gang approached:

> They looked so young, hardly more than children themselves. And their uniforms were in tatters. And they were so thin, so pale, so fragile-looking…The boys who were going to throw stones at them, just dropped them. We just turned around and walked back in stunned silence. When the grown-ups asked what I had seen, I just burst into tears.[61]

Rather than something to fear, the 'enemy' is to be pitied.

Young Henri Dillot recorded his impressions of the 'Boches' who were working at a woodyard near to his grandparents. Having been taught to mind his manners, he would go into the workshop and say, 'Bonjour Boches'. He began to see them as *his* Boches. As friendship developed, the prisoners began to carve Henri toys. Although neighbours and friends told him to 'Chuck that away, it's from a Boche', his grandparents did not say anything and even if he did initially discard the item, he would retrieve it later. He would look at the prisoners' photos of their own children who were so often his age and (at least with hindsight) understood that he had become their surrogate child. Afterwards, 'however many times I was told that the Boche cut off children's hands I refused to believe it.'[62] Ironically, Henri had been told he was being sent to his grandparents in the country to prevent him having his hands cut off. He felt that the adult view of the Germans was nonsensical.

While many children observed or lived alongside POWs, some 2,500 children from East Prussia suffered this fate.[63] Elisabeth Sczuka (b.1904) lived with her younger sister Hildegarde and widowed schoolmaster father, Johann, in Popowen (now Poland, then Germany), close to the Russian border. While French children dreaded the arrival of the Uhlans, Eastern German children dreaded the Cossacks. On 28 August 1914, 'a cyclist arrived from Protsken, "Children, go back indoors, the Russians are coming," he yelled. We tore across the fields and reached the canal. While we were doing this, the Russians surrounded the cyclist and started beating him up [and killed him] … We will never forget the sight.' A catalogue of atrocities that Elisabeth has heard about or witnessed follows, 'The entire district was burning day and night' (7 September 1914). With the villagers taking refuge in the school, 'day and night Russian patrols swarmed around'.

A GUIDING HAND

On 14 September 1914, along with many others, the Sczuka family were arrested, 'armed soldiers escorted us to the station'. Twenty days in a cattle truck to an unknown destination followed; their first meal was only provided on 18 September. The journey acquired a nightmare quality: lice, the soldiers' constant companion, soon proliferated and water for washing, if it could be found, had to be used by four or five people.[64] As the train ploughed ever further east, the word '"Where?" was going round and round in everyone's head.' Child-like, she longed for an 'Aladdin's magic lamp' to assist her compatriots.[65] With the guards having stolen most of their possessions, the deportees arrived in Krasnojarsk (Siberia). She feels that they were considered 'trophies of war', but trophies with which no one quite knew what to do.

Krasnojarsk, a former military base built in the aftermath of the Japanese–Russian war, was one of the largest internment camps in Russia. Perched on a barren plateau, it was soon surrounded by barbed wire. The enemy within soon proved to be infectious diseases and during the winter of their first year's internment, Elisabeth lists the numbers of fatalities but also how internees found ways of adapting to life behind the barbed wire. Held as POWs but without military rank, no one knew what to do with them – were they dependent on the Russian War or Home Offices? In the winter of 1914–15, life 'shrinks to hunger, want and death'. Exacerbated by extreme cold (with temperatures below -45 degrees Celsius), their lack of defined status constantly impacted upon them. Frequently 'lodged in the prison camp [where] we get rations, but at times [we are] forced to seek accommodation outside and lose rations' (11 February 1916), which they then have to buy for themselves.

Like countless children, Elisabeth longed for Christmas – and in similar fashion to Yves in Sedan who counted each wartime Christmas under the enemy's boot, she noted that Christmas 1915 was her 'second' in captivity. The precious tree which the prisoners erected kept the hope of better Christmases to come alive as did singing 'Stille Nacht'.

In spring 1916, the family definitively left the camp for nearby Narwalsk (Norilsk) where, as Elisabeth acknowledged, their slightly elevated social status enabled them to purchase some of the necessities of life. Her heart bled for the poorest families who have nothing, 'Mrs. Gardaike came to Dad in tears and told him of her sufferings. Hunger is so painful that here in Siberia a child born today does not have milk. Dad gave her 5 rubles. He can't help everyone'.[66]

Following her schoolmaster father's suggestion, Elisabeth recorded her gradual return to life. Rather than any palpable Russophobia, the awakening adolescent observed and was intrigued by her surroundings. She is struck by how, with their 'fair hair and blue eyes, [Siberians] are far from the barbarians of German discourse [...] We have had the opportunity to enter into closer relations with [them] and to get to know their customs' (25 March 1917).

In May 1918, the family was 'liberated' under the terms of the treaty of Brest-Litovsk. Initially traumatised, this child POW, had come to identify with the 'enemy' amid whom she had lived for over three years. During their two-year return journey, mainly in carts and troikas, she was touched by Russian generosity, 'If we are not frozen, we owe it to the pitiful Russian women who gave us furs and felt boots. Everywhere, we were welcomed in a hospitable way. Far from the Front [these people] know nothing of the hatred of war.'

Back in Popowen in October 1920, schoolmaster Johann was accused of being a collaborator (an accusation also levied against 15-year-old deportee Emma Knuth whose parents had initially found it hard to believe that the invading Russians who had 'behaved in a peaceful way' would harm them) and a petition for his expulsion from his school organised. With his name eventually cleared, in 1922, he was awarded the German Croix du Mérite. By now, Elisabeth really did not know who was her enemy and who her friend.

In late November 1918, shivering in their 'old thin coat[s]', and cardboard shoes, accompanied by Gretel, 16-year-old Piete, now grieving for the dead young airman with whom she had fallen in love, trudged through deep snow to the Sandsee woods 'to cut some spruce and other greenery for an Advent wreath [...] I could no longer feel my toes for snow' on this 'typical last-but-one day of November'. Their ultimate destination not 'our "heroes' cemetery"', but one whose distance seemed 'never-ending'. As dusk fell it was nevertheless not too dark to 'read the names of the dead, not only Russians ... but also French and English and [...] Mohammedans'...In death all are, so to speak, just like the others.' Exactly three years and eleven months after she first defied her mother by writing her war diary in her own words rather than reproducing the jingoistic pro-German 'lies' her mother had guided her to write, Piete paid homage to all who had suffered in the war. Reverently she placed 'our green fir wreath' on an unknown Frenchman's grave. With him representing all whom the war had destroyed, she vowed, 'My thoughts are with you, and my tears, every day'.

Piete would have instantly related to the words of a Russian peasant woman who, like many others, had thronged to Krasnojarsk to gawp at the infamous 'Germanskis,' including Elisabeth Sczuka, as they began their two-year journey home from captivity, 'Eto Llyudi Kak i my [Why, they are people like us]'.[67]

Unintended Consequences

When in 1909 Baden-Powell passed the 'girl problem' over to his sister Agnes, he would never have imagined that a decade later, in recognition of Girl Guides' role at the heart of MI5, they would serve at the 1919 Peace Conference and witness the signing of the Peace Treaty. Similarly, the education reformers of the late nineteenth century could not have foreseen that their vision of universal literacy would, for the very first time, enable ordinary children to write about this most terrible war in their own handwriting, using their own words, and rendering audible their own voices.

CHAPTER THREE

'What was Done to Us Was Wrong'[1]

Children were constantly being told that the war was being fought for them, to ensure that they did not grow up under the heel of a vicious oppressor, that those fighting overseas were doing so to keep them from harm. Yet war was visited upon society's most vulnerable citizens, on some occasions as the direct result of enemy action, on others from actions taken by children's own governments. Using, wherever possible, the children's own voices or of those who had contact with them, the stories of these innocent victims can be brought at times graphically, almost always painfully, to life.

RMS *Lusitania*: Precious Cargo

At the entrance to New York Harbour's Pier 54 on 1 May 1915, passengers were preparing for Cunard Line *Lusitania*'s crossing to Liverpool; a picture vendor was busy touting his wares: black-bordered, 'Pictures of the *Lusitania's last* departure. It's your last chance to buy one, folks'.[2] We will never know if anyone noticed his use of the word 'last'. Other more informed warnings than this about the mighty ship's 202nd crossing had been received – and discounted.

Meanwhile *Lusitania*'s captain, William Turner, had been breakfasting on the bridge. Glancing at the *New York Tribune,* he espied on an inside page adjacent to Cunard's advertisement for this crossing by the 'fastest and largest steamer now in Atlantic Service', a black-bordered warning first issued by the Imperial German Embassy in Washington on 22 April 1915. This reminded travellers that a,

> state of war exists between Germany and her allies and Great Britain and her allies ... vessels flying the flag of Great Britain or any of her allies are liable to destruction ... and travellers sailing in the war zone of ships of Great Britain or her allies do so at their own risk.'

As a result, two hours later, telegrams addressed 'to prominent passengers' started arriving in *Lusitania*'s Marconi room which dealt with telegraphic and radio communications. These warned against sailing on *Lusitania*. Realising that these originated from a newspaper (the American press was not unanimously pro-Britain), they were held back while Turner sought instructions. Would the crossing be cancelled?[3] It would not, although departure would be delayed by 2½ hours to allow cargo, crew and passengers from SS *Cameronia*, (possibly suddenly requisitioned as a troopship) destined for Glasgow, to be transferred to *Lusitania*. Whatever the reason, another forty-one souls, including at least three children, were thus doomed. It was obvious that despite some looking nervous, no passengers heeded Germany's warnings. The band played rousing tunes, the turbines rotated and with 1,264 passengers (including 189 US, thus neutral, citizens of whom 128 perished), 693 crew and 3 German spies who had been apprehended and locked in a cabin, not to mention the unbeknownst to all but a very select few, 4 million .303 bullets, shrapnel shells, plus fuses for artillery shells, *Lusitania* sailed into the history books.[4]

On 4 June 1915, survivor Margaret Mackworth told *Western Mail* that she did not think she had 'ever seen so many small children on board a ship ... Everyone noticed it and commented on it.' *New York Times* (8 June 1915) quoted one stewardess' belief that there were a 'record number' of children. Saloon-class youngsters, accompanied by nannies and nurses who did their utmost to preserve the young lives entrusted to their care, even had their own nursery and dining-room.[5]

Nigel Booth: 'Nobody thought it would sink so soon.'[6]

Among the youngest of Margaret Mackworth's 'defenceless babies' was 8-month-old Canadian-born Nigel Booth. His parents originated from Leicestershire but had lived in Canada since 1913. In the spring of 1915, Emily Booth decided to visit her seriously ill mother and introduce Nigel to her family. With her husband Henry remaining in Canada, she and Nigel shared their second-class cabin with teenager Molly Mainman. Emily must have been delighted that Molly, who had younger siblings, was good with babies. So good, that Nigel owed her his life.

Learning of the disaster, Emily's sisters immediately rushed to the Cunard offices seeking news of Emily and Nigel's fate. None of the traumatised survivors arriving in Liverpool knew anything, saying it was all 'too horrible to explain', and that 'nobody had thought it would sink so soon'. It was soon obvious that although some passengers had initially jumped clear of the sinking vessel, many were sucked under. Fearing the worst, Emily's sisters returned home to discover a telegram; miraculously, Nigel had survived and was safe in Queenstown. As hopes that there would be news of Emily, or even a body to bury, receded, Nigel's aunt and uncle brought him back to his grandparents' home at Hugglescote Post Office to await his father's arrival from Ottawa. Cared for in the meantime by his Aunt Louisa, whom Henry married in August 1916, the reconstituted family braved the Atlantic again, returning to Canada where Nigel spent the rest of his relatively short life, dying in 1966. *The Coalville Times* (Leicestershire 14 May) had interviewed survivors including Molly Mainman who, having grabbed Nigel and being unable to find Emily, 'threw [him] into the arms of a boatman'. (Parenthetically, 16-year-old Molly lost both her parents and her two elder brothers leaving her to care for her younger twin siblings.)

Elizabeth 'Betty' Bretherton: 'likes to walk and talk.'[7]

American-born Betty was 15 months old when she, her 3-year-old brother Paul and their pregnant mother Norah bade their father farewell and embarked on a visit to Norah's family in Bexhill-on-Sea, Sussex. While many survivors subsequently recounted tales which demonstrate the best in human nature, Norah saw only the worst for, when the ship was struck, although Betty was with her, Paul was asleep in their second-class cabin. Norah's pleas to various male passengers to rush down for Paul fell on deaf ears, even among acquaintances. Increasingly frantic for both her children, she recalled, 'I forced [my] baby into some man's arms who had got to the stairs.' She then made her perilous way down for Paul. When they returned to the deck, although the man was still there, Betty was not. Anxious to save Paul, she tried to board one lifeboat only to be turned away and, but for the intervention of one Helen Secchi, would have been denied entry to a second, Lifeboat 13, which, belying its unlucky number, was rescued by government ship *Stormcock*. Norah may have looked enviously at 3-month-old Audrey Pearl who, with her 18-year-old nurse Alice Lines, was also aboard.[8]

On 10 May 1915, *The Cork Examiner* carried a poignant advertisement:

MISSING A BABY GIRL, 15 months old; very fair hair, curled; fit and rosy complexion; in white woollen jersey and white woollen leggings. Tries to walk and talk. Name Betty Bretherton.

It yielded no leads. With hope of finding Betty's body fading, and doubtless seeking consolation and help in caring for Paul, Norah continued to Sussex. Against the odds, Betty's body was recovered from the sea – the descriptive advertisement may have helped to identify her. No one will ever know whether the man had abandoned her or placed her in a lifeboat that subsequently sank. On 12 May, Betty was buried at The Ursuline Convent, Cork, where her aunt was a nun and her mother had been educated. According to Convent archives, 'the afflicted mother begged to have it [*sic*] buried here and the community would not refuse her the sad consolation.' Betty's headstone reminds passers-by to 'Suffer the Little Children to Come unto Me.'[9]

Barbara Anderson: 'I always knew that she loved me.'[10]

No doubt when Emily Anderson, five months pregnant with her second child, boarded *Lusitania*, her daughter, Barbara, was looking forward to spending her approaching third birthday with her English grandparents in Darlington. Having been born in America, this was probably her first visit to England and her mother had bought her a new dress for when she met her relations; she was allowed to wear this on one special shipboard occasion.

Interviewed for the last time three years before her death in 2005, Barbara, who never gave details that she could not personally remember, vividly described the moments before *Lusitania* left New York, 'I was standing at a railing looking down at all the people, trying to see my father. I am sure he waved up to me'. She firmly believed, 'If my father had seen the warning from the Germans, he would not have let us sail.[11] With so many children on board, she enjoyed the crossing. Their cabin made an indelible impression upon her, 'one bed was above the other', and she felt very grown-up, 'sitting at a very small table for two, opposite my mother, for our meals. I think it was on a balcony as I could see other people sitting at tables below us.' Barbara believed this table, facing a doorway leading to a corridor, almost certainly saved their lives 'because when we were torpedoed ... We just went flying out away from the table and out on the deck and the next thing I knew the first mate [Assistant Purser William Harkness] picked me up'. Far luckier than little Betty Bretherton, for whom no one would take responsibility, Harkness spotted Barbara clinging to the rail. 'Gathering [me] up in his arms, he leaped over the rail of the ship and into a life boat. My mother jumped and missed and they fished her out of the water.'[12] After terrifying hours at sea and having finally made land, mother and daughter set sail from Queenstown to Liverpool and onwards to Darlington.

Barbara's brother, Frank, born in September 1915, died in March 1916, Emily herself in 1917. Barbara retained and cherished memories of her mother, 'She was very kind. A good person. I was not with her long, but I do remember her and I'm glad that I can. Because no matter what happened I always knew that she loved me'. She kept Emily's last gift, a doll's pram, throughout her life. Sadly, her souvenir of the *Lusitania*, a dining-room spoon that she had been clutching when they were shipwrecked, was lost many years later, much to her chagrin.

Barbara remained with her grandparents, attending a local school. Then in December 1919, her now remarried father sent for his 7-year-old daughter. Despite her grandparents' and her own reluctance, she boarded *Lusitania*'s sister ship, *Mauretania*. She could not have guessed that it would be another fifty-five years before she returned to England. Perhaps due to their survivor status, she and three other *Lusitania* survivors were all seated at the captain's table.

A child as young as Barbara obviously could not travel alone and a companion was found,

> Oh, that woman was horrible! ... She was supposed to keep an eye on me until we got to New York. She said to me 'How do you expect to recognise your father when we get to New York? You won't remember him'... Of course I would recognise my father. When we got to New York, on Christmas Day, they were waiting ... on the pier. And I knew right away who my father was, and that woman tried to hold me back but I ran to him. And they had a doll for me, and they took me home.[13]

Helen Smith: 'Please, mister, will you take me with you?'[14]

A little girl wearing a white hat and clutching a doll became an iconic image of the *Lusitania* . Few were untouched by this photograph which simultaneously succeeded in portraying both childhood innocence and the dastardly Hun. That the young child was now an orphan increased the poignancy.

Six-year-old Helen had moved with her parents from Swansea to America before her first birthday. However, for the family which now included 6-month-old Hubert, the New World had not fulfilled its promise and Alfred and Elizabeth Smith decided to return to Wales. Elizabeth's sister-in-law, Cecelia Owens with her sons Reginald and Roland, would accompany them and visit family. The cousins played together throughout the crossing and at 2 pm on 7 May, 10-year-old Reginald asked his mother, who was still dining, if they could continue 'playing on deck … Helen is with us, and it is such fun!' The boys ran to rejoin Helen, who had remained on deck alone. At almost the precise moment as Reginald was talking to his mother, up on the ship's bridge, Captain William Turner received a dreaded telephone warning from the lookout, 'Torpedo coming on the starboard side!' *Lusitania* was hit at 2.12 pm.[15]

Clutching baby Hubert, Elizabeth, Alfred and Cecelia (who later recalled seeing 'Elizabeth running around frantically, with her hair falling loose around her shoulders'), separated as they searched for the three children of whom, in the stampede of terrified passengers, there was no sign.[16] Almost thrown into a lifeboat, which subsequently overturned, Cecelia spent hours in the water. Meanwhile, showing presence of mind beyond her six years, Helen who 'was at risk of being trampled', approached a lone gentleman (Toronto journalist Ernest Cowper).[17] Explaining she could not find her parents, she begged, 'please, mister, will you take me with you'. Assuring her he would be back, Cowper rushed to search (unsuccessfully) for lifebelts. When he returned, the relieved Helen exclaimed, 'You came back to me, just like you said you would!' Fearing that the ship was about to sink, Cowper picked Helen up, ran to the starboard deck and handed her into Lifeboat 13, one of only six lifeboats successfully lowered, apparently saying, 'She asked me to save her. Says she can't find her mother or father … but her grandparents'll be waiting for her in Liverpool.' With Ernest ordered into the boat, the men started rowing for their lives to try to escape the sinking liner's suction. While in the lifeboat Helen reportedly turned to the woman on whose knee she was sitting and said, 'If I can't find my Mamma and Daddy, I'll go with you ladies.'

In Queenstown, with his fears over Helen's parents' fate confirmed, Ernest served as her de facto guardian. A photograph of him holding the child appeared in dozens of newspapers. Against the odds, while still in Queenstown, Helen suddenly announced, 'Why here is Auntie!' Rather than being, as Ernest feared, a 'wealthy woman who read the story and wanted to adopt her,' this was in fact Cecelia. Seen as one of the heroes of the hour and with Helen's image splashed across newspapers on both sides of the Atlantic, Ernest was inundated with offers from people wanting to take Helen. Before returning to Canada, Ernest even 'received a letter from Queen Dowager Alexandra, asking me to take her to Sandringham, but I could not go as I did not know where the child was, and my wardrobe was not exactly fit for making calls on Queens living in royal palaces.' Even had his wardrobe been up to standard, he could not have obliged, Helen was now with her mother's family in Swansea who kept her out of the public eye.

Poignantly, it took Helen a long time to understand the terrible fate that had befallen her parents, her baby brother and her cousins, whose return she had been awaiting just as the torpedo struck. 'Everybody is sorry for me because my mummy and daddy have gone,' Helen told well-wishers, adding, 'they're coming on another boat'. She remained in touch with the man to whom she almost certainly owed her life. In the 1920s, he declared himself 'proud that she had received an award for academic excellence'. Interviewed on the centenary of the sinking, Helen's daughter Elizabeth remembered, 'She was terrified of water, she had a fear of water.' She added that in keeping with the mores of the day, 'She'd been encouraged to forget and most of what we know comes from letters from Mr Cowper who stayed in contact with my mother, and from books.'[18]

Frank Hook: 'Pitched overboard'; Elsie Hook – 'I shall bring you a rose after lunch.'[19]

When Elsie and Frank Hook boarded *Lusitania* with their father George, this was not their first trans-Atlantic crossing. In 1907, George had emigrated to Canada, no doubt hoping to find greater opportunities for himself and, in due course 3-year-old Frank, a 'small but adventurous' lad, and 'shy' 4-year-old Elsie. With the children's mother having died in 1913, George, despite having been reasonably successful business-wise, decided to return to England. Their house sold, they spent a week in New York by which they were unimpressed, before boarding what the children called 'the big ship'.

Having swapped their second cabin berths for third ones in order to travel with friends, when they boarded, George turned to Elsie saying, 'Duck down, Elsie! Make yourself as small as possible.' This was because he had only paid the half-fare to which she was no longer entitled being 12 years old. With this small piece of subterfuge successful, the family enjoyed their crossing, Frank participating in the children's games and races and Elsie making new friends. Just before lunch on 7 May, Elsie was discussing flowers with her friends when a young man, hearing their conversation promised, 'I shall bring you a rose after lunch.' An excited Elsie waited for him, now accompanied (perhaps chaperoned) by her father and brother until another passenger almost ordered her to run and post a letter for her. Elsie reluctantly acquiesced. She was on the staircase when she felt the ship lurch. Not fully aware of any danger and doubtless wondering if her rose had appeared, she raced back to her father and brother. She bent to pick up a wad of money which she had espied, but her father told her to 'Throw them away ... They may cost you your life.' She believed subsequently that this was the moment she realised the danger.

Like most children of her era, Elsie had had a Christian upbringing and she now began to pray, attempting to comfort other passengers by reassuring them 'God will save you.' Aware that the crowded lifeboats were spilling their loads into the sea instead of lowering successfully, and that passengers were being lost in the melee, George reached a rapid decision. They would take their chance and jump into the sea together. Although Elsie and her father managed against all the odds to stay together until they were rescued, they lost Frank.

For three endless days, George and Elsie scoured Queenstown. When their search proved fruitless, they turned their attention to the mortuaries. Perhaps at least there would be a body to bury. Then to their amazement they learned that Frank was alive in a nearby hospital; 11-year-old Frank, who himself thought that his father and sister were among the dead and to whom a survivor from Leeds had offered a home, had his own story to tell.

He had been found in the sea. Some newspapers report a boat had come down on top of him and broken his arm, others state that he 'was pitched overboard' as *Lusitania* sank, others that his leg was broken by striking a piece of wreckage. Despite sinking, he surfaced again and clutched an upturned boat until, like George and Elsie, he too was found by a patrol boat where another survivor, a Dr Moore, 'splinted his leg'. Several newspapers report that at this point the child asked if there were 'a funny paper [comic] on the boat'.

The Hook family's near miraculous survival and a photograph of Frank in his hospital bed watched over by Elsie and George, featured in newspapers on both sides of the Atlantic, including 30 May's *New York Times,* the city which, less than a week but a lifetime ago, they had considered 'noisy and dirty'.

Thomas Quinn: 'grabbed his sister's favourite doll.'[20]
Born in Liverpool in June 1900, Thomas, the eldest of five children, was a bright boy. While many working-class parents needed their offspring to leave school on reaching the official leaving age, Thomas' parents wanted him to continue his education, no doubt hoping that he would be able to do better for himself than his father, who had run away to sea at the age of 14. By 1915, able seaman Thomas Quinn Sr, a professional merchant sailor with the Cunard Steam Ship Company, was due to sail in *Lusitania*'s Deck Department.

Whatever his parents' aspirations, 14-year-old Thomas had the sea in his blood. One morning in April 1915, he left home for school but never arrived. When the boy did not return in the evening, his father went out looking for him. Perhaps recognising his own younger self, Thomas Sr caved in. On 12 April, Thomas signed on as a Boatswain's Boy on *Lusitania*'s Deck Department; at least the father would be able to keep an eye on his headstrong son. To young Thomas, the monthly £1 pay must have seemed a fortune. Five days later, accompanied by all the family, the two Quinns left Liverpool on *Lusitania*'s outward journey. One of young Thomas' sisters begged him not to go. To distract her, he grabbed the doll she was holding and threw it in the opposite direction. As she ran after it, he darted away and onto the ship.[21]

In the early afternoon of 7 May, Thomas Sr was in the 'crow's nest'. In his evidence at the official inquiry, he confirmed that 'at 2.10 pm, he noticed a white wake away on the starboard side about 200 yards away ... it seemed to be, at about 35 knots racing for the forward. Deponent [Quinn] instantly said to his mate, "Good God, Frank, here's a torpedo!"'[22] Having been shouted at by his father to follow him to the deck, young Tom ran the opposite way – the last time he was seen alive. His body never being recovered, *Lusitania*'s youngest crew member is remembered, along with all other hands who have no known grave but the sea, on the Mercantile Marine Memorial, Tower Hill, London. One can only wonder at the burden of guilt his father laboured under for the rest of his life.

Anna Allan: 'Where she goes the angels bend to her.'[23]
Fourteen-year-old Anna and her 16-year-old sister Gwendolyn were accompanying their parents Sir Montagu and Lady Marguerite Allan to meet their older siblings in Liverpool. Eighteen-year-old Hugh attended

Eton while, thanks to familial influence and affluence (as well as being vice chairman of the Allan Steamship Line, Sir Montagu was president of The Merchants' Bank of Canada and the Montreal Telegraph Company), 20-year-old Martha had purchased her own ambulance and intended to serve overseas.[24] To 53-year-old Sir Montagu's dismay, despite being an honorary lieutenant colonel, he had been refused permission to command a battalion of the Black Watch of Canada overseas. Lady Marguerite planned to establish a hospital in England for wounded Canadians.

The couple, their younger daughters, servants, and personal friends including Frederick Orr-Lewis and, to Anna and Gwen's delight, Frederick's valet George Slingsby, settled into their luxurious Saloon Class accommodation. George subsequently gave the press information both about the Allan girls and the torpedo which he noticed 'as a long white streak coming towards the ship in the water, it suddenly struck me as [being] from a submarine.'[25] Having dashed to find lifebelts and with the ship listing ominously, George struggled to get back on deck. No doubt all members of the party were finding it hard to believe their cabin steward's assurance that 'the water-tight compartments had been closed and there was no call for alarm'. Lady Allan later told a Cork newspaper that none of the party was able to get into a lifeboat before the deck was awash with water. In a subsequent letter to his family, Frederick explained how, 'in the twinkling of an eye, [*Lusitania*] took the most awful dive and we all went down with her.' Although, 'I had Gwen by the hand and Lady Allan had Anna', Canadian press reports give the mother holding both her daughters' hands. What seems clear is her statement that they would all jump and die together.[26] Tragically, due to being severely injured when struck by the keel of another boat, Marguerite somehow lost Anna's (and perhaps Gwen's) hand(s) – or maybe Frederick lost Gwen's. We will never know for sure. That both girls could swim must have provided some consolation, another family friend, 15-year-old Robert Holt had been seen swimming successfully to a boat.[27] With his wife having survived and having been invited by the Vice Admiral of the Port to stay at his residence, Sir Montagu began scouring Queenstown for his daughters.[28]

Although, George Slingsby later recounted seeing both girls' bloated and mottled corpses in one of the temporary mortuaries in Queenstown, this was either an understandable mistake or wishful thinking. Eventually, on 18 May, the sea gave up Gwen's body. Labelled 218, she was repatriated and lies in Montreal's Mount Royal Cemetery. Anna was never found.

Commemorated in the same cemetery as two of her three siblings, Anna's memorial includes the words, 'where she goes the angels bend to her'. A tragic footnote to the Allan story is that Flight Sub-Lieutenant Hugh RNAS (KIA 6 July 1917) lies far from home in Coxyde Military Cemetery, Belgium, while Martha predeceased both her parents in 1942.

Chrissie Aitken: 'standing laughing at something when the crash came.'[29]

Four years after his wife died in 1908 leaving 9-year old Chrissie motherless, James Aitken decided that the two of them would emigrate and join Chrissie's brothers, including Jarvie, and his wife in Canada. Bad luck plagued the family as James developed a serious heart condition and then in 1914 Jarvie was also widowed leaving him with an infant son. The two widowers decided to return permanently to Scotland and were no doubt relieved that Chrissie would able to help with 2-year-old Jarvie Jnr during the crossing. Booked on SS *Cameronia* they were among those transferred to *Lusitania*. Chrissie must have been excited to discover her second-class passage had been upgraded to first class, sharing with another initially *Cameronia* girl.[30]

Chrissie made friends with several of the other teenagers and was 'standing laughing at something when the crash came.' The 15-year-old recounted her subsequent ordeal in a long letter to her brothers published in the Canadian *The Nicola Valley News* (4 June 1915). She was pleased with herself for 'keeping calm' largely because 'the girl friend who was with me got very excited, and in trying to calm her I forgot my own excitement', although they lost contact with each other in the seething crush, with 'desperate parents [running] frantically around the deck, lost children scream[ing] for their parents, mothers with more than one child begging strangers to look after some of them.' Those unable to do so found that their 'face would haunt them' for the rest of their lives.[31]

Doubtless hoping or assuming that her toddler nephew was with his father and grandfather, Chrissie helped haul the ropes that were bringing lifeboats closer to the deck. Finally, with *Lusitania* nearly under water, she obeyed the order to get into one herself, jumping some 4ft and landing safely as it pitched downwards. To everyone aboard's horror, the sinking liner was sucking lifeboats under with her. Preferring to take her chance in the sea, Chrissie jumped out, 'As I left the lifeboat the big boat sank; and I was carried down and down. It seemed ages before … my belt brought me up, but I was severely knocked about among wreckage'. At this point, as she remembered in an interview when she was in her 90s, 'I was so sure I was going to die that I just shut my eyes and accepted death. Then I must have blacked out.'[32] Spotted 'on an upturned boat' by three men who succeeded in hauling her up with them, 'we sat huddled together', trying to counter the effects of bitterly cold water and shock, 'It was a sight I'll never forget, passing people ... crying for help, and not able to help or save them.' After some three hours this part of Chrissie's ordeal ended as they were picked up and taken to Queenstown.

The sad task of touring the multiple places of refuge offered to survivors and the countless makeshift mortuaries, seeking news of her father, brother and infant nephew, soon began. Her fears about her father confirmed as she identified his body, two days later she returned to Scotland, the other Jarvies remained lost or unidentified.

Chrissie crept back to Scotland. With understanding of the psychology of grief in its infancy, a (no doubt well-meaning) Edinburgh doctor advised this adolescent who, as well as losing a mother and sister-in-law in the space of seven years, had lost a father, brother and nephew in the most terrifying of circumstances and had herself stared death in the face, 'to go out and find myself a job and work the grief off.'[33] At least with the army absorbing more and more men, jobs were easy to find. She worked in a post office, earning 10s a week (£55 today). She was awarded a total of £7 (£770) from various funds established for *Lusitania* survivors facing difficulties but, being a British national, could not apply to the Mixed Claims Commission for reparations for either the loss of her family's personal possessions or their lives.[34] The girl who, according to *The Scotsman* (10 May 1915), had 'told her story with wonderful calmness and courage,' continued to display identical courage throughout her long life.

Kathleen Kaye: 'Smiling words and reassurances.'[35]

In 1855, Jacob Kirschbaum left increasingly anti-Semitic Cracow in Austro-Hungary and settled in Great Britain. Sometime after Kathleen's birth in 1898, the family changed their name to Kaye, thus Hannah Kathleen Kirschbaum boarded *Lusitania* as Kathleen Kaye. The 16-year-old (not 14 as she was reported in some newspapers) must have been independent and resourceful as she was crossing the Atlantic alone after visiting relatives in Toronto and New York. George Lane, manager of the

Royal Gwent Glee singers, told an interviewer from the *Huntington Press* (Indiana 11 August) that he had 'undertaken at New York to see her safely into her parents' hands at Liverpool'. However, Lane is not mentioned in sources relating to Kathleen and it seems unlikely that in 1915 a 16-year-old Jewish girl travelling alone would have been entrusted to the care of a 26-year-old [Gentile] bachelor. Little has been preserved about Kathleen's time on board other than her being a 'second cabin passenger', but by 9 May her part in the disaster was appearing on both sides of the Atlantic and continued for several months.

On that fateful sunny Friday, Kathleen and George were 'chatting gaily' when George remarked that the ship seemed to be travelling below her maximum speed of 25 knots.[36] Once the torpedo struck, George claimed Kathleen 'clung to me for a moment', but concedes that after that she was 'splendid'. We will never know whether George was in some way seeking publicity for himself and the singers, or the press airbrushed him out of the story. Whether or not she initially 'clung to' her companion before he set off on a brief, fruitless search for lifebelts, her subsequent actions were remarkable for so young a girl for, as 10 May *New York Times* (and many other papers) noted, 'the brief time elapsing between the torpedoing and sinking of the *Lusitania* was enough to develop a heroine in the person of Miss Kathleen Kaye'. According to numerous reports, the 16-year-old smilingly helped 'stewards in filling a boat with women and children. When all were in, she climbed aboard the lifeboat as coolly as an able seaman.' *Lusitania* was now listing so heavily that the boat only needed to be lowered some 2ft before hitting the sea. The crew then began rowing, quite literally, for their lives, in a race against swamping when the doomed liner sank eighteen minutes after first being hit; received wisdom had been that even if the worst happened *Lusitania* would 'take five or six hours to sink'.[37] When one of the exhausted sailors fainted at his oar, Kathleen calmly took his place and 'rowed until the boat was out of danger.'

The 10 May *Birmingham Gazette,* referring to her as a 'little Heroine with her hair down her back', quotes one survivor's praise of her coolness and calmness in the face of the panic around her, 'I saw her afterwards, this little schoolgirl, in one of the boats nursing and comforting the babies and calming their mothers'. In Queenstown, Kathleen was seen still trying to 'comfort and assist her sisters in misfortune'. According to 5 June *Tampa Tribune* (Florida), she attended the large funeral held for victims in Queenstown before setting off for Liverpool.

Back in England, Kathleen's photograph and story were soon circulating, including in the widely-read 15 May *Illustrated London News* and the *Daily Mirror*. In the pictures, her calm demeanour is apparent. Would the jingoistic press have heaped praise on 'the little heroine' if her name had remained the Germanic-sounding Kirschbaum rather than Kaye?

George Wynne: 'I had nothing on – just a singlet.'[38]

In April 1915, George Wynne had found his father Joseph a job aboard *Lusitania*. The 16-year-old who had already completed five trips was proud of his work as a sculleryman for the first-class cabin, considering himself a cut above those who peeled vegetables for less elevated passengers. A dutiful son, he tried to cheer his homesick father who was not enjoying his job and sent some of his £6 a month pay (£660 today) home to his mother who still had six children to care for.

While those he cooked for were finishing their lunch, George was in the kitchen preparing Jerusalem artichokes for dinner when the shout, 'We've been hit!' went up. Father and son rushed up to the port side deck when, remembering George could not swim, Joseph told him 'to hang on' while he searched the 'glory hole' (crew's sleeping quarters) for a lifebelt. When minutes passed with no sign of Joseph, a passer-by urged George to get into the lifeboat that was being lowered, 'wearing just a singlet' (part of his uniform which was completed by regulation trousers) and flimsy slippers. Once on Lifeboat 14, whose plug had either come out or not been put in, George and other passengers used their shoes to bail the water – they were fighting a losing battle and she capsized, spilling everyone. When she was righted, George was one of only four of the boat's original complement of fifty to clamber back, only to capsize again. This time the exhausted lad lost consciousness; he subsequently learned he had been tied to the lifeboat wreckage. After seven hours in the 13°C sea, he was picked up by the trawler *Indian Empire*. Seventy years later he remembered, 'when I came to, there was a crowd there around me and they were pumping water from me, and the next thing they gave me a cup of tea and put a blanket around me.'

With no sign of his father in Queenstown, George began the grim task of scouring the makeshift mortuaries. Deeply shocked and unable to control his hand enough to write a telegram for his mother, he asked another crew member to do so, handing over a slip which read, 'BOTH SAVED. HOME LATER.' The Cunard Line paid all members of staff up until 8 May 1915, the day *Lusitania* was due to dock – George was owed

£5.50. Having been paid and given passage to Liverpool, to George's dismay he saw his mother had come to meet both the supposedly rescued seafarers. Unable to face her, he ducked through the throngs at Lime Street train station. While sitting on the steps of St George's Hall a priest whom George knew came by, the distraught lad confessed the truth. The clergyman suggested that he accompany George home and help break the news to Mary Wynne.

Still keen to cook at sea, George next signed on with *SS Hesperian*. His desperately anxious, perhaps prescient, mother, 'burned all his clothes, hid his kit bag and then did not wake him up in enough time to join the vessel.' On 4 September 1915, *Hesperian* was torpedoed by the same U Boat 20, still commanded by Walther Schwieger, that had sent *Lusitania* to her doom. Ironically, she was transporting at least one *Lusitania* body, that of Frances Stephen who, along with her infant grandson, had been drowned.[39] Despite being wounded numerous times, George survived military service with The King's (Liverpool) Regiment.[40] Seemingly, he was born under a lucky star.

'Precious Lives'

Still a century later, reading the names and some individual stories of those 129 children on board is heart-breaking. Ninety-four children perished (73 per cent, where the overall casualty rate across the whole ship's complement was 39 per cent) including thirty-one of the thirty-nine infants under the age of 2.[41] In some instances, entire families were wiped out. Although in 1915 First Lord of the Admiralty Winston Churchill saw the sinking and loss of these precious lives as a 'sever[ing] of the underlying bonds which sustained civilisation',[42] twenty years later he concluded, 'In spite of all its horror, we must regard the sinking of *Lusitania* as an event most important and favourable to the Allies, the poor babies who perished in the ocean attack struck a blow at German power more deadly than could have been achieved by the sacrifice of 100,000 men.'[43] Would parents have agreed that their beloved children's lives were a price worth paying for this 'deadly blow'?

Silvertown: 'A little boy stood holding an empty bird-cage in his hand.'[44]

Disasters attract sightseers. On Saturday 20 January 1917, cars filled with 'well-dressed sightseers slipped along' several of the East End of

London's poorest roads. While some may have come to offer what help they could, the majority, according to a Mrs Drake, appear to have come out of ghoulish curiosity for the night before a terrible explosion had occurred at the Brunner Mond Factory at Silvertown.[45] How these disaster tourists knew where to go is a mystery, for that morning's *Times* had simply reported that 'an explosion had occurred [yesterday] evening … at a munitions factory in the neighbourhood of London'. Although casualty numbers were then unknown, seventy-three people, including twenty children aged between 18 months and 17 years lost their lives, others were severely injured and even in the 1920s, deaths were still being reported.

The Metropolitan Building Act of 1844 had made it illegal to carry out 'harmful trades' inside the boundaries of London. But, fortuitously for a government that had been facing a munitions crisis almost since the outbreak of the war, Silvertown, which it was popularly agreed would have been more aptly named 'Smoketown' or 'Sulphurtown', lay just outside this boundary. With its teeming tenements housing the poorest labourers and its easy access to London's docklands, the location was simply too good to overlook. By 1914, the area was a hellhole of factories where a cocktail of highly flammable substances including rubber and rubber by-products were manufactured; Tate and Lyle's sugar factory was then, as now, in the vicinity. With the army's shortage of munitions and the 1915 'Shell Crisis' having brought down the Asquith government and contributed to Sir John French, Commander in Chief of the British Expeditionary Force being recalled, the new coalition was determined to dramatically increase munitions production. It decreed that one of Silvertown's factories, Brunner Mond and Company, which manufactured caustic soda, should switch to producing highly explosive trinitrotoluene (TNT).

Despite Brunner Mond directors being horribly aware of the consequential hazards, exacerbated by Woolwich Arsenal being almost directly opposite on the other side of the Thames – an explosion in one factory could endanger the other – they nevertheless, reluctantly, caved in to government pressure. In September 1915, the plant began churning out 9 tons of TNT a day. Increasing the risks, the 'danger buildings' (as sheds handling the most noxious substances were termed) were situated a mere 200 yards 'from the dense row of workers' houses and right in the middle of other factories and wharves … containing highly combustible materials'.[46] Writing in 1964, Dr Freeth, chief chemist at Brunner Mond in 1916 remembered, 'Every month we used to write to Silvertown to say

71

their plant would go up sooner or later, and we were told it was worth the risk.'[47]

Staff, including teenagers, worked across three shifts day and night to ensure continuous production. At 6.52 pm on Friday 19 January 1917, the inevitable happened. A fire in the 'melt pot' room at the Crescent Wharf factory ignited some 50 tons of TNT. The ensuing earth-shattering explosion ripped a large area of Silvertown from the face of the Earth. Shockwaves were felt all over London and Essex. The ensuing fires were visible in Guildford and Maidstone. The explosion was even heard over 100 miles away in Southampton and Norwich, some claim it was audible in France.

In language that could have been used to describe villages on the Western Front, the following Saturday, P[atricia] Lynch wrote in suffragette Sylvia Pankhurst's weekly newspaper *Woman's Dreadnought* of 'whole streets, containing just shells of houses, the windows broken, the doors gone, the ceilings and floors fallen in.' Among the many sights that struck Lynch was of a small boy, 'holding an empty bird cage in his hand', the cage somehow representing a connection to the life which had instantaneously been destroyed. Lynch's article, 'EXPLOSION', is full of what we would term 'human interest' stories, although the mores of the time mean, frustratingly, no names are given. What might have been the psychological impact on the 'red-cheeked factory girl' who told Lynch that, as she ran away from the fire, 'we heard a roar ... There was a crash and something hit me in the chest. I looked down and it was a man's head. I couldn't run any further then.'?

Touring the area, Lynch noted 'heaps of bricks, broken glass, twisted iron covering the bodies of those that had perished.' Among that night's many tragedies, a few stand out a century later. The Betts family had firefighting in their blood, for which they paid a heavy price. Seven Betts men worked at Silvertown, living with their families in accommodation adjacent to the fire station. Fifty-four-year old Samuel was station commander (his wife Mary Ann was killed) while another Betts, Fireman J.J., was a gifted writer who describes in painstaking detail the scene just before the disaster occurred with, 'Children carrying baskets of provisions and enamel tea-cans, the evening meal of parents working overtime, hastened on their way.'[48] When one fireman rushed in shouting, 'Brunner Mond's alight!' those on duty at Silvertown Fire Station instantly realised 'the terrible implications'. They knew with gut-wrenching certainty that, 'Once those rising flames reached the danger buildings, there was little hope for the lives and property in the vicinity'. Having 'yelled' to his wife Polly (subsequently rendered stone-deaf, probably from PTSD) and their 12-year-old son to dash to safety, a third Betts, George, strode into the inferno. 'The factory had gone. There were fearful sounds in the air, the screams of injured women and children, the groans of those imprisoned under the debris. In all, nine factories and mills had caught alight, ignited by the red-hot iron girders flung sky high by the explosion falling in their midst.'[49] Betts does not say whether he himself escaped unharmed but George's family were less lucky; injured himself, George identified the remains of his 4-month-old daughter Ethel. Like some *Lusitania* parents who only managed to save some of their children, Mrs Betts had rescued two children but could not reach Ethel.

According to J.J. Betts, 'every available fire-engine ... from all parts of London converged on Silvertown'. Two local firemen perished, including Frederick Sell; his wife, Caroline and four sons survived, but daughter Winifred, was killed. Aged 15, she attended Central Secondary School. That the Sells allowed Winifred to take up the scholarship she was awarded indicates that they valued her education and achievements. The explosion had broken her back, and her body, identified by her eldest brother Harold, had been blown into a field. Harold told the inquest held at the London Hospital that two of his brothers were injured and his now widowed mother was in hospital suffering from shock; their home at the fire station had been destroyed.[50] Although father and daughter were not killed together, they share a grave with fireman Henry Vickers and George Betts' daughter Ethel. After a service at which the Bishop of Chelmsford officiated, their coffins were 'borne on motor engines' in front of a crowd estimated to have reached 1,000. *Manchester Evening News* (30 January) reported the impressive funeral attended by representatives of every London and more distant Fire Brigades, 'in gleaming helmets and wearing medals'.[51]

Even more unfortunate than Catherine Sell, Alice Croft had been sitting in her kitchen alongside her husband, nursing her only child, 18-month-old Edward, when the house simply collapsed around them. Rescuing Edward and despite being injured herself, she managed to get him to Poplar Hospital where he died on the Sunday, her husband was only dug out of the ruins the following day. It is perhaps unsurprising that she 'collapsed' when giving evidence at the inquest and 'had to be carried from the court in a swoon'.[52]

The 3 February 1917 bi-weekly *Stratford Express* reported in considerable detail a funeral service held at the Public Hall attended, to the journalist's gratification, by a representative of the King, the 'Hon. Henry Stoner'. '[H]undreds of women many of them accompanied by young children assembled at the burial ground.' The Bishop of Chelmsford again delivered the address. Perhaps endeavouring to point a subtle finger of blame at those who had deemed that using Brunner Mond's factory for TNT was worth the risk, he stated, 'This explosion could in no way be said to have come from or by the will of God. Surely it was the product of man. It was due to the wrong-mindedness and selfishness of man.' He did however add that 'such an occurrence made [people] all the more determined to carry on the war'. Suitably sombre music and hymns accompanied four coffins to the West Ham Cemetery where a single grave awaited the remains of 11-year-old Elsie Wass, whose mill-hand father had found her unconscious in the rubble of the house, as well as those of her mother 32-year-old Mary, and Elsie's 10-year-old bother, Stanley; mother and son had been identified in different mortuaries.[53] The East London Cemetery was the final resting place of Leonard and Ada Patrick's two sons and two daughters, aged between 10 and 2. One can only wonder how the parents and their one surviving child, 7-year-old Cyril, negotiated this loss. Perhaps as a damage limitation exercise, the Ministry of Munitions took it upon itself 'to pay for the funerals of the victims'. They also offered those rendered jobless, 'first chance of employment at Woolwich Arsenal' just over the river.[54]

As the identification of the dead continued so too did the inquests, many of the witnesses bearing physical as well as emotional signs of their traumatic experience. Nineteen of the deceased discussed on 5 February were 'under 20 years of age, ten under 10'.[55] Flour mill labourer James Preston explained how he was working on the night shift, but his wife, Elizabeth was at home at 6 Mill Road with baby Dorothy and 3-year-old Eric. The distraught widower explained that 'the only one he could speak with certainty about' was his son, whose body he had identified. He could only presume that the mother and baby were dead together. Occasionally, it fell to siblings to identify a body. Having identified his body, teenage Clara Gardner confirmed that although her and 5-year-old Norman's father had carried him out of the ruins of their home alive, by 24 January, Norman had succumbed to his injuries.[56]

The sad litany continued; 15-year-old Lilian Davey was, like so many working-class girls, employed as a servant. Her employer George

Cartwright told the inquest that she had, 'called his attention to the fact that a fire was taking place'. She then left to return to her home at Victoria Docks; stepping into the inferno, she was never again seen alive.[57] Sixteen-year-old Catherine Hogg (also known as Lizzie Lawrence) worked in the factory itself. Her foster father Albert Lawrence told the inquest that she was working the 2 to 10 pm shift at the top of the factory, sending down 'crude material to put in the melting pot.' Albert had recognised the two rings shown him by a doctor, all that remained of the teenager was her charred trunk.[58]

Death can be random. On 19 January, James Oates was at work at Tate & Lyle while his wife Catherine and children were at home in West Silvertown. Escaping outside, she realised that one of her six offspring, Tommy, was missing. Rushing back inside, by the light of a borrowed candle she saw 'the lad lying in the passage. A large piece of iron had come through the roof and was lying on the body of the boy.' Her eldest child, 7-year-old Catherine, had her arm severed – seemingly by the same piece of iron. Young Catherine learned to live with her devastating injury, subsequently marrying a local boy, George Gammans.

As in all disasters, the Silvertown explosion showed up all facets of human nature. There are countless stories of East End inhabitants, themselves the poorest of the poor, sharing what little they had with strangers. There are other tales of 'Despicable conduct' for which harsh sentences were handed out. One adult looter was 'staggered' by being sentenced to three months' hard labour.[59] One case at West Ham Children's Court involved a group of boys pulling a barrow containing a number of obviously looted items, some having been 'stolen from a home the occupiers of which were injured and are now in hospital'.[60] When Constable Challis approached them, the older boys ran off but 12-year-old Harry C. and 13-year-old Thomas J., both from nearby Canning Town, 'were roped to the barrow and could not get away'.[61] They 'denied all knowledge of what was in the barrow but were remanded with a view to being charged with theft.'[62] As female school teachers were frequently blamed for increases in juvenile crime, was the finger of blame pointed at women in this case?

Harry and Thomas were undoubtedly roaming the streets because 'many of the schools in the southern part of the borough had been significantly damaged'. One so badly that 'its restoration would probably take four to six months'. The Chairman of the Local Education Committee pointed out that it was deeply fortuitous that 'the accident was at the time when the schools were not in session, something of an understatement as the damage to the buildings included 'large casements blown in and lodged across the desks where the children would have been sitting.' Grimly, another school was being used as a mortuary. It was calculated that it would be 'several weeks' before any of the schools were fit for use.[63] *Stratford Express* may not have been exaggerating when it commented that 'thousands of children for the time being [are] without school places'.

Friday 19 January was the day of St Barnabas Church's eagerly awaited Band of Hope treat with tea and games. Between sixty and seventy children were playing 'kiss-in-the ring', when helper 'Miss Griffiths noticed a flare in the sky.'[64] The mission hall, little more than a tin hut, 'caught some of the fury' of the explosion. 'The walls parted outwards and the apex of the roof fell to the floor ... the place was plunged into darkness.' Sickeningly aware of the danger, Miss Griffiths and other female helpers found superhuman strength, they successfully held up the lowest part of the roof while 'all the little ones were removed from the place.'[65] Of the three injured, only one child needed hospitalising. The children's 'miraculous escape' was subsequently recorded on a memorial tablet. Many would have been among those rendered homeless and orphaned by the explosion.

To try to assist with their emotional recovery and their schooling, in February youngsters from West Silvertown were sent to various convalescent homes acting as boarding schools, including some 240 children and their teachers who were accommodated in a 'beautiful convalescent home in Kent' which was turned into a makeshift school. Organised by the Mansfield University Settlement, the author of the in-house magazine was gratified that 'some of our East End children will taste the joys of a boarding school in the country [Parkwood, Swanley, Kent] and watch the coming of spring'.[66] A few quickly returned suffering from homesickness. Despite the obvious dedication of the staff, it is impossible to know whether further emotional damage was inflicted on these traumatised children, some of whom were noted as suffering from 'psychological shock', by removing them from their own environment and placing them into an undeniably middle-class one with its insistence on cleanliness and godliness.[67] Although no copies of their school work remain, a number of activities were undoubtedly undertaken for therapeutic reasons including drawing and petting furry animals.

Significantly, when playing out of doors, several youngsters pretended to build houses. One group of children whose lives may have been saved by their attending Parkwood were the ten pupils of Upper North Street School, Poplar, whose school received a direct 'hit' on 13 June 1917 with 18 children killed. Just under 400 children passed through Parkwood; they returned to the East End in July 1917. The cost was met by 'funds given by a generous public aided by a Grant from H.M.Treasury'.[68]

These little East Enders returned home, one group who did not do so were the orphaned girls and boys 'between the ages of 5 and 13 and a half' who were sent to the Shaftesbury Homes, and in particular the 'boys of suitable age who have been rendered fatherless by the explosion' who were sent to the Training Ship *Arethusa*. Unusually, no payment was required from 'the widows'. Widows with younger children, battling for compensation, housing, and even fighting demands for rent on houses that no longer existed, may have welcomed this opportunity for their slightly older sons to learn a trade, be fed and clothed. Arguably this was of greater practical use than the messages of sympathy sent by Their Majesties, who contributed £250 and Queen Alexandra £100 'for the poor sufferers', of which there were thousands.[69]

Inevitably, conspiracy theories abounded, some people believed camouflaged German Zeppelins had bombed the factory while others suspected it was the work of foreigners granted permission to work at Brunner Mond, despite there being none at the plant.[70] Silence was the order of the day. Initially, although this soon broke, even the name of the factory was censored. The 'Report of the Government Inquiry into The Cause of the Explosion which occurred on Friday 19th January 1917 at the Chemical World of Messrs. Brunner Mond and Company Limited, Crescent Wharf, Silvertown in the County of Essex', which found inter alia, a 'very unsatisfactory state of affairs' was labelled 'SECRET'.

This 'unsatisfactory state of affairs' had led to damage amounting to over £1 million. In addition to the loss of homes, life and livelihoods, 'nearly a thousand people' were 'maimed or injured' in an 'orgy of blood' comparable to the Front Line, but, rather than their being soldiers, this orgy's dead, wounded and psychologically traumatised included 'helpless children.'[71]

'If that is an air-raid, I never want to see another.'[72]
25 May 1917

If *Lusitania* and her sister ship *Mauretania* were 'the largest, most powerful and fastest transatlantic liners of their day', the Gotha bomber could make a similar claim to being king of the air. Able to fly at '15,000 feet, above contemporary fighter's maximum height. With a range of 800km (500 miles) and a bomb load of up to 500 kg (1,100 lb), the Gothas were designed to carry out attacks across the channel against Britain.'[73] With four squadrons established in Belgium, from May 1917 these machines brought death and destruction to British civilians, including children, in a never hitherto experienced fashion.

One late May day, Arthur Sullivan, famed for his collaboration with W.S. Gilbert on many popular operettas, was travelling to Paris. Crossing the Channel, he witnessed, an 'unfortunate vessel slowly go over and disappear under the water in clear, bright sunshine ... It was too horrible – and then we saw all the boats moving about picking up the survivors, some so exhausted they had to be lifted on to the ships.'[74] Despite rescuers from Sandgate and Folkestone's valiant efforts, only eighty-five men were saved, 284 mariners lost their lives; a memorial subsequently erected in Cheriton Road Cemetery, Folkestone records the tragedy. The rescue was widely lauded in both the English and the German press, for the ship in question was the German iron-clad turret-ship *Grosser Kurfürst* and the episode took place on 31 May 1878 – a month that would again enter into Folkestone annals.[75]

Between December 1914 and May 1917, the Kent coast towns of Dover, Margate and Ramsgate suffered significant attention from German bombers. Folkestone, despite being a frontline military town with troops departing for the Western Front and a large Canadian camp at nearby Shorncliffe (over 100,000 troops passed through), had been spared. Folkestonians attributed this to German appreciation for their actions on that fateful day in May 1878.

Friday 25 May 1917 dawned bright and sunny, the weather looked promising for the coming Bank Holiday weekend. As well as it being payday, the news that potatoes had been delivered to Stokes Greengrocers, Tontine Street, increased the sense of wellbeing. At around six o'clock in the evening, the street was full of chatting women and playing children queuing to make their purchases. No one batted an eyelid at the sound of distant gunfire and crashes. With Shorncliffe camp so close by, such sounds were part of the backdrop to daily life.[76] Perhaps sharing the town's complacency, the military had done nothing to protect it: there was no air-raid warning system or anti-aircraft defences in place and when townspeople such as Mrs Helen Coxon, on her way to visit friends, heard 'a very large flight of about twenty aeroplanes circling and pirouetting over my head', she, like fellow citizens, assumed that British airmen were finally 'up and doing' something about the raiders that had targeted the other towns on the Kent coast. To her horror, almost as she watched the planes' 'graceful actions', a bomb was dropped, killing a woman who was just behind her in the road. Now horribly aware that these were not the friendly aircraft she had assumed, she rushed to Brampton Down, the school of her 14-year-old daughter, Doreen. To her relief, all was well and the mistress said that all pupils had 'behaved uncommonly well' and followed instructions to the letter.[77] Mrs Coxon would soon discover that others had been less lucky for the 'pirouetting' planes were Germany's latest weapon in aerial warfare, the Gotha GIV bomber. A squadron of no fewer than twenty-one bombers under the command of 34-year-old Hauptmann Ernst Brandenburg, had successfully crossed the Channel from Belgium. They had circled London but the cloud cover was such that, following agreed guidelines in the event of poor weather over London, bombers would target 'military sites, lines of communication and coastal towns', on this occasion following the South Eastern and Chatham Railway Company's line to the Channel Ports.[78] There are claims that the bombers 'headed where they could see the most civilians, mostly women and children, which was outside Stokes in Tontine Street, although some argued they were actually aiming for the harbour.'[79] The local authorities had not received any warnings as the 'London warning control centre had lost track of the Gothas'.[80]

By the time bombs began raining down on Tontine Street, young victims had already been both claimed and miraculously spared. Sixteen-year-old Doris Walton had been playing tennis in the grounds of Athelstan School. Killed by flying shrapnel, Doris holds the sad honour of being Folkestone's first child victim. Badly injured in the stomach, she died the next day in hospital. Her tennis partner was unscathed although her racket 'was riddled with shrapnel'.[81] Three bombs had just exploded in the Shorncliffe Road area, one, apparently intended for the station, had missed its target and fallen straight into the cot of an infant who had just been removed from it.[82]

In the Edwardian and early Georgian years, Folkestone was a popular holiday destination boasting hotels for the more affluent, and boarding-houses for the less so. These provided employment across the area. Kathleen Chapman, a 16-year-old chambermaid from Chilham Lees, 22 miles away, worked at Bates Hotel. Having some precious time off-duty, she and Private George Bloodworth had turned into Bouverie Road to collect a friend's shoes from the cobbler. Both were killed by shrapnel from the bomb that had destroyed 19 and 21 Bouverie Road – also killing the shop owner.[83] The hotel manager considered Kathleen 'cheerful and conscientious' as well as being popular with guests.[84] Although the bombs in these areas caused enormous destruction and cost a number of lives, the worst was still to come as the bulk of the casualties were confined to the Tontine Street area, in particular around Stokes stores where two bombs fell; although one was a dud, the other exploded outside the shop at 6.22 pm.

The shoppers included (Canadian) Private George Moss's wife and baby son. A devout member of the Salvation Army, George longed to become a chaplain. He had been quick to enlist in the Canadian Expeditionary Force and had been at Shorncliffe. The blast tore off Jane's legs, and baby Walter, the first of the many casualties to be taken to the Royal Victoria Hospital, received a terrible chest wound. While George survived the war, his four brothers were killed; even more devastatingly, both his wife and son succumbed to their injuries. The scene on Tontine Street resembled one on the Western Front: 'In a moment the street was filled with dead and dying, some torn limb from limb, intermingled with human bodies being the lifeless and mangled carcases of horses'.[85] A fractured gas main shot a huge sheet of flame across the pavement. Giving evidence at the inquest, Chief Constable Harry Reeve declared it was 'the most appalling sight', which would haunt him till his 'dying day'. He also confirmed having received no warning from the military authorities about an imminent raid.

George Moss was not the only husband and father who would receive notice of his loss while serving with His Majesty's Armed Forces. Annie Beer's husband Ernest served with the Royal Garrison Artillery; his brother Harry was a coal porter and marine fireman. Annie was caring for Harry's sons, 9-year-old William and 11-year-old Arthur, who had accompanied her and her 2-year-old daughter Annie to the shop. Bored by queuing, the boys had started kicking a ball to each other when the bomb fell. Baby Annie's face was simply blown away; Annie Sr and Arthur were also killed instantly, William subsequently died from a chest wound. It was Harry who informed Ernest of their family's terrible losses. Like many of his generation, Ernest appears to have buried his double bereavement deep in his heart. Subsequently remarrying, a locket with Annie's picture was found upon him after his death.[86]

Little girls are often the apple of their father's eye, none more so than 2-year-old Florrie Norris. She and her 1-year-old brother William were with their mother outside Stokes; little Florrie's head with its golden curls was severed from her shoulders. Albert Taylor, the 'Brewery Tap' publicans' 16-year-old son, remembered how 'the street was like a river of blood, and arms and legs ... were blown onto the flat roof of the [pub].' Haunted by 'seeing little Florrie's head on the saloon bar tap', decades later, Albert would 'scrub and whitewash the step every morning and he could still see the stain where the small head had lain.' It was many years before those who had witnessed the tragedy could stop themselves from crossing the road rather than walking on the discoloured spot.'[87]

Tragically, double, triple and inter-generational losses were not uncommon. Widowed Nellie Feist's second son Arthur had joined up on 1 September 1914, serving with the Buffs in France. During the war, Nellie lodged with her brother and his family at Coombe Farm. On 25 May she had brought her 5-year-old grandson and her 12-year-old nephew Albert Daniels into Folkestone in a horse and cart. Nellie had stepped in to help look after baby Stanley when his mother died following his birth. Unlike many of the victims, Nellie and the two boys were simply passing through Tontine Street when the bomb fell. All three were found dead in their cart. Arthur himself was killed on 17 July 1917. Nellie and Stanley share a grave on which Arthur is also commemorated.[88]

Arthur Stokes, 14-year-old son of joint shop owner and prominent Folkestone businessman William, had been picking bluebells but had returned to the shop, keen to help with the Friday rush. Despite his legs being 'shredded by shrapnel', Arthur managed to crawl outside into to the street. Taken to Shorncliffe Military Hospital, he survived for three days but died as dawn broke on 28 May. He and his father William share a grave.[89] The newspaper comment that, 'They have lost their lives equally with those that have served at the Front', seems particularly apt in Arthur's case as, like so many wounded soldiers, he succumbed to gangrene.[90]

Arthur was not the only victim inside Stokes. With a bomb weighing some 50 kg having landed just outside, the premises were 'completely flattened. All that was left was a mass of splintered wood and masonry'.[91] Among the young employees was Edith Eales. Having been taken, still just alive, to the Royal Victoria Hospital, she died of wounds the next day, one day short of her eighteenth birthday. With her father a marine porter, she may have hoped to 'better herself' by becoming a bookkeeper at Stokes. A few months younger than Edith, fellow bookkeeper Florrie Rumsey was terribly wounded in the head; she was transferred from Royal Victoria to Shorncliffe Military Hospital, more experienced in dealing with the types of war wounds inflicted upon her. To no avail, she outlived her colleague by a day.

On 30 May 1917 *The Scotsman* reported how Queen Alexandra had contacted Folkestone's mayor,

> I cannot say how deeply distressed I am at this tragedy which has caused the deaths of so many innocent and harmless women and children and which has brought such sadness and suffering into so many quiet homes. Please give the poor sufferers my deepest sympathy and tell them how greatly I feel for them.

The sufferers would of course have included not only the dead, injured and bereaved, but those who had witnessed the unfolding horror – some of whom had a lucky escape showing, just like at the Front, the randomness of war deaths.

Friends, 15-year-old Kate Featherbe and Anne Pegden, intended to visit Folkestone Pier. Unluckily they were at the end of Tontine Street when the bomb fell. Anne's leg was torn off and Kate had all her clothes stripped off. 'Cut and bloodied and suffering from severe shock', both girls were taken to the Royal Victoria Hospital. Now their sufferings would have exceeded many of those similarly injured on the Western Front who would have been transported by modern motorised ambulances, frequently driven by women and sometimes funded by children's fundraising activities. Kate and Anne were simply loaded onto a horse and cart. With the overwhelmed Royal Victoria unable to cope, Kate was loaded back onto the horse and cart and sent to Shorncliffe. Almost against the odds, both survived. Anne's injuries were life-changing, which may explain why she appears on the 1939 Register as 'single', undertaking 'unpaid domestic duties' for her younger brother Thomas.[92]

While many children living close to the Front had exposure to the horrific sights of the Great War, English children were better protected – but not those who experienced that fateful death-filled Friday evening. Decades later, Edith Vye recounted how she was walking in Tontine Street with two friends when the planes arrived. Just as they were pulled into shelter in the Brewery Tap, the bomb fell killing Edith's (unnamed) friends. She almost certainly witnessed Florrie Norris' death,

> There were babies in prams outside the shops and some of them had their heads blown off. It was an awful sight, a carnage, there were horses lying in the street, cut to pieces. I was so shaken I didn't know what to do. Eventually I ran home ... sobbing all the way.

Like service personnel, memories haunted survivors for years, for decades, for ever; summed up by Helen Coxon, who had so admired the 'circling and pirouetting planes' on the 'exquisite' summer evening. 'I do not think many people will be likely to forget the first visit the cultured Hun paid on the undefended town of Folkestone'.[93]

'It Never Happened.'

In the late nineteenth century, the Canadian government sought immigrants to populate its vast territory in the West. Many of those 1.5 million individuals of multiple religious faiths and ethnic background, enticed by the promised '160 acres of free land', came from Germany and the 'ramshackle Austro-Hungarian Empire including the Ukraine', not then an independent country with 80 per cent of the area ruled by Russia and the remaining 20 per cent lying in the Austro-Hungarian provinces of Galicia, Bukovina and Transcarpathia.[94] The immigrants put down roots and raised families, Canada becoming their long-term home. After three years residency, they could apply for Canadian nationality – although many did not do so. Not all Canadians welcomed these new arrivals with open arms; the Canadian West 'held stronger anti-alien sentiments than anywhere else in Canada and in British Columbia, local resentment was, by 1914, at its peak because unemployment rates were typically much greater among foreigners.'[95]

Immediately war was declared, the Dominion of Canada threw its support behind the 'Mother Country'. As in all belligerent nations, initial distrust of citizens originating from Canada's enemies, be these real or perceived, rapidly hardened into visceral hatred; all were assumed to be potential spies and saboteurs whose nefarious activities needed controlling. On 22 August 1914, the Canadian *War Measures Act* allowed the authorities to arrest, detain, censor, exclude, deport, control and capture all persons and property considered as potential threats to Canada. Immigrants who still had military obligations as reservists in their birth countries and who might therefore feel obliged to return and join the forces of His Majesty's enemies were forbidden to leave Canada; steps were immediately taken to prevent reservists possessing firearms or explosives.[96] There were further fears that these individuals might undertake 'act[s] injurious to Canada or the Empire'.[97]

The 150,000 non-naturalised residents whose birth country lay within the Central Powers' territories were now considered 'enemies'. On 28 October 1914, the registration and even the internment of enemy nationals was authorised.[98] Within a matter of weeks internment camps under the direction of illustrious General Sir William Otter (retired) began to spring up. Anyone *thought* to be an enemy sympathiser could be arrested and interned without trial.

German immigrants to Canada included teacher Karl Schwarze and his wife Victoria who arrived in Nanaimo (BC) in 1910. A son, Günter, was born soon after, Karla followed in 1913, Nanaimo the only home they knew. Karl found employment as a school principal and a mortgage enabled them to buy a house. War would put an end to their comfortable existence for, despite being eligible for naturalisation and loving Canada, Karl remained proud of his German heritage. Fired by his school's board, Karl, like hundreds of his fellow 'enemy aliens', could not find other employment. The Schwarzes soon found that more than the school board had turned against them.[99] If they did not initially know that on 18 September 1914 an internment camp for 'enemy aliens' had opened in Vernon (BC) some 200 miles away, they soon would.

In March 1916 Karl was arrested (without charge) while working in his garden.[100] Now dubbed #835, Prisoner Schwarze was sent to Vernon Camp. Worse soon followed. Unable to pay his mortgage or taxes, the family's home was repossessed. In April 1916, 6-year-old Günter, 3-year-old Karla, and newborn baby Vera's new home was a wood-framed hut 'covered in tarpaper' behind Vernon's barbed wire.[101] In 1917, doubtless seeking to remove himself and his family from internment, and because having a job 'helped make prisoners eligible for parole', Schwarze applied for a post at the University of British Columbia.[102] For some reason, he withdrew his application and in October 1919, with no home to return to and with four children – including Helmut who had been born in the camp – to support, Karl requested his family be deported to Germany, home still perhaps to him but not to the children. The four uprooted children lost their mother three years later. Although Karl again became a school teacher, the rise of the Nazis led him to lose his job again – he was imprisoned by the Nazis in 1944.[103]

Hugo and Anna Rack and their three children arrived in Alberta in 1910. That Hugo had remained a member of a German militia unit placed him, in October 1914, on the authorities' radar.[104] His so-called 'irritating attitude' towards the British Empire led to his arrest. A series of imprisonments and paroles followed; he spent time in five different camps leaving his wife Anna to care for their now five children, her father-in-law and their homestead. Perhaps Hugo being a difficult detainee, unafraid of demonstrating his anti-British attitude, who suffered both abuse at the hands of the guards and several spells of imprisonment (one in what he called Morrissey Camp's notorious 'Black Hole of India', about which he wrote to Anna), led to scant material assistance being offered to her and the children, despite police promises that they would be provided for by the Internment Camp Operations.[105] Hugo's sins continued to be visited upon his family. Eventually at her wits' end, Anna abandoned the family homestead. Despite Hugo being in another camp (Kapukasing), she and the children moved behind the wire at Vernon. They were deported with Hugo to Germany in 1920.

Newly married Rochus and Else-Freda von Lüttwitz arrived in Canada just six days before war was declared. By 30 April 1915, Rochus and the now pregnant Else-Freda were among Vernon's earliest inmates, Rochus only the ninety-second male, Else-Freda the second female to arrive at the camp. Vernon would eventually house 250–350 mostly single, German men as well as some eighty women and children.[106] The camp followed the 1907 Hague Convention's guide-lines on the treatment of prisoners-of-war, including recognition of an internee's social class. German internees were deemed First Class. They enjoyed better conditions, clothing and food and were housed well away from Second Class Austro-Hungarians.

Although the von Lüttwitz were comfortably housed in the top floor of the camp office, they would have been acutely aware that their liberty was curtailed and that their baby son Siegfried's first sight of the world was of the triple strands of barbed wire which encircled the camp and divided up particular areas: notices warned the public to 'Stay 10 Feet Away', guards drawn from local militia units circled the perimeter and marched working prisoners to their duties. Generally working with bayonets fixed to their rifles, there were ample guards, at Vernon the ratio was approximately one per 4-5 prisoners.[107] Having spent almost the first two years of his life in an internment camp, Siegfried and Else-Freda were released to live with family in America in October 1917, returning to Germany in June/July 1919. Whether they voluntarily left Canada or were among the prisoners who were forcibly repatriated at the end of the war is unknown.

Unsurprisingly, with some 250–350 individuals held against their will, tensions of all sorts ran high and bitter disputes broke out. It appears that the twenty children who lived in the camp (between eight and ten were born there) were shielded from these and doted on by the adult prisoners. Conscious that, unlike their compatriots outside the wire, these children were being deprived of an education, one man ran a school and activities were arranged for them. All belligerent countries had the right to request 'their' prisoners be visited by a consul of a neutral country.[108] Vancouver's Swiss Consul Samuel Gintzburger was a regular inspector and a strong advocate for all internees irrespective of nationality. He went so far as to submit internees' letters of complaint directly to his government, thereby bypassing the tight censorship meted out by officials in Ottawa.[109] Gintzburger worked, 'tirelessly on behalf of all the prisoners' including the children and, on at least one occasion, drove some of them into town to visit the cinema, the first time these innocent detainees (none aged over 10) had set foot outside the wire since their parents' internment.[110] Jewish Gintzburger was invited to a Christmas party at Vernon in 1917; prisoner #97, Paul Kopp presented him with a plaque, now held in the Swiss National Archives, depicting a mother encircling two small children.

With anti-German sentiments becoming increasingly virulent, life in Canada became exponentially harder for those who were, or appeared to be, German. One family (believed to be Leo, Martha and their son Alfred Mueller), requested internment, staging a 'sit-in' until they were accommodated within the camp after townsfolk wrecked hairdresser Leo's business.[111] The Mueller's second son was born behind the wire in 1918. Sadly in 1919, when tensions among prisoners reached fever pitch, a quarrel between one of Leo and one of a Carl Wagner's sons embroiled

Des uhlans fusillent un jeune berger de 13 ans qui s'opposait au rapt de son troupeau

'Uhlans shooting a 13-year-old cowherd who tried to protect his beasts'. This card, sent by a poilu on 3 October 1914, is part of a 'German Atrocities' series aiming to rouse anti-German feelings. (*Author's own collection*)

177· LA GRANDE GUERRE 1914-16. — TRIAUCOURT (Meuse .
La rue Haute-d'Evres brûlée par les Boches le 7 Septembre 1914.
Visé Paris 177
Benoist, Edit. - Bar-le-Duc

Another propaganda-type card carries the sender's ironic comment, 'How beautiful my country now is'. Child victims were frequently portrayed. (*Author's own collection*)

(*Above*) The *Histoire d'un brave petit soldat* proved popular with both French and English pre-readers and their parents. (*Portail Palanca - Occitanie Livre & Lecture*)

(*Left*) *Hurra Ein Kriegs Bilderbuch* was equally popular with those on the Central Powers' side. (*www.Spiegel.de*)

Lieb Vaterland magst ruhig sein!
Ein Kriegsbilderbuch mit Knüttelversen von
Arpad Schmidhammer

...ring von Jos. Scholz, Mainz

(*Above*) *Lieb Vaterland magst ruhig sein* was another popular pre-reader for German and Austrian infants. (*www.zeitlupe.co.at/werbung/propaganda1.html*)

(*Right*) *The Child's ABC of the War* enabled war-time infants to learn the alphabet and patriotism at one and the same time. (*The-SaleRoom.com*)

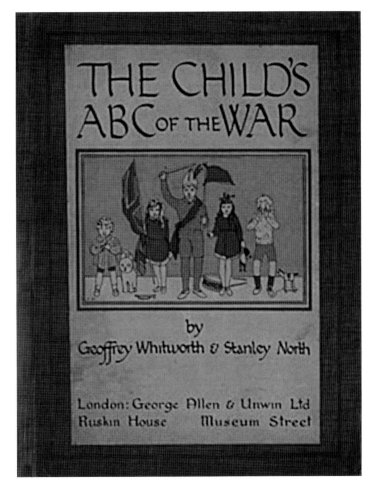

THE CHILD'S ABC OF THE WAR

by
Geoffrey Whitworth & Stanley North

London: George Allen & Unwin Ltd
Ruskin House   Museum Street

- les Fugitifs -

Belgian and French refugee children fleeing the Occupied Territories were a common sight in the early days. This card is part of a series sold in aid of French Army Orphans. (*Author's own collection*)

THE NEW PATENT
EXPLODING
TRENCH

This game proved too gruesome for all but the strongest stomachs and was withdrawn from sale. (*Antique Toy World Trader*)

Children frequently received certificates commending them for their patriotic efforts. These were often cherished by the recipients for years or decades, as was the case for this one awarded to Clara Whittaker. (*Author's own collection*)

'*Das Machinengewehr*'. This German Red Cross card shows how imaginative children could be in playing war. Unusually, the girl is 'firing' the sewing-machine gun which destroys whatever stands in its way. (*Author's own collection*)

Das Maſchinengewehr.
Hurrah! Jetzt kommt der Verbündeten Heer
Sogar mit einem Maſchinengewehr!
Das rattert und wirft blaue Bohnen
Auf die Koſakenſchwadronen.

Aus dem Bilderbuch: „Wie ſpielen Weltkrieg!" Verlag des Kriegshilfsbüreos des k. k. Ministeriums
des Innern. — In allen Buchhandlungen erhältlich zum Preiſe von 3 Kronen.

Encouraged to write to their serving fathers, countless children mention writing and receiving such letters; this postcard is part of a popular series sold on both sides of the Channel. (*Author's own collection*)

Diarist and subsequent pacifist Piete Kuhr with mother, brother and grandmother c. 1915. Piete's relationship with her jingoistic mother became increasingly problematic. (*Piła NaszeMiasto.pl*)

(*Above left*) Yves Congar at his wartime First Communion. He entered the priesthood in 1930, becoming a Cardinal shortly before his death. (*Conseil Départemental des Ardennes*)

(*Above right*) Simone de Beauvoir (c. 1914) became a leading feminist and renowned author. She soon understood that children could be exploited to raise money for the war effort. (*Pinterest*)

(*Below left*) Françoise Marette (b. 1908, seen here aged two). Headstrong from an early age, her diary shows how incomprehensible the war seemed to so young a child. (*Association Archives et Documentation Françoise-Dolto*)

(*Below right*) Germaine Paruit, aged 14. Her wartime diary gives a sensitive account both of living under occupation in Sedan and of her repatriation, via Evian, in December 1917. (*14ansen1914.wordpress.com*)

Libre et compatissante,
la Suisse accueille les veuves
et les orphelins de la Belgique
héroïque et meurtrie.

(*Left*) Switzerland had a well-established reputation for offering compassion and sanctuary to refugees in time of war. Here Helvetica welcomes a Belgian widow and children. (*Author's own collection*)

(*Below*) 500,000 civilians were repatriated from Occupied to Free France. Their journey to Evian on Lac Léman [Lake Geneva] was often harrowing, but they were warmly welcomed, despite the pressures refugees placed on the town's infrastructure. (*Author's own collection*)

This little boy became the face of the 2014 exhibition held at Evian to commemorate the town's wartime charitable reception of repatriates from Occupied France. (*Author's own collection*)

Lusitania survivor Helen Smith – she became the face of the *Lusitania*. (*Gare maritime*)

Tontine Street, Folkestone, May 1917. The raid shook Folkestone to the core and claimed many young lives. (*Kentonline.co.uk*)

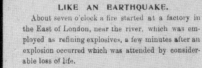

LIKE AN EARTHQUAKE.

About seven o'clock a fire started at a factory in the East of London, near the river, which was employed as refining explosives, a few minutes after an explosion occurred which was attended by considerable loss of life.

His Majesty the King has made inquiries as to the extent of the damage and loss of life, and has expressed his solicitude for the victims and their families.

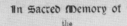

In Sacred Memory of

the

VICTIMS of the GREAT

EXPLOSION

in the East End of London
on Friday evening, January 19th, 1917.

MAY THEIR SOULS REST IN PEACE.

With sincere sympathy to the friends and relatives.

Mourning card serving as a reminder of the Silvertown Explosion. These types of cards often appeared after calamities. (*Author's own collection*)

Considered 'enemy aliens', Fred Kohse (L) and Victor Heiny (R) were amongst the German internees held at Vernon Camp, Canada. (*Vernon Morning Star, 18 September 2011*)

Interned for the simple reason that they were immigrants from the Ukraine, women and children were transported hundreds of miles from their homes in Canada and held as virtual Prisoners of War. (*Ukrainian Canadian Civil Liberties Association*)

This statue of the 'Interned Madonna' (Felicia and Mary Hancharak) was commissioned by the Ukrainian Canadian Civil Liberties Association (UCCLA). The sculpture is by John Boxtel and was unveiled in July 2001. It serves to remind that 'What was done to us was wrong'.

(*Above left and right*) Yvonne Vieslet was shot, aged 10, in October 1918 for giving her lunchtime bun to a French POW. A memorial was raised to her in Marchienne by public subscription. Sadly, the road named after her was recently renamed, this time in honour of a Belgian boxer! (*Author's own collection; original photograph by Ivan Newman*)

(*Below left*) Mabel Lethbridge suffered horrendous injuries in a munitions factory disaster. She became the youngest recipient of the OBE. (*Wikipedia*)

(*Below right*) Emilienne Moreau was awarded the British Military Medal for information given about German machine gun posts around Loos and, somewhat against her will, became France's 'Golden Girl'. (*Author's own collection*)

Fourteen-year-old Marina Yurlova followed her Cossack father to war. She served under a false name from 1914 to 1919 and was decorated three times for bravery. (*Pinterest*)

Thirteen-year-old disobedient Désiré Bianco made it to war on his third attempt. Stowing away on a Gallipoli-bound ship, he became a regimental mascot. (*Wikipedia*)

(*Right*) Underage Jean-Corentin Carré came to symbolize the French youngsters who, putting 'Duty Before Homework', ran away to serve. His actions are still celebrated in France. (*Wikipedia*)

(*Below*) A sanitized view of the Battle of Lemburg by Polish artist Wojciech Kossak. A number of teenage boys and girls fought with the Poles and became known as the 'Eaglets'. (*Wikipedia*)

Jean-Corentin CARRÉ
1900-1918
Engagé volontaire au 410ᵉ R. I., à 15 ans.
Mort en combat aérien, à 18 ans.

'Uncle Sam's' youngest doughboy, American boy soldier Ernest Wrentmore served in some of the US Army's fiercest actions. (*Findagrave.com*)

Illiterate, under age Thomas Ricketts was the only Newfoundland soldier to be awarded the VC. King George referred to him as 'splendid'. He returned to Canada to learn to read and write. (*Wikipedia*)

the fathers; Leo broke his neck in the ensuing fight. In 1920, widowed Martha and the children were deported to Germany; like all internees, they would have been released with only the clothes they were wearing. In Germany, former internees were treated to a 'heroes' welcome'.[112]

Although it was long assumed that families were held only at Vernon and Spirit Lake, a picture of a man holding a young toddler within Morrissey Camp's barbed wire confines, led researcher Sarah Beaulieu to discover that two First Class German prisoners' families lived alongside the internment camp, spending much time there during the day. Just before curfew, the POWs and guards would escort the family back to their quarters outside the wire. Detainee Leon Sauver's wife Charlotte and their young sons Ingo and Helgi, lived inside Morrissey.[113] It is impossible to know if these 'First Class' children were aware of the brutality meted out to Second Class prisoners or if their father's social status shielded them from the severity of the punishments at Morissey which led the indefatigable Consul Gintzburger to again submit complaints directly to the Swiss Government.

In the early twentieth century, a woman automatically assumed her husband's nationality upon marriage. This would have a significant impact upon many German and British-born women during the war. One was English-born Hilda Kohse who had emigrated to Canada around 1911 and married German boatbuilder Frederic. Now she was an enemy alien.[114] When her husband was detained, the family's property and money were confiscated leaving mother and infant son, Fred, destitute. With Frederic interned, Hilda took matters into her own hands. She put baby Fred into a boat and 'rowed up the gorge to the detaining centre where her husband was held and asked to be with him.'[115] The nonplussed authorities declared a detainment centre was 'no place for an Englishwoman'.[116] Penniless and homeless, mother and son moved behind Vernon's wire, which became their and Fred's cousin and age-contemporary Victor Heiny's 'home' for much longer than they could ever have anticipated.[117]

If Hilda had seen internment as a solution to her problems in 1914, she came to regret her actions. Requesting release due to her English birth, camp staff simply tore 'up her letters in front of her'.[118] She next appealed to a higher authority. Having made friends with an Englishwoman outside the wire and knowing that internees' post was censored, sometime in 1916, a letter addressed to the British House of Lords was smuggled out. However, their lordships' wheels turn slowly and the war had been over for almost two years before her letter was processed. Post-war, the family moved to Vancouver Island where Fred eventually became a fisherman.

In 1997 memorial plaques were unveiled at Vernon. Fred Kohse attended and shared memories of the place where he had spent his young childhood surrounded by a vista of barbed wire and where whole families were interned for who they were, not for what they had done. Fred could still recall 'the dry hills round the camp' where he and his cousin had spent so many formative years simply because his mother had married a man born in Germany.

With the Allies victorious and German nationals posing no conceivable threat, one might have imagined that popular and official attitudes towards them would have softened; not so. When word spread in Kelowna that several families were planning to move there, rumours of their ethnicity spread and a crowd of returned soldiers forcibly prevented their arrival. Ironically all twenty-nine of them were Canadian nationals. Kent West Ontario MP Herbert S. Clements' speech on 24 March 1919 demonstrates the extent of the xenophobia:

> I say unhesitatingly that every enemy alien who was interned during the war is today just as much an enemy as he was during the war, and I demand of this Government that each and every alien in this dominion should be deported at the earliest opportunity ... Cattle ships are good enough for them.[119]

He would have doubtless been cheered by the (Canada) Great War Veterans Association who were vigorously lobbying against these wrongly called aliens.[120]

A total of 8,759 individuals (including 81 women and 126 children) were interned; 3,138 of these could properly be classed as Prisoners of War, 5,441 internees were from the Ukrainian ethnographic territories.[121] Yet the majority of these, described in 1916 by City of Quebec American Consul G. Willrich as 'good, sturdy, inoffensive men, able and willing to work', would have felt no love for the Austro-Hungarian Empire they had left behind.[122] Instructions sent to the Canadian Government from London on 8 February 1915 gave a list of races 'considered to be *hostile* to Austro-Hungarian rule' (and thus friendly to Canada).[123] The list included those classed as Ukrainian. Ignoring these instructions, thousands of Ukrainians were sent to primitive and remote camps across the country including Spirit Lake. The Canadian government's draconian actions had a drastic effect on the lives of many children, even infants were targeted. On one occasion, 'under the order recently passed by the City Council an [8-week-old] tiny scrap of humanity being an alien enemy ... has been denied civic assistance at one of the hospitals'.[124] The *Daily British Whig* of 8 September 1917 anticipated that the treatment meted out to internees 'will have sown in their hearts the seeds of a bitterness that can never be extirpated'. Such 'seeds' grow in children's as well as adults' hearts.

Spirit Lake Camp, Abitibi region, separated from the rest of Quebec by 300 miles of virgin forest, was the second camp to house a significant number of the 156 children whom Canada interned. Surrounded by high barbed-wire fencing, it was the only Quebecois camp which could be classed as a 'concentration camp'.[125] Opened on 13 January 1915, on 19 April the first group of twenty married couples and children (ninety-two people), predominantly Ukrainian Catholics, were forcibly entrained in Montreal, their destination distant Spirit Lake. They, and occasionally their accompanying families, suffered significant abuse, some lost their lives and many their livelihoods as the small amount of wealth that they had accumulated through hard work since arriving in Canada was confiscated, never to be returned.

With unemployment sky high among Ukrainian men, and families dependent on soup kitchens, perhaps some of these hapless individuals initially believed William Pradley, Montreal's American Consul-General (then overseeing Austro-Hungary's affairs), who assured them that they were heading for guaranteed work, 'houses with gardens [which] would provide women and children with a healthy contrast to the city slums they currently endured.'[126] The reality turned out to be tarpaper shacks (for families), labouring for local road construction, or expanding the national park system for a pitiful 25c a day; the 'perimeter of the camp [was] surrounded by a high wire fence with large lamps at each corner [and] the gates [being] closed at night to prevent escapes'.[127] These men's labour, as opposed to the money they received was, according to contemporary documents 'computed at $1,500,000 a year.'[128] Money they never received. Although 177 military guards under Lieutenant Colonel William Rodden oversaw the 1,144 prisoners' every movement (at the camp's peak), about fifty men escaped.[129] A number of internees remained until 1920 because post-war these Ukrainians, who hadn't even left their camps during the war and who had been considered Austro-Hungarian, were now somehow deemed a 'Bolshevik' threat.[130]

With so many military personnel, it is unsurprising that some soldiers' families accompanied them. They appear to have been accommodated in separate lodgings but other than two infants' names, Arthur and Ethel, nothing further is known about them and their strange existence at the edge of Spirit Lake.[131]

On 13 January 2008, the 93rd anniversary of the opening of Spirit Lake Camp, 93-year-old Mary Bayrak, the last known survivor of any of the internment camps, died. The Hancharak (Hanczaruk) family, including her father Nkolay, had arrived at Spirit Lake in early 1915. He married internee Felicia Heilik.[132] One iconic internment photograph depicts a small, anxious looking be-scarfed woman cradling a swaddled infant against a backdrop of a stone wall and a military guard. Other small children gaze warily at the cameraman. The mother is Felicia, the infant Mary, born December 1915. Three generations were now confined behind Spirit Lake's wire.

Mary was one of the fifteen children born in the prisoners' village baptised by the Roman Catholic priest from Amos, the nearest settlement to Spirit Lake in March 1916. He also baptised two soldiers' infants, including a granddaughter of the camp commander. Was Mary the former internee who told her son that she was born 'in a little village just outside of Montreal'? This son, who like so many descendants initially knew nothing about the internment, as many internees found this shameful, eventually discovered that his mother had seen the light of day not in the fictionalised pleasant-sounding 'little village', but in 'a concentration camp in a tarpaper shack in the middle of nowhere'.[133] He added, 'They were concerned they were thrown in prison for nothing. There was barbed wire, soldiers, rifles, bayonets. It wasn't a subject they discussed.'[134]

The camps cast dark shadows, physical as well as mental, over internees. In his 1916 report, American Consul G. Willrich mentioned that tuberculosis was rife. One wartime victim was Mary's grandmother. Then, post-internment, 32-year-old Felicia died and little Mary spent two years in Edmonton Hospital. Mary was not alone in losing a parent to TB. The disease, contracted in the camps, blighted many family's post-camp life, even going down the generations as happened with Mary's own children.

WHAT WAS DONE TO US WAS WRONG

American Vice-Consul Marsh visited Spirit Lake in October 1915. Families would have lived in what Marsh called the 'married prisoners' village' with 'rudimentary' log bunkhouses accommodating one to four families.[135] Marsh refers to the 'Austro-Hungarians' of the 'laboring class' as 'prisoners', showing he had accepted the dominant view of internees. There is no evidence whether his plans to open a school for the 114 children ever materialised.

When Consul Willrich visited Spirit Lake in November 1916, by then in the grips of a strike, his comments on 'deplorable' conditions, with the 'prisoners huddled together like a herd of sheep in winter – cold and shivering from exposure' make grim reading.[136] Despite living in families' quarters, children would have been all too aware of the way the men, including their own fathers, were treated. Morning and evening roll-call, where all internees had to line up and, judging by a photograph, stand to attention, not to mention a 9 pm curfew, would have been added reminders that their day was bound by military rules.[137]

One of the most heart-rending of the litany of complaints Willrich documented came from a man interned without his family. Arrested in March 1916, H. Domytryk was not alone in leaving distraught children (aged between 9 and 1) behind. Fearful that his wife would be forced to beg for bread and that his children would starve and suffer from exposure in the small house he was purchasing in Edmonton, he could only leave his family a few dollars to live on, a situation the government forced upon detainees.[138] Transferred to Spirit Lake, over 2,500 kilometres away, Domytryk was among the fathers who 'just disappeared when coming home from work ... leaving children fatherless until the end of the war when they were freed from the prison camps.'[139] Consul Willrich described their first meeting when Domytryk handed him a 'pathetic letter' written by 9-year-old Katie. With tight censorship of both outgoing and incoming letters, it is amazing that hers reached him.[140]

My dear father:
We haven't nothing to eat and they do not want to give us no wood. My mother has to go four times to get something to eat. It is better with you, because we had everything to eat. This shack is no good, my mother is going down town every day and I have to go with her and I don't go to school at winter. It is cold in that shack. We your

91

small children Kiss your hands my dear father. Goodbye my dear father. Come home right away.[141]

The young Domytrks were among 5,439 children living in Canada with so-called enemy alien fathers. On 1 June 1915, it was calculated that there were also 14,304 children left in 'the Old Country' (Ukraine). Remittances from their 6,126 fathers were now cut off as few if any of these men had work – and no way of sending money back even if they had any.[142] The hardship these families suffered would have been even greater than those in Canada – and even less documented.

Mary Manko was born in Montreal in 1909. Like most Ukrainian internees, her parents had 'been invited [to Canada]. They worked hard. They contributed to this country, with their blood, sweat and tears'. But when war came, 'thousands of Ukrainian Canadians [were] rounded up as "enemy aliens"'. [143] The family's nightmare started in early 1915, when André and Catherine, their Canadian-citizen children, 6-year-old Mary, John, Annie and 2-year-old Nellie arrived at Spirit Lake, to be interned as Second Class Prisoners of War. Nellie died on 22 May 1915. Seventy-nine years after her sister's death, Mary attempted to find her grave, 'I would like to go back and visit Nellie's grave, one last time. But I'm told it's no longer there. Her body was moved. Why, or when, or how, I don't know. No one seems to know where she rests'. Officially, 'Proper records of all deaths are kept, burials made with due decorum and the identity of graves established.'[144] Mary who planned to be buried with her parents wished Nellie could be with them. 'But that will never be. Ottawa interned our family together in life. In death Ottawa will keep us apart.' Thinking both of the Ukrainians and of those whom Canada interned in the Second World War, Mary concluded, 'Because no one bothered to remember or learn about the wrong that was done to us, it was done to others again and yet again. Maybe there's an even greater wrong in that.'[145]

If baby Nellie Manko's grave, and hundreds of others, disappeared, so too did the internment story. Collective amnesia descended on the government, aided by a meeting of the Honourable Treasury Board on 5 March 1954 which agreed that any remaining archival records were to be destroyed.[146] Perhaps these gentlemen were unaware that the reports sent by Swiss and American inspectors were, and are still, retained in the Swiss Federal Archives.

Internees' property was not returned, those who had worked for a pitiful 25c a day were not paid their full wages, nor did they receive any compensation. 'Thousands of dollars and valuables were confiscated … without record, which made theft possible. Upon each individual's arrest, whatever valuables they might have had were seized.'[147] It has been estimated that nearly $30,000 in cash 'was left in the Receiver-General's Office at the end of the internment operations. The value of all other assets held has not been calculated.'[148] Those who have now made claims against the Canadian government point out that the $10million fund set up a century later to compensate descendants is not government money but is simply what rightfully belongs to internees' families.

Quebecois writer J-Ulric Dumont's novel *Le Pays du Domaine*, based on Spirit Lake, epitomises the internment programme; its 'sinister shadows, echoing cries of women', and its overwhelming sense of melancholy endure to this day, serving as a reminder of all the 'restless souls who were interned and kept at gunpoint' during a black period in Canadian history'.[149] A period so dark that for ninety years officialdom claimed, 'that never happened'.

The Ukrainian Canadian Restitution Act received Royal Assent on 28 November 2005. Finally, it was acknowledged that the unlawful internment of innocent men, women and children had indeed happened.[150]

CHAPTER FOUR

Courage Beyond Their Years

While most children in belligerent nations spent the war years living on what the British poet Rose Macauley termed 'the rim of the shadow of Hell', the deliberate actions of some youngsters brought them inside the rim. Demonstrating courage beyond their years, they earned recognition from their peers and their nation.[1]

Yvonne Vieslet: 'Shot for a bun.'

Born on 8 June 1908 in Marchienne au Pont, a small commune 4 kilometres from Charleroi (Belgium), the German army's inexorable advance into Belgium shattered Yvonne Vieslet's childhood on 22 August 1914. Charleroi was in flames; dozens of buildings, including Yvonne's home, were little more than smouldering ruins, numerous citizens were executed and hundreds of workers deported to Germany as slave labourers, a fate which Yvonne's father Emile, a metal worker in nearby Monceau-sur-Sambre, miraculously escaped. Yvonne, known as playful and conscientious, attended school in Monceau.[2] By 1918, most Belgians were living barely above starvation levels and the Comité de Secours distributed a daily 'coque' (brioche bun) to school children, this constituted their lunch.

On Saturday 12 October 1918, with hopes of an Allied victory gathering force, Yvonne's classmates heard that a group of some twenty-five French prisoners of war were being temporarily held in a requisitioned mansion in the Cercle Saint Edouard which, surrounded by iron railings, had been turned into a makeshift transit camp where they were closely guarded by German soldiers. Despite being in retreat in many parts of the line, the Germans were taking prisoners with them – and closely guarding them. Although POWs were a common sight in Brussels, they were a novelty in the smaller communes. The young pupils were eager to see them after school finished, and Yvonne persuaded her mother to let her go before they went to meet her father. When Yvonne and her mother Adeline arrived at the Cercle, despite the interdiction on making contact, people were trying to reach through the bars to give the starving Frenchmen something to eat and drink. Although with a less disastrous outcome, on the very same day in Brussels, English governess Mary Thorp witnessed similar scenes, 'Belgians cheered them, brought them food, tobacco ... plundered the adjacent fruit barrows'; in Monceau, German sentries tried to restrain the spectators and tempers ran high.[3] Distressed by the prisoners' plight, Yvonne, who like many pupils had imbibed the lesson taught at school that soldiers had sacrificed themselves for the sake of the children, wanted to do something in return.[4] She went forward holding out her bread to one of the prisoners; a soldier drew his Mauser and fired. Seriously wounded in the stomach, Yvonne crumpled at her mother's feet; three other bystanders were also wounded. Taken to hospital, Yvonne died in the late morning of the following day with the priest who had administered the Last Rites assuring her distraught parents that their child had died for Belgium.[5] Buried on 16 October, school children lined the funeral route and accompanied her body to its resting place among the sixty-six citizens of Monceau shot in 1914 by the Germans.[6] The bed in which she had died subsequently carried her name, while on 12 October 1919, a plaque was unveiled at her school with the bust of a smiling child holding out her bun.

Although a different account of the episode began circulating in 1984 (thus sixty odd years after the event), which suggests that the shooting was unintentional, the version which entered – and has largely remained – in the Belgian national consciousness, was that the child had performed an act of pure Christian charity. The tale of her actions, not to mention a poem composed by one of the prisoners, spread rapidly across the region and, following the Armistice, numerous pictures, additional poems and even commemorative coins/medals, as well as a 1937 film *La Tragédie de Marchienne,* appeared in her honour.[7]

On 11 September 1919, President Raymond Poincaré posthumously awarded her the Médaille de la Reconnaissance Française. Nine years later, her remains were exhumed and transferred to the Carré d'Honneur to be reburied on 1 July 1928, close to the spot where the atrocity occurred. Following a requiem mass, an elaborate tombstone, depicting Yvonne stretching out her hand holding the bread with an inscription reading, 'To Yvonne Vieslet, shot at the age of ten for having given her school bun to a French prisoner', was unveiled in the presence of Princess Marie-José of Belgium who, to the delight of the crowds, had previously visited the hospital where Yvonne had been cared for. The Belgian Ambassador to the UK attended and, representing the French Army, General Lacapelle, General Officer Commanding the 1st Army Corps at Lille. On a platform adjacent to where Yvonne was shot, Lacapelle conferred on the child a posthumous Croix de Guerre, giving the decoration to her older sister to whom Princess Marie-José also handed the Cross of the Order of Leopold. Local poet G. Moulin's long dramatic hyperbolic poem recounting her deeds was read at the unveiling.[8] Soon, roads, buildings, a creche, and a hostel for young girls in Brussels bore her name.[9] In a country which had lived under the heel of a brutal invader and whose citizens had struggled merely to survive the 1,561 days of war, there were relatively few national heroes to revere. Starvation, deportation and 'civil disobedience' do not lend themselves to heroization. Her act of simple charity, the brutality of her death and the innocence of her ten years, gave Yvonne Vieslet a place among Belgium's national heroes.

Although during the second occupation the Nazis removed and broke up the monument, illicit flowers appeared at the spot every 12 October. With the tombstone restored in 1956, a bronze sculpture, commissioned by the Fédération Nationale des Combatants, depicting Yvonne handing her bun through the bars was erected outside her school at Monceau sur-Sambre encouraging children to revere and preserve the memory of their own little heroine.

Violet Buckthorpe: 'A Heroine in Pinafores.'

Born in Walthamstow in 1902, sometime after 1911, Violet Buckthorpe's silversmith father Frederick moved his family to the City of London's Bartholomew Close, a move that would have significant repercussions once war was declared. Although Stoke Newington had been bombed on 31 May 1915, it was only in August 1915 that the Kaiser agreed that London could be systematically targeted. Although several attacks were carried out in August, none, as far as the German aircrews were concerned, achieved spectacular success. This changed when, on the evening of 8 September 1915, 31-year-old Kapitänleutnant Heinrich Mathy, among Germany's most successful and highly decorated airship commanders, took command of Zeppelin L13 with its massive payload of incendiary bombs. He inflicted an estimated £534,287 (£58,771,570 today) of damage (one sixth of total air raid damage in the UK during the First World War), on the area around the City. Starting in Golders Green where he dropped two explosive and ten incendiary bombs, Mathy then headed for central London. Picked up by searchlights, 'twenty-six guns in and around London opened fire but without scoring a hit', allowing him to indulge in 'promiscuous' bombing.[10] Having dropped a bomb in Bloomsbury, narrowly missing the British Museum, he continued through Holborn, over the Clerkenwell Road, Leather Lane and Hatton Garden, dropping bombs on the way.

Once over St Bartholomew's Hospital which, parenthetically, still carries reminders of this fateful night with one wall scarred by the shrapnel damage it sustained, Mathy unleashed what he termed his 'love gift to England': a 660lb bomb which exploded over Bartholomew Close creating an 8ft-deep crater and flattening or significantly damaging the nearby buildings, some of which were business premises; the others were residential or mixed use. With the amount of incendiaries dropped, unsurprisingly, fires raged for several hours; twenty-two people were killed and eighty-seven injured, including Violet Buckthorpe.[11] In his subsequent report, Mathy described looking down from the control gondola of L13 and watching as 'a whole cluster of lights vanished in the crater'.[12] When walking around the area early the next morning, Bomber Pilot Donald Harkness observed,

Two huge six storey buildings on one side of the street and one on the other [still] burning fiercely while flames poured out of every window and met in a fiery furnace above, lighting up the town for miles around and making the golden cross on St Paul's glitter and sparkle'.[13]

Unaware of the drama soon to take place in the skies above their home, Frederick and Daisy Buckthorpe had gone out for the evening, leaving their four children, 13-year-old Violet, 12-year-old Rose and 10-year-old Frederick in the care of their grandmother. The children were playing quietly on the first floor and baby Marjorie was asleep on the floor above when Mathy unleashed his 'gift'.

The force of the bomb was such that the whole of the window in the room where the youngsters were playing was blown over their heads, landing against the opposite wall, strewing bricks, mortar and debris around the room. Outside, the stairs both to the bedroom above and to the street below were rocking as though they would give way any moment. Aware that Marjorie was in considerable danger, Violet scrambled up the 'insecure stairs, some of which had disappeared, leaving wide gaps. She found the little child in bed covered by debris from the falling ceiling.'[14] Clutching her sister in her arms, she turned around to discover that most of the stairs had now disappeared and the staircase was about to give way. Making her way down by means of jumping over the gaps where a stair should have been and clinging to the shaking banister, she was convinced that the baby was wounded as she could see blood. Once outside, she took off her own dress, wrapped it round the child and knelt down to pray. She then 'hurried to the nearest hospital [presumably St Barth's] where the baby was taken care of and she herself was found to be sorely wounded and bleeding, something she had not noticed in her concern for her sister'. Subsequently, a piece of glass was taken from her ear.

While the human drama was played out below, Mathy was making his way safely across the channel. Almost immediately summoned by the Kaiser and Kaiserin to Berlin, who wished to be certain that no harm had been done to Buckingham Palace (his first cousin George V's home), churches or historic buildings. The pilot assured them 'all bombs were accurately aimed' – a point which he knew was, at best, economical with the truth because an ability to pinpoint targets was far beyond the technology of the day. The Kaiser may have been less pleased to know that Mathy's actions added recruits to Kitchener's New Army, as recruiting sergeants were soon roaming the nearby streets taking the names of men, suitably outraged by what had happened, now eager to volunteer. Violet's father did not however feel similarly moved; he only entered the Royal Flying Corps as a conscript in January 1918.

While Mathy was being lauded in Berlin, the British government, fearing panic among the civilian population, had taken steps to insure that no details of the raid were published beyond the fact that it had occurred, several fires had broken out and the casualty list was 106. It would be some considerable time before Violet's heroism reached beyond a very limited audience and her actions publicly acknowledged.

One wonders whether the Buckthorpe family read in *Sunday Mirror* on 29 October 1916 that 'Knight of the Sky' Kapitänleutnant Heinrich Mathy was no more. Having completed '14 combat flights in the course of which he had dropped about 34,000 kg of bombs', he and the crew of L31 had been brought down over Potter's Bar.[15] Having chosen to jump rather than burn to death, the following day, crowds from far and wide paid a shilling to see the wreckage of the Zeppelin and the imprint of Mathy's body in the soft earth.

Four weeks later, it was Violet who featured in newspapers; on Saturday 25 November 1916, *Birmingham Daily Mail* published details of 'the little Heroine of the Zeppelin Raid'. The story was rapidly syndicated, some newspapers referring to her as the 'heroine in pinafores'; she also featured in the (to modern readers irritatingly) didactic *The Children's War.* On 23 November, in the prestigious surroundings of London's Mansion House, the Lord Mayor of London, Sir William Treloar, had presented the child with a gold wrist watch, the gift of the Carnegie Hero Trust Fund, established in Britain in 1908 to recognise that while 'The false heroes of barbarous man are those who can only boast of the destruction of their fellows. The true heroes of civilisation are those alone who save or greatly serve them.' To qualify for the award, 'The heroic act must have been voluntary and have involved risk to the rescuer's life.' In addition, 'the Trustees will maintain a continuing interest in the welfare of the person recognised and/or their family'.[16] Violet's award cited her 'exceptionally heroic conduct on the occasion of a Zeppelin raid'. In addition to the watch, in itself an unusual possession for a child, she was also presented with a £30 (just under £3,000 today) educational grant which she used to prepare for the Civil Service entrance examinations.

Featuring in several Australian newspapers' sections relating to 'Some Wonderful Kiddies. Gallant Acts that have been performed by Children in many places and many circumstances', journalists echoed the Lord Mayor's 'hope that [Violet] will grow up ever having before her the ideal which she has already displayed so well – performance of duty and thought for those who are weak and helpless.'[17] Every newspaper was keen to stress the Lord Mayor's peroration praising Violet's youth, her gender and her actions, convinced that such 'pluck by a girl of such tender years must arouse a thrill of pride throughout the country'. By saving her infant sister,

> she had displayed the spirit of Britain in its determination to defeat the power of might against right, and by her immediate and tender thought she had shown all those qualities which had produced in England the Florence Nightingales of the present war. Her action will be the admiration of the motherhood of the country.

Violet's name is inscribed on the Carnegie Hero Trust Fund's Roll of Honour held at the Andrew Carnegie Birthplace Museum in Dunfermline, Scotland.

Eric Bush: 'Dining with the General.'

Sometime in late May or early June 1915, Royal Navy officer Eric Wheeler Bush, serving on armoured cruiser *Bacchante*, flagship of the 7th Cruiser Squadron, had been invited to dine with General William Birdwood, (commander of the Australia and New Zealand forces) at Gallipoli. The British officer was suitably impressed, 'To prepare for this great event, I scrounged some fresh water and tried to get my hands clean and improved my shirt by rinsing it with sea water'. The invitation and his fellow diners surprised him for, when, 'I reached the dug-out, I discovered I was his only guest'.[18]

Apart from both having been born in India, the two men had little in common; after all, General Birdwood was tipped by some as a future commander-in-chief and Eric Bush was a 15-year-old midshipman, or 'snotty' (so-called because the buttons on the cuffs of their monkey jackets were allegedly to prevent them wiping their noses on their sleeves!). Nevertheless, the boy could hold his head up in such distinguished company for while his host wore the ribbon of the Distinguished Service Order, the child could put up that of the Distinguished Service Cross, a decoration awarded for his 'Gallantry during active operations against the enemy at sea', the youngest person ever to have been so honoured. Although Eric is tantalisingly silent about the dinner conversation between him and the 49-year-old general, it is safe to assume that his part in the ill-fated 25 April 1915 landings on the beach known as Anzac would have featured. For seventy-two heart-breaking hours from dawn on 25 April 1915, with fatalities sustained among the crew as well as those they were landing, the picket boat – of which the teenager was in charge – had ferried soldiers to the beach and the wounded back to ships. And his duties continued almost without a break, for a month. Thus, there would have been plenty to discuss.

Eric's very presence on that ill-fated day had caused jealousy among his fellow snotties who, learning of the responsibilities falling on his very young shoulders, had taunted him with being 'Favoured! Favoured!'[19] He had been placed in charge of *Bacchante*'s picket boat which was to 'tow the launch, the first cutter and a merchant ship's lifeboat which we have borrowed for the occasion'. With 160 soldiers and a crew of eight (at least nominally) under his orders, it was not, as he put it, 'a bad command for a Midshipman', and one which more senior midshipmen hankered after, hence the taunting.[20] He modestly concluded that his selection owed much to practicality because, standing at barely 5ft tall, 'I was the least likely to stop bullet or shell'.[21]

Young as he was, by the time he took charge of the picket boat, Eric had seen more action than many an older man for he had been mobilised before war was declared. Yet this mobilisation – and the distinguished naval career that followed, could so nearly not have happened. When interviewed for a place at the Royal Naval College Osborne in April 1912, 'I could not find Tasmania or Madagascar on the map'. Then to further reduce his chances, 'I tripped over an electric light lead' when leaving the room. When his anxious parents assessed the likelihood of Eric being accepted, 'gloom descended over the Vicarage'.[22] The interviewers undoubtedly felt that his lack of geographical knowledge could be remedied and for two years he underwent the gruelling training programme ('if we put a foot wrong we had our backsides beaten') which was the first step in turning a 12-year-old boy into an officer in His Majesty's Navy. In peacetime, youths were generally appointed to the Fleet as midshipmen at about the age of 17½.

This leisurely progression from college to training ship to sea, changed on 1 August 1914 when a telegram bearing the one word 'Mobilise' was received. Appointed to ships of the Second Fleet, 'where it was hoped that we could make ourselves useful and continue with our training in comparative safety, 434 excited boys got away, complete with their sea chests, in six hours.' Posted to *Bacchante*, Eric was too small to lift his own sea chest.[23] But the 'comparative safety' element proved illusory. He and his comrades would soon undergo their baptism of fire at the 28 August 1914 Battle of Heligoland Bight. Like so many of his contemporaries across all belligerent nations, Eric's idea of a naval (or indeed a land) battle was,

> based on a serial I had read in *Chums* … Now I was to witness the aftermath of the real thing. The fo'c'sle of one of the destroyers had received a direct hit, killing most of the crew … I was horrified to see streaks of blood on the upper deck and down the ship's side.

When some of the wounded and dying were brought on board, ghoulish curiosity soon got the better of many of the children who 'had never seen a dead man before [so] we had a peep at them. Later on, we had a look at some of the amputated limbs hidden behind a cushion in the Captain's cabin.'[24]

While Eric was merely observing an action, his classmate and contemporary midshipman, Christopher (Kit) Wykeham-Musgrave (b. 4 April 1899) – known to be 'keen and trustworthy, keen at all games and sports', was aboard HMS *Aboukir*.[25] He would soon earn himself a place in the Royal Navy's annals. On 22 September 1914, *Aboukir,* along with sister ships *Hogue* and *Cressy* (largely crewed by reservists and boy sailors) were patrolling off the Dutch coast when, with deadly effect, U-Boat 9 commanded by Otto Weddigen, torpedoed *Aboukir,* blasting a hole in her starboard hull. Kit, asleep 'in the gunroom when the explosion happened', was soon swimming for his life in the unwelcoming North Sea.[26] Spotted by lookouts aboard *Hogue*, which was scouring the sea for survivors, a rope was lowered. But, 'just as the dazed teenager was being hauled aboard, a pair of torpedoes from U-9 slammed into the ship's hull.' Within fifteen minutes *Hogue* joined *Aboukir* on the seabed. Once again, with seconds to spare, Kit dived back into the sea and, 'with a group of survivors from both ships began paddling frantically for *Cressy,* the last remaining British vessel.' Plucked again from the sea, Kit must surely have thought that this time his luck would hold, particularly as he was brought a steaming mug of hot cocoa. The enemy had different ideas and U-boat 9's remaining two torpedoes found their target: *Cressy*. Doubtless drawing on strength he did not know he had and clinging to a small plank of wood, for the third time in little over an hour, the boy 'battled for his life' for over three hours in the inhospitable sea. His local newspaper, *Warwickshire Advertiser and Leamington Gazette* 26 September 1914, asserted that, had he not then been picked up by a Dutch fishing vessel *Titan*, he would have joined the 1,300 casualties of the triple attacks who have no known grave but the sea. His letter to his grandmother informed her that 'I had the most thrilling experience'. The newspaper's hopes of a 'long and distinguished career in the service of his country' for the child described by one survivor who glimpsed him clinging to his plank as 'a little light-haired boy' were prescient. Lieutenant Commander Wykeham-Musgrove died in 1989 aged 90.[27]

No doubt some of Kit's classmates envied the escapades of the Navy's 'luckiest mariner'. Envy that turned to anxiety when the loss of so many cadets 'caused outcry in the Press'. To their relief, on 30 November 1914 Winston Churchill, then First Lord of the Admiralty, defended the decision to send these very young lads 'to sea in time of war... They would learn incomparably more of their profession in war than any educational establishment could teach them ...They render useful service.'[28] Supporting Churchill's views, Wykeham-Musgrave's mother argued that if boy sailors were expected to put their lives at risk at sea, then boys of the officer class should do no less. The snotties (if not all their parents) concurred. Reflecting decades later on the part the boys played in the Gallipoli landings, Bush was adamant,

> It would have been disastrous to our morale if we midshipmen had been deprived of our part in the landings because we were so young. After all it was in the boats that midshipmen belonged ... To have been kept back would have meant a complete loss of face and heart. We were in a manner of speaking just as expendable as anyone else.[29]

Expendable or not, diminutive midshipman Eric Bush was not feeling totally relaxed on the night of 24 April 1915, hours before the dawn landings. In his hammock trying to snatch some sleep, 'I put my hands together. I felt scared for the first time'. Hearing the cry, 'Midshipman of the picket boat', he knew that zero hour had come.[30] Nowadays the level of responsibility placed on such young shoulders appears breathtaking. Decades later, he recalled,

> The shore is about two miles away. The moon has set and it is one of the darkest nights I can remember... We are alone: twelve picket boats with their tows steaming in line abreast, spearhead of the invasion. It's 4.20 now. Soon it will all be over.

Grimly aware that something is going horribly wrong,

> We've been seen! ... The enemy opens fire and down comes a rain of bullets ...The time is 4.30 am ...There is no cover for our soldiers and several are wounded before the shore is reached. I see some of them fall back into the crowded boats as they stand to jump out.[31]

If casualties among the landing troops were horrendous, the boats and tows bringing them in were far from immune,

> Our picket boat had received a direct hit from a shell which had not exploded; otherwise I might not be here.[32]

It was obvious, even to Eric's young inexperienced eyes, that things were not going to plan, 'There are hundreds [of wounded] to be taken off and many have been lying in the sun all day. It is a long and painful task.[33] Dawn turns to day turns to night and then, 'it is daylight again and we are concentrating on landing water and ammunition and evacuating casualties', often desperately trying to find hospital ships with space for yet another cargo of fearfully wounded men, some, as army nurse Anna Cameron recalled with horror in her diary, being 'shot further in the boats which took them to us' – boats 'commanded' for the most part by teenage middies.

Night falls again, 'We are just beginning to wonder how much longer our boat's crew can keep going. Some of us can hardly keep our eyes open from lack of sleep.' Eventually with the 'three boats in tow, we are steaming back to the ship. We can see her ahead of us.' At midnight on 27 April, having been 'on our legs for seventy-two hours', Eric was put to bed in 'Lieutenant Tom Phillips' cabin'. Some kind soul had laid out his pyjamas and provided hot water. Schoolboy that he still was, he was 'too weary to wash', and tumbled between the sheets. Waking what he imagined to be a few hours later as it was 'still dark', to the amusement of the quartermaster and other sailors, he discovered, 'I've slept the clock round'.[34]

Soon Eric was back on duty evacuating the wounded. 'This became increasingly heart-breaking.' With casualty numbers having been totally underestimated, the wounded were almost touted round the hospital ships. 'Sorry old chap, full up here!' said the first ship. 'We can take three walking cases' said the second, and so it went on, sometimes pleading, other times insisting that a few more could be squeezed aboard. 'When cot cases were hoisted in, we had to wait for the stretchers to be returned as they were urgently needed ashore. [Then] we were back at the pier again with blood-stained stretchers.'[35] 'No one at Anzac will ever forget the terrible smell of rotting corpses which was worse at night as far as we were concerned because of the offshore wind. Hundreds of bodies, friend and foe, lay between the trenches, frizzled by the sun and black with flies.'[36]

With things going increasingly badly at Anzac and further south at Krithia, further landings were planned at Suvla Bay in early August 1915. Eric was again commanding *Bacchante's* picket boat. 'There was not a sound ashore except from a dog barking some distance inland', doubtless an ancestor of the wild dogs that still roam Suvla today.[37] These troops' reception would be as hostile and the plight of those at Suvla as desperate as that of the men still refusing to surrender their few yards of land at Anzac and Sedd el-Bahr.

Few teenagers can have spent the days immediately preceding their sixteenth birthday in a more unusual way than Midshipman Eric Bush DSC. Just after the Suvla landings, on 9 August 1915,

> I was taken up to the trenches below Chunuk Bair and saw through a trench periscope heaps of casualties – friend and foe – lying on the ground. Such is the impressionable nature of a boy of that age that the memory of the scene [...] remained imprinted on my mind.[38]

By mid-August his services were requested back at Anzac and its stream of wounded which 'we thought would never end', often sleeping in dug-outs when *Bacchante* was out of reach. The blissful night in Lieutenant Philips' bed but a distant memory.[39]

Although troops remained in Gallipoli until 8 January 1916, 'we in *Bacchante* took no part in the famously successful evacuation because we had been ordered to Malta ... We couldn't get there fast enough.'[40] Like the teenagers they were, *Bacchante's* midshipmen soon painted Malta red. One sailor was, however, sympathetic when seeing the hungover Eric 'hanging on to the guard rails for dear life and feed[ing] the fishes generously, "Corf it up, Sir", he said, "We'll soon be back in dear old Blighty."'[41] Complaints about their drunken and loutish behaviour reached the commander, 'there was a frightful row afterwards and most of us had our backsides beaten'. Being General Birdwood's dinner guest and the nation's youngest recipient of the DSC did not spare Midshipman Bush's posterior!

Back in 'dear old Blighty' in early 1916, once home in Bathford,

> I went straight away to the toy cupboard and opened the doors wide. My fort was on the middle shelf together with a lot of soldiers ...

My Red Cross ambulance lay among them complete with nurses, stretchers and wounded soldiers and a little hospital tent. I arranged the soldiers in "column of route", a formation I had learnt about in *Bacchante.* It was strange to be able to play with soldiers again although I hoped no one would see me … I arranged a couple of 15-pounder shell-cases and some bullets I had found at Anzac and I put two Turkish bayonets crosswise on the wall.' [42]

The fusion of man and boy was complete.

With leave over, Eric joined *Revenge* in time for the Battle of Jutland where another teenager, 16-year-old Jack Cornwell, Bush's junior by four months, would make history as the youngest recipient of the VC. Yet Jutland made far less impression than Gallipoli, 'I have taken part in many naval actions in both World Wars, but, looking back now, none of them has such a place in my memory and in my heart as Gallipoli.'[43]

Having been present at the scuttling of the German Fleet at Scapa Flow and with 'nearly all those who had slept at my end of [the] dormitory [at Osborne] gone', Eric and 370 young naval officers arrived in Cambridge to finish the education which had been so drastically curtailed on 1 August 1914. Hearing of the youngsters' arrival and still mourning the loss of his own underage son John (KIA Loos September 1915), Rudyard Kipling wrote a prayer/poem for these old young men who had served their country well. May 'the Soul of the Child at last let fall the unjust load it bore.'[44]

Mabel Lethbridge: 'hurled through the air, falling down, down into the darkness.'

Born on 19 May 1900 in Somerset, Mabel's baptismal records indicate her father John served with Paget's Horse, known for their service in the Boer War. The 1901 UK census records Mabel's American-born mother Florence as 'living on her own means', while John was overseas. With a butler, a cook and two nursery nurses, the family lived in comfortable circumstances. In 1903, very unusually for the time, John successfully sued for divorce, the decree nisi granted in March gave the co-respondent as 'Harold Webber', whom Mabel refers to as 'a friend of the family'; he would come to impact significantly upon Mabel's life. In 1907, John was living in Kenya where he was declared bankrupt and although his children spent seven months with him, he appears to have had no further contact with his six offspring. Following this rupture, by 1911, Mabel who suffered from 'a wasting illness', was living with her mother and two brothers in County Cork, Ireland; the 1911 Ireland census records Harold as a 'visitor'. As a punishment for unladylike behaviour, in 1915 she arrived at Haberdasher's Aske's School (Hertfordshire), an establishment she considered 'dreadful' and from which she narrowly escaped being expelled.[45]

Back in London, Mabel's stormy relationship with her mother and their diametrically opposed views about appropriate behaviour led her, 'on a wet dreary Monday in February 1917' to leave home, bound for the voluntary subscription Royal Eye and Ear Hospital, Bradford, where her elder sister had arranged for her to undertake nursing training. She was 'immensely contented when at the end of my month's trial Matron announced she would keep me. My salary was to be £15 [about £1,500] pa'.[46] Either forgetting Mabel's youth, or simply because the hospital was chronically short-staffed, matron soon moved her to a soldiers' ward with horrifically injured soldiers. Initially 'distracted with terror and anguish by all I saw. Some terribly blinded, others with unspeakable facial disfigurement or terrible head wounds … I found myself brought face to face with war … the ugly side of war', the 16-year-old soon 'rejoiced that I was permitted to take so active a part at last.'[47]

Mabel might have rejoiced at her active part; her mother was unimpressed. Deeming Mabel too young to be on night duty in a soldiers' ward, she demanded her return to Ealing. Nevertheless, Mabel remained convinced that 'there was a place for me in this war [where] I could be of service to my country'.[48] She found that place when Harold, who was 'making shells at the Napier Munition Factory at Acton', told her that there was a 'terrible shortage of shells'; when he explained 'every pair of hands counted', Mabel felt, 'I could do no less than offer mine.'[49]

Full of teenage enthusiasm, and despite her mother thinking she should become a 'Voluntary Worker' where she could 'mak[e] bandages, knit and [do] goodness knows what', Mabel headed to the local Labour Exchange; she was offered paid employment 'sewing wings of aeroplanes at the White City'. 'Sewing' sounding suitably ladylike, her mother agreed, 'if it is a part time job'.[50]

Although children as young as 13 and 14 worked legitimately in factories, there were strict rules relating to where they could be employed; they were excluded from areas known as the 'Danger Sheds', where workers handled high explosives and other dangerous materials. However, just as teenage boys lied about their age in their endeavours to enlist, girls were up to the same tricks in the factories and one such was Mabel. At the Labour Exchange, she calmly gave her age as 18. The slightly sceptical clerk questioned her, explaining, 'We have to be so careful here', particularly as that morning's batch of prospective workers were destined for 'Number 7 National Filling Factory at Hayes'. She added that this factory was 'very particular' about not employing girls under 18.[51] However, she accepted Mabel's assurance; without confessing to her mother, Mabel was now a hand at Hayes.

Mabel's first day at work proved an eyeopener for one as gently reared as she. Having put to the back of her mind the grim words of a woman who waited with her at the bus stop that her daughter had worked at Hayes, and the previous year had been 'all blowed to bits', and successfully negotiated her way through the 'soldiers with fixed bayonets [who] guarded the gates and challenged my entry', she was sent to the Inspection Shed where nurses checked on the health of potential workers and whether they had head lice – again quite a shock for a person of her social class.[52] She was instructed to report to C Shed for a lecture on the safe handling of explosives and the issuing of magazine clothes which 'are handed out utterly irrespective of size'.[53]

With her unsuspecting family believing that she was daintily sewing wings at White City, 12129 Lethbridge was getting to grips with the reality of working at Hayes surrounded by a '10-foot corrugated iron fence', with its 'military guard consisting of a colonel, a captain, three subalterns, 190 NCOs and men'. The site covered 5 miles and comprised '397 buildings with a total floor area of 14 acres'.[54] With its thousands of munitions makers, cleaners, carpenters, not to mention its own fire-brigade staffed by sixty women, Mabel was a tiny cog in an immense wheel.

Still eager to 'do her bit', on her sixth day at work (23 October), Mabel saw a notice requesting volunteers for the 'Danger Zone'. Only those graded, as Mabel was, A1 for health could apply.[55] To cheers of her colleagues, 'Good Luck! Don't let the lads go short', the 17-year-old joined 300 other men and women who had volunteered to work in the filling sheds using Amatol and TNT, where security to prevent workers inadvertently causing accidents was intense. In her Shed, No. 22, four female workers stood at 'four huge cauldrons containing the "filling mixture'", which they ladled into scoops which were then tipped into 'an empty 18-pounder shell. Hot dry amatol' was then 'pressed firmly down inside the shell [to make] room for the fuses'.[56] Mabel and her friend Louie had to carry two filled shells (weighing 5.5 kg each) about 50 yards to the so-called 'monkey machine', which pressed the amatol down into the shell to make room for the fuses. 'Hour after hour went by and I felt my arms were being pulled out of their sockets and that my back must surely crack beneath the weight.'[57]

Although these 'monkey machines' had been condemned as unsafe a year earlier and new ones had arrived, much to the workers' indignation, these had not yet replaced the faulty ones and an accident occurred during the morning shift, 'We knew [it] had been a serious one and were all more or less unnerved'.[58] At lunchtime, the conversation was gruesome with workers discussing previous, at times fatal, accidents caused by the condemned machines. Mabel's colleagues unsuccessfully tried to dissuade her from returning to her post. Instead, in a manner reminiscent of some under-age soldiers who also volunteered for dangerous forays into No Man's Land, when volunteers were called for to continue working the shift, Mabel raised her hand, declaring, that the recent accident 'wasn't the fault of the machine.'[59] Delighted to have solved his workforce problem, the foreman tells her it was 'very decent of you coming forward like that'.[60] The afternoon dragged on, with her friend Louie concerned about the shortcuts they were being instructed to make to boost the factory's output. Mabel had just turned to reply when,

> A dull flash, a deafening roar and I felt myself being hurled through the air, falling down, down into the darkness. Mother! ... Mother! I cried in my terror. Wouldn't someone come, wouldn't someone speak to me? I lay quietly on my side. Now a blinding flash and I felt my body being torn asunder. Darkness, that terrifying darkness, and the agonised cries of the workers pierced my consciousness.[61]

Mabel's desire for her mother is identical to young (not necessarily under age) seriously wounded soldiers who frequently called for their mothers, even believing that the nurse who was caring for them was that dearly loved person.

Mabel never fully erased from her memory the fire in the shed and the workers' agonised screams.[62]

> In the glare, I saw girls rise and fall shrieking with terror, their clothing alight, blood pouring from their wounds. I made a last effort to get to the ... huge sliding doors of steel. I crawled through the blazing boxes which had surrounded my machine ... the agony was indescribable.

To her horror, 'Swiftly, surely the flames crept nearer'. Feeling that something was lying across her legs, 'I tried desperately to free them, tugging at the left one which appeared buried in a wet mass of blood and earth.' Her leg had been blown off, 'and I held in my hands the dripping thigh and knee'.[63] All around her, the chorus of desperate workers were shouting to the firefighters who were doing everything in their power to reach those who were 'burning to death'. Mabel realised they were all 'trapped in a burning furnace, a crucible of death', and then when the firefighters turned their powerful water hoses on the shed, 'now in our agony, we were to be drowned'.[64] At last, 'up came the fire-girls flinging themselves bravely into the furnace dragging their hose-pipes ... water poured over my mutilated body ... then ... blessed oblivion'.[65]

Mabel was one of only two workers in her shed to be pulled out alive – at enormous personal risk to the sixty female firefighters who had fought their way into the blazing building. The other survivor, Louie, suffering from what was undoubtedly Post Traumatic Stress Disorder, was taken to what Mabel called, 'a hospital more suited to the repair of her mental wreckage' where she, like many shell-shocked soldiers, appears to have ended her days.[66] The catalogue of the teenager's own forty-seven injuries, thirteen of which could have proved fatal, was lengthy, including: left leg severed, double fracture of the skull, right leg and thigh fractured, both arms fractured, right foot badly broken, left ear drum destroyed (leaving her stone deaf in that ear), one lung damaged beyond repair, temporarily blinded by flame, hands badly burned, countless small wounds and injuries, and huge emotional shock. On 27 November 1917, the king and queen expressed their concern to the hospital (St Mary's Paddington), inquiring about her progress; Queen Mary sent flowers and a copy of *The Soldier*.[67] Inevitably, there were lasting effects both physical and mental from many of these injuries. After months in hospital, her wooden 'peg leg' finally arrived, 'the sight of its nakedness' appalled her. 'Painted a sickly pink shade and held together by numerous heavy leather straps and buckles, the whole attached to myself by a leather belt that did not look unlike a horse's halter.'[68]

On 1 January 1918, Mabel became the then youngest person ever to be gazetted Officer of the British Empire (OBE) 'For courage and high example shown on the occasion of an explosion during which she lost a leg and sustained severe injuries'. With the investing marquess kneeling to her as she was unable to stand, she received the award at a ceremony in Maidstone on 15 May, still just short of her eighteenth birthday.[69]

After a long battle with officialdom, Mabel learned that she was not entitled to a pension and the maximum amount payable under the Workmen's Compensation Scheme was £1 a week. Apparently, she was fortunate to obtain compensation at all because girls under 18 were not allowed in the Danger Zone.[70] Her difficulties in adapting to life as 'a young cripple' were exacerbated by her mother who, however well-meaning, could not understand her daughter's desire to find work rather than be treated as an invalid. Forbidding her to continue with a romantic attachment started via correspondence she explained, 'Girls in your station in life do not write to strangers; they do not become factory hands or struggle out to work in your state of health'.[71]

With the war over, Mabel was far from at peace within herself, finally publishing her autobiography in 1934. The 21 February 1935 *Sydney Morning Herald* reviewer concluded, 'One can marvel at this story of immense and unscrupulous pluck and can but admire the dauntless [Mabel]'. Her exasperated mother was surely right when she accused Mabel of being 'the most extraordinary girl'.[72]

Emilienne Moreau: 'A price on her head.'
Between November 1915 and early 1916, numerous British newspapers featured stories about a heroic young woman whose 'experiences' were among the most terrible of the war. Indeed, 'no nobler story of a young girl's devotion [had] ever [been] written.'[73] Yet when Emilienne Moreau was born into a mining family in Wingles (100km from Calais) on 4 June 1898, none would have anticipated the fame which would descend upon her. After her adored father, a fiercely Germanophobe veteran of the 1870–71 Franco-Prussian War retired, the family moved to the mining community of Loos-en-Ghoselle; he kept the local grocery store. An ambitious girl,

Emilienne had just begun studying to become an elementary-school teacher when war broke out.

In October 1914, the dreaded Uhlans invaded Loos-en-Ghoselle, pillaging and sacking everything including the Moreau shop; many of the town's 5,000 traumatised inhabitants fled, but not the Moreaus. When the French dragoons arrived in pursuit, the town became a battleground. The French soldiers had good reason to be grateful to sharp-eyed Emilienne who informed them that a machine gun was concealed by some nearby pylons and provided information about the enemies' movements.[74] But, as the early war of movement settled into static warfare, Loos was encircled by German trenches, 'Death is everywhere; corpses of men and beasts putrefy in the village. We are cut off from the rest of the world', living in semi-siege conditions.[75] With many of the remaining village men deported, and her father about to be executed for breaking the strict curfew (*Washington Herald*, 23 January 1916, implied that, having 'a genius for the diplomatic gesture', she negotiated his release), Emilienne hid him in the pigeon loft. In December 1914, he died 'as a result of privations and anguish' at his homeland being once again occupied by the detested Germans.[76] With no undertakers, carpenters or even wood available, Emillienne filched planks from under the Germans' noses and fashioned a coffin herself.

Aware of the dangers faced by local children who roamed the village when the two sides exchanged shellfire, Emilienne established a school for the forty-two remaining youngsters aged between 3 and 16 in an abandoned house that was 'still just about standing'.[77] The lessons included how to file safely down to the cellar when bombing started. Her self-appointed tasks included searching for coal on the slag heaps – but there was a motive beyond trying to keep her schoolroom warm. Clambering around, she kept her eyes 'wide open' and became aware that 'among other improvements' the Germans had dug 'new communication trenches, installed more machine guns, and even electricity and a telephone line', Loos was becoming as she put it, 'a veritable fortress' which the Germans were determined to defend and, as it turned out, the French to regain.[78]

By September 1915, Maréchal Joffre had opted for a Franco-British offensive to push back the Germans in the Artois region. What would become the biggest British attack of 1915 opened on 25 September when the British First Army attacked in the early morning. With an immense battle being fought around them with devastating casualties on both sides, the inhabitants of Loos-en-Ghohelle were subjected to 'two days of bombardment. We live in cellars as what is left of the town is shelled'.[79] Instinctively realising that this was a titanic struggle, Emilienne, known for her sharp eyes, crouched in her attic for three days taking note of all that was unfolding. When Highlanders of the Black Watch, 'monstrous' in her eyes in their gas masks and kilts (which she had never previously seen), appeared, she knew that she must warn them about the murderous still-concealed machine gun. Putting her own life at considerable risk, she pointed out a little-known route around the town.[80]

With hand-to-hand fighting in the streets (and her own young sister wounded), Emilienne turned her home into a makeshift field hospital. RAMC medic Dr Burns showed her how to apply field dressings and bandages. When she saw a sniper hiding in a nearby house firing on a wounded soldier who was trying to make his way to the dressing station, she rushed into the street armed with a grenade and a revolver. By hurling the grenade 'at their vantage point' and killing several (numbers vary between two and five) German soldiers, she enabled the man to struggle in. When two others threatened her with bayonets, she turned the revolver on them, with 'no time to examine my feelings. I only know that I felt hatred, pain and disgust', she continued assisting the medics.[81]

With Loos in Allied hands and concerned about her wounded sister, Emilienne, her mother and her younger brother 'leave our skeleton of a house to take her to hospital'; en route, they learnt that Henri, her elder brother, had been killed on 4 June 1915, Emilienne's seventeenth birthday.[82] To her surprise, she heard that General Rawlinson, commander of IV Corps, wished to meet her at La Buissière near Béthune. Then a letter from Douglas Haig's ADC informed her that Haig had advised the French authorities of her 'bravery and devotion'. Emilienne was unaware that her life was about to change dramatically as the press, desperate for some good news, eagerly transformed her into the 'heroine of Loos'.

On 27 November 1915, a ceremony took place at the Place d'Armes in front of Versailles. Among the soldiers being decorated with the Croix de Guerre was one black-clad female, Emilienne Moreau. The investiture had been moved from the more usual Les Invalides due to a tip-off from the Spanish Ambassador that the Germans, considering her a 'franc-tireur', had put a price on her head and, doubly outraged by her gender, would execute her if they caught her.[83] General de Sailly assured her and the ecstatic crowd that, 'You honour the women of France. For them you are a magnificent and reassuring example.' President Poincaré's voice was added to the plaudits.[84] Eight months later, Emilienne became the first woman to receive the British Military Medal, invested by Lord Bertie, British Ambassador to France and, in recognition of her assistance to the wounded, she received the Royal Red Cross and the rarely awarded Medal of the Order of St John of Jerusalem.[85]

Eager for a first-hand account of the actions performed by this 'magnificent and reassuring' young woman, and only too aware that with the French still sustaining enormous losses, morale-boosting stories were in short supply, E. de Feuquières (who wrote for the extremely popular newspaper *Le Petit Parisien*) approached Mme Moreau enquiring if her daughter were literate. When the proud mother assured him that Emilienne had been training to be a teacher, an eyewatering offer was made. Having lost all but the clothes they stood up in when fleeing Loos and subsisting on 5 francs a day (Henri's army pension), the Moreau family would be lodged in the luxurious mansion, La Maye near Versailles, and given 5,000 francs for Emilienne's serialised account of her life and actions. She was 'set to work', writing her memoirs, her whereabouts closely guarded for fear that other journalists would approach her. Coiffed and dressed (albeit in mourning black) at the newspaper's expense, the miner's daughter became a celebrity with foreign newspapers acquiring rights to publish her story. With the amount of advance publicity in British newspapers, these must have come with a heavy price-tag.

With photographers flocking to immortalise France's second 'Jeanne d'Arc', Emilienne became a pin-up girl, her pensive image adorned postcards and soldiers' dug-outs. A photograph was taken in order that she might be added to the Staircase of Heroes in what was already being prepared as a Pantheon of War, a 402ft circumference, 45ft tall work of art depicting some 6,000 heroes of the Allied War Effort; an Australian film *The Joan of Arc of Loos* sealed her place as a representative of the new entente between France and her anglophone allies.[86] Before long her poster-size image gazed down upon Paris metro users.

War is hugely expensive, both of a nation's treasure and its blood. From the earliest days, France, like all belligerents, needed to raise money from the general population to fund the war and care for the wounded. Posters instructing citizens to buy war bonds or subscribe to War Savings schemes were all very well, children roaming the streets with collecting tins brought in funds but a bigger, more dramatic drive was essential. Needing figureheads, the authorities turned to three heroes of the air, René Fonck, Georges Guynemer and Charles Nungeseer, and to Emilienne Moreau. As she put it cynically, 'Our role was to collect money from wherever it could be found, that is to say from the rich'.[87] As a hint of romance appeals, still more so in wartime, wearing a 'pretty dress' – doubtless in black to increase the poignancy, she and Guynemer were sent to high society balls, to the Opéra, and other social occasions. Together this youthful golden couple seemed to represent all that was noble in France. Nevertheless, 'we were on a long leash; we present cheques, always with the required smile'.[88] She makes no comment on her feelings about Guynemer's death in September 1917, or whether her escort was merely changed to one of the surviving two 'Knights of the Air'.

Towards the end of the war, Emilienne was permitted to return to her studies and, using money earned from *Le Petit Parisien,* fulfilled her pre-war dream of qualifying as an institutrice, teaching in Paris before she and her family returned to their war-ravaged home.[89] There is conflicting evidence about their immediate post-war lives, British and American newspapers indicate that the shop kept by her and her mother in her birthplace, Wingles, was purchased through a subscription organised by British soldiers as 'a tribute of their unforgettable admiration'. She makes no mention of this in her autobiography, simply stating that the shop was acquired from her aunt, Zélie Moreau. What is in no doubt is that, to her relief, 'slowly I faded from public sight and memory'.[90] Then in 1941, the now married Emilienne Moreau Evrard proved that her teenage bravery was but a precursor to the fortitude and humanitarianism she would demonstrate in France's second struggle against the nation her father had so loathed and feared.

CHAPTER FIVE

A Very Teenage Rebellion

In August 1914, poet Winifred Letts recognised that, for children and young people, 'it's fine to play at soldiers...'. While millions played, some youngsters took the game one step further and found ways to get to the Front. In doing so, they kicked against the traces of authority which prevented children bearing arms in combat.[1]

Marina Yurlova: 'A little fool ... but a good Cossack.'

Born on 25 February 1900, Marina Yurlova's father, Prince Obolemskya, was a Kuban Cossack Colonel. In July 1914, she was at the family's summer home in Raevskaya, near the Black Sea. With little idea of how completely this would impact upon her life, the 14-year-old heard the bells ringing out for mobilisation (29 July): 'there were Cossacks riding over the field, crying out as they rode ..."War! War!"' If news of war was greeted with horror by some and elation by others, most Cossacks, true to their heritage, expressed their enthusiasm, 'For centuries my people have been noted fighters; a military nation within the great Russian Empire.'[2]

Leaving Raevskaya proved easy. Traditionally, Cossack women accompanied their fighting men, encamping as near the army as possible. Following what she later termed a 'blind instinct', Marina accompanied the other women to the station where they were permitted to follow the troop train to 'the border'.[3] Aware that her father's elevated status may lead to her being unceremoniously returned home, she claimed to be 'Maria Kolesnikova' – a fiction she maintained for many years. 'What lay ahead of me I neither knew nor cared, so long as it brought me nearer to the war.'[4] After days in the crowded train which had penetrated ever further into the Southern Caucasus (border area of Europe and Asia), 'a little girl in a grimy, blue dotted frock, very small for [her] age and very slight' emerged; her family, including her father who was 'somewhere in the troop train ahead', having no idea as to her whereabouts and her mother, who did not like her to 'walk alone along the highway', doubtless frantic with worry. Marina herself, with the selfishness of youth, 'had no regrets ... Adventure lay just ahead ... And war.'[5] A war that would hold her in its vice.

Marina's metamorphosis from grimy schoolgirl to Cossack fighter was relatively slow. Initially, she remained with the women who, now on foot, were attempting to reach their husbands. To her horror, at one point, Russian soldiers – no lovers of Cossacks, attempted to rape them. 'That night we slept by the roadside under the cold stars with no blankets. I have never been so miserable in my life.'[6] When the women finally reached the Cossack regiments, it dawned on her that she was totally alone; 'with little grimy channels down my cheeks where the tears had fallen', no one cared what happened to her.[7]

Hearing her sobbing, a Cossack sergeant named Kosel threw his blanket to this 'scared ragged little girl ... It was not long before I worshipped him'. Having told Kosel her 'name', she explains that her father is one of the grooms up ahead and wonders if she can help with the horses until she can track her father down – a fiction she maintained for many months for now she had 'only one ambition – to stay with Kosel until we reached the war.'[8] Obligingly, Kosel produced a uniform, which unsurprisingly, needed altering – he unsuccessfully attempted to cut it down with his sabre. Seeing her rolled up 'pigtails under the *shapka* (cap), an amused Kosel vowed, 'Before I die, I'll make a Cossack out of you.'[9] Prophetic words.

That her father was one of the grooms may have been mendacious, that she was good with horses was not. A true Cossack, she could ride one horse while leading seven which quickly earned her platoon's respect. Eager to be more than a glorified groom, she begged to be taught the rudiments of drill, although ruefully acknowledging that initially, 'my horse knew far more about it than I ... so in the end I left things to him.'[10] News of this unusual groom, whom the men had turned into some sort of mascot, having reached his ears, an officer arrived to assess the situation. 'When I had dismounted and saluted, my knees were knocking together ... I felt very small and frightened and terribly afraid that I was going to ... burst into tears.'[11] Conquering her emotions, to her joy, she was given a sabre and accepted into the Reconnaissance Sotnia (100 Horse Squadron) of the 3rd Ekaterinodar Regiment.

As summer 1914 turned to autumn, Marina moved into huts with the men – and the strangeness of her situation struck her, that 'I, a colonel's daughter, should be here in this place that smelled so horribly of bad air ... of unwashed bodies and feet ... I thought I would never get used to it.'[12] That she herself smelled equally bad dawned on her when, with her comrades, she entered a dug-out with its 'darkness, damp earth, unwashed bodies'. Having not had a bath herself, 'I was beginning to be a soldier'.[13] Like other youngsters, with little awareness of what awaited her, she was eager to accompany the men on a scouting foray, 'I jumped to my feet, flushing with pride' at being chosen.[14] However, when left alone holding five horses, she realised that this was no longer make believe,

> Somewhere beyond lay ... the Turks and the Germans ... I was sure I could hear my heart thumping. Horrid stories came crowding into my mind ... about Turks and what they did to their captives. My hands were full of bridle straps. My fear communicated itself to the horses ... I screamed but my terror was so great that the scream came out of my throat like a sort of coughing choke,

which, luckily for her self-respect, no one heard.[15] Sentry duty was less exciting than it sounded,

> After a little while it began to dawn on me that there was far more discomfort than honour in doing sentry duty. The next hour seemed as though it would never end ... Patrol duty at least had the excitement of terror; this was merely blank and hideous.[16]

Unable to escape the other bane of all Great War soldiers' life, cooties, the helpless task of trying to remove these became a campaign in its own right – one that no soldier was known to win. When a Red Cross nurse arranged a bath for her, she ruefully commented that, 'it looked like a mud pool before I got out of it.' Now with her clothes disintegrating, the kindly Kosel purloined others – albeit of the wrong size; reluctantly they both realised, 'You cannot make the largest underpants in the Russian army fit a girl of fourteen however hard you try'![17] The pants altered and her hair shorn, 'I doubt that anybody who did not know me would have taken me for anything but a boy.'[18]

Most soldiers agree that their life is made up of boredom and terror and, initially, the squadron suffered much of the former and no sign of action. This changed suddenly when 'beside the muddy waters of the

Araxes', the Turks 'a great black sea of men', caught up with them, although she took some consolation from the fact that, 'my comrades [also] stood frozen beside their horses.'[19]

Following a call for volunteers to blow up a bridge to stop the Turks advancing across the Araxes River, near Erevan, Marina, to Kosel's despair, was the first to raise her hand, prompting the greatest compliment he could give, or she receive, 'Marina … you're a little fool but you're a good Cossack.'[20] Inevitably, heavy casualties ensued.

> The enemy was bearing down …There was a sound I shall never forget and could not describe even if I would. Kosel plunged forward, blood spouting like a fountain from his forehead, blood on the grass … My cries were lost in a terrific explosion … there was a blow on my leg … I pitched forward, close to Kosel. I tried to crawl near him and found that I had no strength to move…trying to reach his hand and grasp it. Then the unanswering darkness.[21]

Carried back to Cossack lines, the hundreds of casualties were left without attention. 'The air stank of blood. I was violently sick.'[22] Without even rudimentary first aid, her privileged childhood with 'my own nurse who used to bind up my little scratches' started to haunt her, leaving her wondering what she was doing so far from her comfortable home.[23] After a nightmare journey to Baku (now capital of Azerbaijan) lying on a hospital cart, 'jolting unmercifully over the rough tracks which served for roads … I have forgotten most of that journey but the fear, the jolting.'[24] For days she dared not look at her barely dressed wound until eventually, 'I screwed up courage and looked at the wound. My whole leg was swollen to three times its normal size and it had turned quite black'. Gangrene had set in and with it the risk of amputation, only her own obstinacy and refusal to submit to the procedure saved her limb. For the first and only (reported) time in her career, she informed the disconcerted surgeon that as a colonel's daughter and a volunteer, he could not operate without her consent. Eventually with the bullet extracted, amputation averted (although the wound pained her throughout the war) and, initially slightly flattered by the attention heaped upon her in hospital which soon began to pall, 'I felt like a caged animal whom people poke'. When one woman started to talk about wanting to adopt her, 'I thought it was high time to go back to my regiment.'[25]

Having been at war for almost exactly a year, on her returning, she heard of her recommendation for the Cross of St George – which neither she nor her jealous comrades felt she deserved, 'She didn't blow up the bridge', one man grumbled. The sergeant who had replaced Kosel pointed out, 'She didn't blow up the bridge, but she was the first one to volunteer and the only one left of them all.'[26]

Summer 1915 saw constant incursions from Kurds, the most brutal of enemies. Close to being raped by the Kurdish leader who had ambushed her squadron, she was forced to 'strip off my jacket ... Through his filthy tatters I caught a glimpse of even filthier skin. His round brown eyes were like an animal's eyes ... His hand wandered downward over my breast and up again. And he laughed so strangely that I could stand it no longer. I jumped back'. Like Scherezade, she kept him at arm's length for many hours telling and retelling her war story,

> I began my story. I shall never tell another one like that in so strange a setting to so hideous an audience ... I noticed they were quite genuinely fascinated by what I was saying. Terror was my guide, I could not have stopped talking even if I had been told to.[27]

Bewitched, the forty listening Kurds were unaware that she was walking them back to her own lines where they, not she, became the prisoners – for which she received a second, to her mind equally undeserved, George Cross.

With the passing of time and an increasing number of actions, she acknowledged that she too had become brutalised, welcoming the opportunity to kill, although saddened by the plight of the starving children in the villages they plundered. In autumn 1915, they were detailed for the bitter, unforgiving terrain of Mount Ararat. The 'adventure' of being a soldier had settled into harsh reality but, 'However terribly I needed my mother at times, yet I had a grim determination to stay on with the army and see things out.'[28]

Seeing 'things out' involved further intense fighting, including the bitter battle for Erzerum. Illusions about the glamour of both war and the Cossacks – a 'crowd of half useless lunatics' evaporated; having seen for herself 'the grossness of which a dispirited Cossack is capable, I was not shocked so much as hardened. I lived inside a shell which nothing could penetrate'. Nevertheless, 'I had become just another soldier too ... waiting to be killed.'[29] Like so many youthful soldiers, Marina served as a runner, dicing with death as she wove her way between posts. As others, including young American doughboy Eric Wrentmore would also find, 'Either your nerves give way altogether or they grow so numb that nothing can break them.'[30] With Erzerum and the Third Turkish Army finally rolled back, on 16 February 1916, nine days short of her sixteenth birthday, she gazed upon the plains to where 'the dead of both armies lay … frozen into sarcastic afterthought upon the whole campaign.'[31]

Caught by an exploding shell, Marina was herself soon among the wounded. After a night listening to the howling of the 'pariah dogs or wolves hunting along the edges of the night … and certain to find me when it was entirely dark', stretcher bearers stumbled across her.[32] Placed in an officers' ward (the nurses were unsympathetic towards someone who had crossed gender and rank boundaries), the officers themselves were amused by her presence. To her surprise, in hospital she received a third, to her mind still undeserved, St George Cross.

Sent to train as an automobile mechanic at Tiflis (now Tiblisi, capital of Georgia), she became as adept a driver as she was rider. The perk of the job was driving officers, who, accompanied by ladies who were not their wives although they 'may well have been somebody else's', often tipped generously.[33] With her privileged girlhood but a distant dream and with a generous tip in her hand, she wondered whether an enticing pastry shop was reserved for 'Officers Only'. Greeted warmly, she concludes, 'Heaven may well be a white table in a shop that smells of fresh pastry with a proprietor that does not discriminate against private soldiers'.[34]

In autumn 1916 she joined a Red Cross unit in Erevan. With starvation rife, she came face to face with the horrors war inflicts upon civilians, 'We used to be assaulted by desperate bands of children, more than half naked, their bellies swollen out of all proportion, their legs so thin you wondered how they could stand upright on them'.[35] Such sufferings led this Cossack girl, who once saw war as being almost written in her DNA, to reflect that this was 'one town among many for which the most brilliant feats of the late war will never provide an excuse'.[36] She wondered how the civilians and her 'weak and staggering comrades fitted in with the mercies of Christian teaching'. Demonstrating the chasm that had opened between the colonel's daughter and the Cossack soldier, there is bitterness when noticing that 'the officers looked as though they had never been deprived of anything'.[37]

Although with no knowledge of the realities of the political situation in Moscow and St Petersburg, 'the very air seemed to be heavy with rumours' – rumours which by the time they reached her (early summer 1917), were fact.[38] Of more immediate concern was the weapon now being used against them on the Persian border. The gas 'through which we moved like ghosts with round black windows for eyes and white spots for faces ... Nobody looked human even when men fell dead ... Deafened and speechless I went about my work [as a driver] automatically, staggering back and forth to the stretchers'.[39] Caught by a gas shell, she just had time to realise that 'gas masks are not always a protection against gas' before being buried alive. Hovering between life and death at a sanatorium in Baku she learnt of the March Revolution and the overthrow of the Czar, 'For the first time in many weeks I thought of Kosel. Kosel had died for a cause that did not exist anymore, that had been overthrown in a night ... Kosel, and my comrades, and a million others'[40]. Now the 17-year-old, who had spent over three years witnessing the horror of war, would be caught in the brutality and savageness of the Revolution – with Cossacks, thanks to their loyalty to the Czar, 'to whom my people had always looked as their only leader under God', a prime target.[41] With the Revolution having 'found its way into our mountain fastness [and] witnessing brutal murders by the blood-crazed mob, I had a vague feeling that the end of the world had come, there in Baku.'[42] Deaf and mute from neurasthenia, exacerbated by the horrors perpetrated in Baku, and subsequently evacuated to a Moscow hospital where although the 'Moscow of 1918 has written itself into history ... to me it is only a darkness.'[43]

While children across Western Europe were celebrating the Armistice or trying to come to terms with defeat, Marina, with all her family killed, was fleeing for her life across Russia, eventually finding refuge in 1919 in an American-run military hospital in Vladivostock, 7,000km from her home in Ekaterinodar. Still suffering from both the mental and physical effects of her wounds, 'Maria Kolesnikova', three times recipient of the Cross of St George, 'drained of hope and of fear', recognised that Marina Yurlova, privileged daughter of the Cossack colonel Prince Obolemskya, no longer existed. She had perished on the blood-soaked plains of Armenia.[44]

Zoya Smironov: 'only a thin girlish voice betrayed her sex.'

On 26 February 1916, an article entitled 'The Twelve Friends: Girl Volunteers at the Front', featured in *The Times* 'Russia Supplement'.[45] The Petrograd correspondent almost apologised for publishing the story. He felt that accounts of young females 'joining the ranks of the Russian

Army in the guise of men' may have begun to pall with English readers. Nevertheless, he believed that the account of the 'twelve friends' as told by Zoya Smironov, might interest readers. Entitled 'Young Girls Fighting on the Russian Front', the article appeared in the May 1916 *New York Times' Current History*. Listening to Zoya, the journalist felt that 'only a thin girlish voice betrayed [her] sex', while her 'close-cropped hair gave her the appearance of a boy.'

According to Zoya, as Russia mobilised, she and eleven Muscovite schoolfriends aged between 14 and 16, hatched a plan. Leaving 'early in the morning without saying a word to their parents', the girls ran away – Zoya admitted that they all felt sorry for their parents but the 'desire to see the war and ourselves kill Germans' overrode any sense of filial duty. Recognising that their chances of getting away from Moscow undetected were slim, they hired 'izvozchiks' (simple horse-drawn carriages) and reached the Muscovite suburbs where they convinced some soldiers to conceal them on a train bound for the Front. Obligingly, the men even provided them with military uniforms.

Once at the Austrian front, the regimental authorities were baffled and disturbed by the presence of these young girls in military attire but as they refused to return home, the staff officers undoubtedly felt that they had more to bother about than twelve runaway girls. While girl soldiers are almost non-existent on the Western Front,

> there are widespread accounts of them on the Eastern Front where the more chaotic the military command, the less strict military bureaucracy and the possibility of recruiting decisions taken at lower levels of command, all contributed to the scattered entry of women in the military system.[46]

The regiment to which the girls were attached proceeded to Lemberg, a city where another teenage girl would, four years later, come to make her mark. Life became increasingly hard for the girls as on foot, they and their regiment, 'traversed the whole of Galicia; scaled the Carpathians and were constantly fighting bitter battles.' Having been taught to shoot and given rifles, these twelve female private soldiers, 'shared' over many months 'all the privations and horrors of the march'. Zoya claimed that most of the time, the girls almost forgot their past – even their feminine names, as they had assumed male ones. In spring 1915, the regiment 'underwent a perfect hell' as heavy guns were consistently used against them. Zoya dismissed the interviewer's rather facile 'Were you afraid?' by simply replying, 'Who wouldn't be?' Although she admitted that the younger ones particularly longed for their mothers – but in this they were no different to many younger men.

Almost miraculously, the twelve had so far survived unscathed, but that changed one night in the Carpathians when 15-year-old Zina Morozov 'was killed outright by a shell'. According to Zoya, 'her small body ... torn into fragments'. Somehow, her schoolfriends managed to collect enough of her remains to bury her and some of her few possessions. The next day they were on the march again; Zoya confessed that within days she would have been unable to locate the grave, 'all I know is that it is in the Carpathians at the foot of a steep rocky incline'.

Now it seemed that the friends' luck had run out; several were injured including Zoya, twice, once in the leg and, far more seriously, in the side. Left unconscious on the battlefield, stretcher bearers who, by a stroke of good fortune found her, initially assumed she was dead. She was in hospital for over a month. Frustratingly, she provides no details as to why or when this occurred but she was promoted to a junior NCO and received the St George's Cross (awarded under her male alias, Evgenii Makarov), for 'a brave and dashing reconnaissance'.

Once back in the trenches, she was unable to locate her own regiment. Surrounded by strange faces, disoriented without the support and familiarity of her unit and schoolmates, she was persuaded to exchange her soldier's uniform for that of a nurse, at least temporarily. When the article appeared, there was still no news of any surviving girls who had been her classmates in what must now have appeared to be another existence. The journalist wondered, 'do graves already cover them, similar to that which was dug for the remnants of poor little Zina who perished so gloriously in the distant Carpathians?' Did a war grave finally also cover Zoya herself?

Disobedient Désiré: 'Grinning with excitement.'[47]

Désiré Bianco saw the light of day on 4 April 1902. Little is known about his early childhood other than his sister was called Alice and that his parents, Jean and Mathilde, were 'day labourers' (*journaliers*) in Marseille picking up work as and when they could find it. His school being near the barracks of the 6th Hussars Regiment, on 6 August 1914, Désiré and his classmates including Raoul Estripaut, watched excitedly as, cheered by enthusiastic crowds, in full uniform and with flowers in their rifles, the Hussars marched to Marseille's St Charles station. Destined for Lorraine, they were eager to avenge France's 1871 defeat and humiliating loss of the twin provinces of Alsace-Lorraine. Raoul remembered how 12-year-old Désiré now had one obsession: to accompany the Hussars to the Front.

In January 1915, 12-year-old Désiré appeared close to fulfilling his dream. He successfully entrained with cyclists and men from the 6th Hussars heading for Nixéville (Meuse). Regimental history confirms that 160 men and twenty cyclists were in the trenches in the Bois de Corbeaux area although no mention is made of the youngster. He seems to have gone undetected, or at least unreported, until March 1915 when he was dispatched to the rear and, after he made a further attempt to reach the Front line, returned to parental control. Still determined to, in his words, 'see the war', or at least more of it than he had already seen, the obstinate lad decided to try his luck on a troopship departing from Toulon with the recently formed (14 March 1915) 1st Battalion of the 8e (subsequently 58e) Régiment d'Infanterie Coloniale (RIC).

With his thirteenth birthday just behind him, on 2 May 1915, young Désiré hid aboard *La France* which was carrying men of the 58e RIC to Cape Helles and the killing fields of the Dardanelles. Doing the rounds of the transport, soldier Louis Nicolas found the young stowaway. As the ship certainly could not be turned around to offload one young fugitive, there was nothing for it as far as the regiment was concerned, but to keep him with them – ideally out of harm's way. A delighted Désiré realised that his plan had worked spectacularly well. Kitted out with a rifle and a sailor's uniform (arguably because with boy sailors [*mousses*] aboard something could be found to fit him), he was designated mascot of the Galinier battalion. It subsequently transpired this battalion was to lead the attack.

On 6 May, under Lieutenant Colonel Frèrejean, the regiment disembarked at Sedd el-Bahr. Just as some of his near contemporary midshipmen serving with the Royal Navy are reported to have done, Désiré grinned in excitement as shells burst around him. Having taken up their positions in the trenches and with barely time to draw breath, on 8 May, the men of the 58e were ordered to attack, and 'irrespective of losses', take a small fort perched on Hill 300, to the east of Krithia.[48] With Nicolas having ordered Désiré to remain in the trench, Lieutenant Asquier took the added precaution of removing the boy's rifle. Perhaps by way of consolation and astutely realising the youngster needed something more military to do than twiddle his thumbs, Asquier instructed Désiré to keep his sword safe. At precisely 1.15 pm, the men leapt out of the trench. Then out of the corner of his eye Nicolas glimpsed a small figure brandishing Asquier's sword and shouting 'Forward with bayonets, men'. Désiré's fate was now beyond Nicolas' control. Sometime before 3.30 pm when the first line of the battalion reached the Turkish trenches, Nicolas 'saw little Désiré totter and fall'. Like battalion commander Galinier, Lieutenant Asquier, sixteen other officers, fifty-four NCOs and 842 men, mascot Bianco had survived barely forty-eight hours after disembarking from *La France*. His body, like those of so many others, never found.

By 10 December 1915, the 58e RIC had been bled white. Back in France, with the disastrous campaign behind them and further bloodbaths still to come, men of what was left of the 58e clamoured for recognition for their gallant, if thoroughly stubborn, little companion. On 30 August 1916 he was, with General Joffre's approval, cited in General Orders 54 of the Day for the Armée de l'Orient. This special citation to the young mascot who died with the sword his officer had entrusted to him in his hand, heads the lists of honours and awards conferred on the officers and men of the 58e for their gallant actions in the Dardanelles. His story largely forgotten during the war years, in time, Désiré's enthusiasm and courage came to be constructed as more important than his obstinacy. On 28 August 1920, it was recognised that, 'killed by the enemy', he had 'died for France' – which entitled his parents to a pension.

In 1935 the Légion des Mille was founded to preserve and honour the memory of the approximately 1,000 French boys and young men, both dead and still alive, who had voluntarily enlisted before their 'Classe' was called up at the age of 20. Heading the list was Désiré Bianco, France's youngest poilu.[49] The Légion was determined that the names of those who put 'Duty before Homework' would be remembered. On 17 May 1936, 21 years and nine days after his death, watched by his parents, this 'kid' from Marseille was posthumously decorated with the Military Medal and the Croix de Guerre and a monument was unveiled in front of Toulon's Grignan Barracks. Only the churlish would suggest that the solemn-faced sculpture bears little resemblance to the mischievous, obstinate lad whose story, as the local newspaper *Var Matin* pointed out on 11 November 2013, owes much to the futile, to the comic, to the tragic.

Désiré is one of 335 known underage personnel to have died in Gallipoli. They include Australia's youngest casualty, James (Jim) Martin. Teenage obstreperousness lies at the heart of his story. Born in Tocumwal, New South Wales in 1901, by 1915 the young farmhand was in thrall to the war fever sweeping Australia. His first step to illegal enlistment was to convince his parents that if they did not give their written parental consent (which in 1915 was required for Australian men aged between 18 and 21 who sought to join the army), he would go anyway and they would never hear from him, whereas, 'If you let me go, I'll write to you'. He then informed the authorities that he was 18. They may have taken little convincing because at 5ft 6 in tall with an appropriate chest measurement, he fulfilled size requirements; he enlisted in April 1915.[50]

With initial training completed, on 28 June 1915, men of the 1st Reinforcements, 21st Battalion of the Australian Imperial Force, including 1553 Private James Martin, set sail for Egypt and more intensive training. Keeping his promise to stay in touch, Jim sent sentimental postcards home and wondered why he never received any letters from his family. With ever more men needed in the Dardanelles, on 2 September 1915, Jim was aboard HMT *Southland*, a captured German passenger ship, bound for Lemnos island and onwards to Gallipoli. Just hours away from Mudros Bay, *Southland* was torpedoed. After four hours in the sea, Jim was among the survivors.[51]

On 8 September, Jim arrived at Anzac Cove. Continuing his promised letters, at one point he told his parents that despite 'the Turks [being] about 70 yards away from us', they were not to worry as 'I am doing splendid over here'. Such optimism was misplaced, he succumbed to the now rampant typhoid and, having been evacuated to HMHS *Glenart Castle* on 25 October, died that same evening; he was buried at sea. Matron Frances Reddock assured Mrs Martin that, the nurses 'did everything possible for him'. His mother may have been comforted to learn that he had 'thanked me *so* nicely for what had been done for him'.[52]

Jean-Corentin Carré: 'The wine is good and the girls friendly'.[53]

On 27 April 1915, one Auguste Duthoy signed on with the French Army at Pau, (Pyrenees area). He explained to the sergeant that with his home department Ardennes occupied by the Germans since August 1914, he had no official identity papers but that he had been born in Rumigny on 10 April 1897. As a loyal Frenchman, he knew his duty was to enlist. The recruiting sergeant was no doubt pleased to have one more recruit for the 410e (Breton [Brittany]) Regiment d'Infanterie (RI). Auguste was a bit small but then weren't so many of these peasants' kids, and this one was highly articulate and deeply patriotic. He would soon prove himself an excellent much decorated soldier rising rapidly through the ranks.

On the surface, there is nothing unusual in the story apart from one crucial fact: Auguste did not exist. He was instead Jean-Corentin Carré, born in the village of Le Faouët in the department of Morbihan on 9 January 1900, the seventh of nine children. Noted as an exceptional scholar, who had even been congratulated by the examiners for his achievements when he passed his School Leaving Certificate examinations aged 12 as opposed to 13, the official examination/leaving age. He had been offered a job as a clerk in the town hall. His schoolmaster, with whom he kept in touch during the war, noted subsequently that he was a brilliant pupil.[54] In 1914, three of the Carré sons were called to the colours. Luckily, Jean-Corentin was far too young, a point the local mayor made to him when he begged that he too be allowed to march off to war with the other, appropriately aged, men from Le Faouët.

Nothing if not persistent, in early April 1915, Jean-Corentin told his parents that he wanted to go to South America, but in fact he headed for Pau where, conveniently, his claim to be Auguste Duthoy was believed. After initial training in Rennes, in October the 410e left for the Front. While still serving, he wrote up his experiences in an exercise book; the opening lines based on his 'carnet de route' read,

I request that these notes made while I served with the army should be returned to my parents who will be able to keep this exercise book as a souvenir of their kid who fell on the field of honour. 'To die for one's country is the most glorious of deaths'.[55]

The first entry (22 October 1915) notes the Regiment's 10 pm arrival at St Menehould, (Marne); the raw recruits were greeted by the sound of gunfire as the French sought to regain a lost trench. Two days later 15-year-old Jean got his first glimpse of the war, 'The men are covered in mud, their weapons so full of earth that they can't fire them. When the Germans got wind of us, we lay down on the road, I wasn't frightened'. The road the men were marching along was cratered by shells and covered in 'a glutinous mud'. He added that, 'it was very hard and my bag seemed so heavy. I'm not used to carrying it when it is full'.

Edging closer to front line duties, on 3 November they arrived in a small village (Somme-Trourbe) where their billet left much to be desired: 'piled in like sardines – no straw and rats running all over us'. Two days later, 'after a 15km march, we arrived in the Front line to relieve a company that seemed exhausted.' His first glimpse of the dugout was far from reassuring; detailed for sentry duty in a 'trench with corpses that stank, for company rats clambering over what was left of them.' After eight days 'in freezing cold, sleeping for about 5 hours in the day but awake every night', with the monotony broken by the occasional fall of shells, on 17 November, he volunteered to 'go scouting'. With his bayonet fixed, 'I went through several old Boche trenches full of corpses which I was forced to walk over … some with smashed skulls, others with bayonets through their stomachs.' With winter setting in and rotating in and out of front line and reserve trenches with mud at times 'up to our shoulders', the 15-year-old even 'started to wonder why on earth I had enlisted' – although he claimed [5 December] that 'this was the only time during my 22 months at the Front that I wondered this. Self-respect and courage stopped this train of thought.'

Promoted corporal in January 1916, on 30 May Jean-Corentin reached Verdun, 'or to be more precise the ruins' of Verdun. By the time the 410e arrived at the citadelle, they would have known what awaited them. This may have prompted the youngster to write to one of his sisters, Marie, explaining that as he had enlisted under a false name, if he were killed, no one would know what had happened to him (worry about their family never knowing what had happened to them weighed heavily upon several adolescents who enlisted under false names). With the additional fear of being tarnished with the name of deserter when his 'classe' was called up, he begged Marie to tell Le Faouët's mayor what he had done. He added that as he had lied about his identity, he did not feel that the government had any responsibility towards him and he should not receive a dole.[56] There is evidence of British parents – and doubtless those of other nationalities, placing advertisements in newspapers informing their underage offspring that they will not approach the authorities and reveal the child's deception if they contact their parents with details of their whereabouts.[57]

Having been involved in relatively minor – although at times terrifying skirmishing, the men of the 410e were about to enter what Jean-Corentin terms Verdun's 'killing fields', including an aptly named 'death valley', 'covered with corpses that might once have been buried but have been unburied by shells which have no respect for a final resting place – truly terrible to behold.'[58] The teenager's graphic descriptions of the miseries and terrors of their troglodyte world explain why he was considered so exceptional a scholar. By 6 June, he was 'staggered to find that I was still alive. We suffered serious losses'. As it was 'impossible to do anything by day, we remain crouched in our sodden holes for 10 hours longing for night to fall.' His company sustained heavy losses but, despite being wounded in both legs, 'this wasn't the time for malingerers, so I refused to be evacuated.'

Alternating between hot and quieter sectors – more of the former than the latter, in mid-September having volunteered to go out on patrol,

> I noticed what looked like a dead Boche in a shell hole. I tapped him on the shoulder and he shot up. I took him by the scruff of his neck and we marched him to our colonel who was delighted to have thus got a prisoner without the loss of any French lives.

He appeared to enjoy the few days well-earned leave granted shortly after the prisoner episode, 'the wine was good and the girls were fun'.

Although Jean-Corentin mentions that he was given a 200 francs reward (his pay as a sergeant would have been around 92cts a day) which he shared with those who had been on patrol with him, he makes no mention of being awarded the Croix de Guerre on 15 November, almost exactly a year after he arrived at the Front. Whether this was through modesty or because he felt that the decoration had little value or was ill-deserved we shall never know, but he is far from the only young combatant to not mention or dismiss a decoration as 'undeserved'.

On 29 December 1916, giving his postal address as 'les Tranchées' (the trenches), and apologising for bypassing official channels and going straight to the top, he composed a letter to Colonel Treillard, commander of the 410e RI, confessing that Auguste Duthoy never existed. He also explained that as he would be 17 in January 1917 – the age at which French adolescents could enlist with parental approval, he felt he should now come clean; the letter suggests that he had already received parental consent. Colonel Treillard acceded to his request to serve under his own name. Perhaps it would have been too awkward to let him stay in the

9th Company and so, no doubt much to his comrades-in-arms' regret, he was moved to the 10th Company. Although he briefly lost rank, Treillard ordered its reinstatement; Sergent Duthoy rapidly became Adjutant (Warrant Officer) Carré.

His papers now 'in order', two weeks' leave and a machine gun course behind him, on 16 April 1917 Jean-Corentin Carré was once again in action, this time for the opening day of the disastrous Chemin des Dames offensive; 'my company is on the left bank of the canal'. Ironically it was the youngster who steadied those who were his seniors in years, but by far his juniors in combat experience. On one occasion he noted that 'we took 4 prisoners, 2km of ground and captured 8 machine guns'. Alternating in and out of the line, he achieved his second 'citation', once again silence reigns over what this was for.

Jean-Corentin's personal memoir, written up in the early summer of 1917 ends on 19 June. He had heard the Armée de l'Air was calling for recruits and, unsurprisingly in view of his war record, he was rapidly accepted into this seemingly dashing service. His decision to change arms was, he explained, less because he wanted to leave the misery of the trenches but because he found 'the weight of responsibility for the 50 human lives now under his command too heavy a burden for my young shoulders'. The Divisional Commander bestowed a rare honour on one of enlisted rank and invited him to dine before he set off for initial training. The nationalistic press considered his story a 'godsend' to a war-weary nation, images of him appeared in several national newspapers. Although the newspaper inaccurately claimed he was France's youngest soldier, what is accurate is that he was the country's highest ranking and most decorated one.

If the teenage pilot kept a record of his service with the Arméé de l'Air, sadly, this has been lost. He is known to have earned his wings in September 1917. Pierre Palaric from Le Faouët, whose father was one of Jean-Corentin's schoolmates and who has done much to keep his memory alive, argues that his transfer to the prestigious Armée de l'Air was a form of reward for his patriotism, superb military record and devotion to duty. Attached to an observation squadron, having survived Verdun and the Chemin des Dames, would he buck the life expectancy trend of three months for pilots? A report on 6 May 1939 in the newspaper *Paris Soir*, claimed that when he came home on leave in March 1918, his mood was dark and just before his departure, he engraved on the table 'Jean Carré killed 22 March 1918'.

On 18 March 1918, flying a Sopwith 1½ Strutter, 18-year-old Adjutant Pilot Jean-Corentin formerly of the 410e RI, now of SO 229 was attacked by three enemy aircraft and, despite putting up a valiant fight, came down above Verdun where he had once led his men in deadly combat. Critically injured, he died the same day in Souilly Military Hospital and is buried at Rembercourt-aux-Pots. Should the story about the dining table be accurate, he had miscalculated by a mere four days. His third and final citation for valour was posthumous.

But if Jean-Corentin Carré were dead, how should his memory be preserved? Suggestions included transferring his remains to the Panthéon in Paris.[59] Seen as a product of all that was good in the 3rd Republic's education system, his letter to a former schoolmaster, Mr Mahébèze, assuring him that it was in his classroom that he had learned that being a French citizen carried with it duties and responsibilities to uphold France's honour and traditions, soon became the stuff of legend. The letter went on to assure his teacher that he had felt it incumbent upon him to turn the lessons he had learnt in the schoolroom into actions and refuse to allow France to fall under the enemy's yoke. It was, he stressed, duty not the hope of personal glorification, which led him to answer the call to arms. After all, 'life is nothing if it is not well lived'.

In 1919, the French Education Board commissioned a dramatic poster which reminded children of their own little hero and his patriotic words; copies soon adorned classrooms the length and breadth of France. Incorporated in the Légion des Mille, his statue was unveiled in Le Faouët on 7 May 1939, serried ranks of schoolchildren and local dignitaries against a backdrop of a sea of French flags, looked on as the mayor praised the young volunteer to whom duty and patriotism were everything. To ensure his memory remains alive, in October 2014, a young person's comic book was published; Jean-Corentin Carré features in the current French school curriculum while Le Faouët's secondary school bears the name of Brittany's favourite, most famous poilu.

Ernest L. Wrentmore: Monroe, did you shave for this inspection?'

On 9 November 1918, a doughboy of 'I' Company, 60th Infantry, 'Red Diamond' Fifth Division of the Regular US Army celebrated his birthday in American Base Hospital No 1, France. Thousands would have spent their birthdays as hospital patients, some at least relishing lying between sheets for the first time in months. Where this soldier's case differed was that, unbeknownst to nurses, the birthday being celebrated was his fourteenth. Records stated that he was Henry Earl Monroe. But, far from being the 18-year-old orphan he claimed to be when he enlisted in September 1917, he was Ernest L. Wrentmore, son of a respected Ohio physician. Young Ernest's idyllic childhood included fishing and hunting, hikes, camping trips and membership of the local Boy Scouts – whose military aspect he had relished. As Ernest approached his thirteenth birthday in September 1917, he measured 5ft 6in and weighed 140lbs, far bulkier than many of the hopefuls seen by recruiting sergeants who were striving to build Uncle Sam's fighting force.[60]

Long before America entered the war in April 1917, many newspapers had fed readers a diet of anti-German atrocity stories while the loss of civilian, particularly American, lives on board *Lusitania*, meant that many Americans (including the Wrentmores) were eager for their country to enter the fray. Like countless other boys, an awestruck Ernest watched America becoming a 'huge military camp'.[61] But Ernest did more than watch, looking back at his youthful self, he believed that something stronger than himself 'drove me on'. Determined to join America's war effort and having bided his time, on the first day of the autumn term, he walked past his school, stowed away on a freight train and began his journey to Europe's blood-drenched fields and America's history books.

On 28 September, having added five years to his age and been told that he was in 'fine physical condition', orphan Henry Earl Monroe was welcomed into the 'big happy family' of the US Army. Torn between terror and elation, it soon dawned on Uncle Sam's youngest doughboy that 'those with whom I had joined up ... were to become my buddies, my comrades-in-arms, and I was determined to ... stay with them through thick and thin'.[62]

Intensive training at Gettysburg turned the raw civvies into a combat team. Like so many underage soldiers, Ernest rapidly gained even more weight and muscle and accepted that having sworn the oath of allegiance, he must take the army's 'rough, tough routine in stride and never know the word failure'.[63] Always fearful of being rumbled for the child he was, his knees shook when on inspection, the captain 'shot at me, "Monroe, did you shave for this inspection?"'. His negative response led to 'Sergeant, take this man's name'. Nevertheless, 'fatigue detail' was preferable to being 'called on the carpet about my age'.[64]

In early April 1918, 'I' Company boarded the USS *Maui*, one of a convoy of battleships destined for St Nazaire, France. Before boarding, each man was given 'an Overseas Card to be forwarded by the Red Cross to our families'. Working out that he was now just a 'number among millions', the youngster completed it with his correct name. After seven months of total silence, the distraught Wrentmores finally learnt that the boy who had failed to turn up at school in early September 1917 was crossing the Atlantic.[65] Acknowledging there was 'no turning back', his last chance to come clean about his deception having passed him by, he almost regretted his decision as *Maui* ploughed through both some of the worst storms in living memory and 'submarine-infested waters'; the 13-year-old was 'scared to death.[66]

Once in France and learning that 'Monroe' was to serve as 'Company runner', 'topkick' platoon sergeant McCart, who had successfully transformed the recruits into a combat team, asked, 'Kid, why don't you come clean? How old are you, anyhow? I could get you out of the hell we are heading into if you'll just say the word.'[67] Ernest/Henry refused. Next to grill him was Captain Shuck who finally conceded, 'you have proved yourself the equal – I might say the superior – to some of the men in the Company ... Report to me in the morning!' Looking back with the hindsight of some forty years, Ernest admitted 'Little did I realise how scared I would be after I became part of that inferno ahead'.[68]

As training in the art of modern warfare continued, including 'the importance of gas masks' – and the need never to lose them, ('I didn't know that the loss of [mine] would spell the end of my career in combat)',[69] he soon had more to worry about than his gas mask. 'With a sick feeling in the pit of my stomach' 'I' Company arrived in the supposedly quiet Anould Sector (Vosges) on 16 June 1918 where the Americans were to gain their first gentle introduction to trench warfare. Having previously held this sector, the French had, in this most rugged terrain of the whole front, developed a 'live and let live' attitude towards those in the opposing trenches.[70] Having never previously seen such 'mountains and heavy forests!', Ernest was relieved that 'we had drawn a soft assignment'.[71] Soft apart from some undesirable visitors,

As we entered the opening of the deep dug out, a few huge rats scampered into the dark corners. [Soon] we became buddies of the rats, cooties and other vermin that never seemed to come forth until we were bedded down for the night on stiff, meshed wire, stretched across a wooden frame with only a blanket to offer the body a bit of padding.[72]

One Sunday, he and his buddy Harry Henz visited Bruyers [*sic*] a few miles behind the lines. In the 'little church there was a serene quietness'. With no one around, homesick Ernest played the "Moonlight Sonata' on the organ. Then 'I saw two nuns and a priest in the fading light [who] were most generous with their thanks'.[73] Subsequently hauled up in front of the 'Skipper', Captain Shuck expressed bemusement, not for the first time, 'For an orphan, Monroe, you do the most amazing things … Your audience could not believe its eyes – such a very young American soldier', adding, 'I am proud of you. I am still amazed, however!'[74]

The sector's quietness soon proved illusory, 'At about 2 am on June 17th, the Boche gave [us] a baptism of well-directed high explosives, together with gas.'[75] The reality of what he had done hit him forcefully, 'I was scared speechless but managed to cover up', but was in 'constant fear and dread – day and night. War does something to you, something that only death can erase … Regardless of the spanning years, you always remember the … inferno of blood and carnage. You can always hear the scream of the wounded, the last gasp of the dying.'[76]

Continually on the run, 'taking messages up and down the mountainside to HQ, every night became a nightmare'.[77] It seemed to his stretched nerves that it was always on the blackest nights with the rain coming down in torrents that he was sent hither and thither with messages, slipping and sliding down the treacherous paths in a maze of old and new trenches, some recently vacated by the Germans. Working in the pitch black, he needed to be totally familiar with the maze of communicating trenches, some of which led directly into the German lines. A runner's sole duty and objective was to deliver the message despite the weather, the darkness of the night or the exposure to enemy crossfire in the daytime. 'Only death or a serious injury held [them] back … Many exhibited courage and bravery "beyond the call of duty". Their reward? A nameless grave somewhere in France.'[78]

On one terrifying occasion, in torrential rain he lost his way in the entanglement of trenches. Then, to his horror, 'I was hearing speech that didn't sound like my kind of American jargon. The voices were guttural.' Himself overheard, a volley of gunfire chased him back to the US lines.

'To be out alone on such a night – covering such a distance with the enemy so close that it seemed you could reach out and touch him – was enough to scare me into shocked immobility. But to run into a nest of Heines to boot', unsurprisingly, the 13-year-old 'was numb with fear'.[79]

Like so many combatants, he retained an abiding memory of his first terrifying night of hand-to-hand combat, with the added horror of the dreaded flamethrowers,

> Again and again down passing years, I awaken from a vivid dream of that night. I hear the shouting and cursing of my buddies above the din of battle and the groan or grunt of a man as bullet meets flesh. Nothing can equal the hideousness of such combat ... when an eternity is lived in the space of minutes.[80]

Transferred to the much tougher St Mihiel sector, struggling to come to terms with the reality of warfare in its naked horror, 'the sight of high explosives on the human body made my insides turn over'; as a runner, his duty was to keep alongside his captain and 'the mighty machine of death.'[81] On one occasion, having worked his way across corpse-strewn, blood-soaked land and delivered his message, the major 'took a good look at me, exclaiming, "You're a hell of a young-looking child to be in this man's war. Must be carryin' a good bunch of guts."'[82]

In late September/early October, serving in the Nixéville area (where Désiré had arrived in early 1915), Ernest finally confessed to Harry Henz; having explained he 'never receive[s] any mail from the USA' because his family had no idea of his whereabouts, things had nevertheless looked up a bit lately because, 'I get a letter now and then from some French girl I've met in some of the villages'.[83] The confessional raised his spirits, it had long preyed on his mind that if he were killed his family would never know what had happened, '[n]ow I knew that if I didn't make it my family would be properly advised.' Although staggered, Harry admitted, 'Everyone of that old gang knows you're just a child ... but you seem to do o.k.'[84]

On 11 October, the regiment entered the Meuse-Argonne Salient to 'become an important part of a series of the most severe battles ever seen on the face of the earth'[85] Accompanying the Skipper up front, Ernest realised, 'We'd passed the point of being human beings long ago.'[86] Time passed in a nightmare of running messages between the Front and the rear; although the significance of each one was impressed upon him;

at one point Captain Allworth turned to him saying, 'I have an important message for you to carry and it must get through. It means the success or failure of this operation'. The message was to advise the CO of the Assault Company that, 'The gap must be closed or our advance will bog down completely. Get going and God be with you.'[87]

God appeared to be with him for although his gas mask was hit and torn to shreds, against all the odds, he himself came through. Learning of the mission's success, Allworth assured him, 'you saved the day!'[88] Despite Allworth's optimism, with men being lost in their thousands, the 'Red Diamond' was reduced to fewer than a brigade. With friends and comrades dropping around him, the 13-year-old was close to break-point. Once again, he was sent back with a message. Still without a gas mask, he heard the dreaded words, 'GAS!' 'This is it I thought' and it very nearly was. Having also been hit in the legs, he came-to lying on the floor in the Ferme de la Madelaine, 'clearly marked with a large Red Cross'.[89] To his horror, the 'Goddamed Boche were firing on the wounded and helpless.- [Then] there would be cries that would end in a blood-curdling gurgle.' Vaguely aware of the horrific wounds surrounding him, he wonders 'if maybe [death] was the quickest way out of this hellish torment.'[90]

Moved to American Base Hospital No. 1 located at Vichy, the medics immediately placed him in the 'Death Ward'. With youth on his side, he pulled through and, to the amazement of many, he was declared well enough to go home. Now he had to fully confront his actions of September 1917. 'I began the most difficult letter I have ever been called upon to write ... I realised that in leaving home, I had committed a terrible wrong and caused my family grief beyond expression. How could I ever atone?[91]

The long journey back to Ohio and adolescence began. Among the first combat troops to be repatriated, although New Yorkers roared greetings to the conquering heroes, in an attempt to shield the public from the worst of the casualties, the American authorities had all stretcher cases, including Ernest, 'hurried off the boat and taken to the hospital at Camp Dix, New Jersey.'[92] On 18 February 1919, discharged from both the hospital and the army, his (first) military career ended.

Having been away nearly two long years during which time he had seen sights no child should see, the boy who had run into a German trench, criss-crossed battle lines, defied death to deliver vital messages, now faced another fear. What reception would he get from those at home who had also suffered 'months of torture'? Collecting him from the station, gazing on the son who appeared to have disappeared off the face of the earth, his father simply said, 'My God! My boy home at last!' Back home, 'There stood the dearest mother in all the world. Her face was pale; her eyes opened so wide; a look of rapture was on her face. I gave one cry, "Mother!" and we were in each other's arms'.[93]

Along with a 'wounded body ... the knowledge of desolation and the sorrow and the agony that is the aftermath of war', 14-year-old Ernest Wrentmore was left with 'memories that can never be erased – memories that bring again and again, visions of an eternity spent [aged 13] in a hell on earth.'[94]

Sofja Nowosielska: 'They put pants on me to punish me.'

Another teenage fighter who has aroused little interest among anglophone historians is Sofja Nowosielska née Lipowicz, born in Poland on 22 January 1900.[95] In August 1914, an independent Poland as we know it today did not exist, partitioned instead in the late eighteenth century between Austro-Hungary, the Kingdom of Prussia and the Russian Empire which had suppressed freedom of speech and education in Polish. Like so many of her contemporaries, Sofja had listened to tales of freedom fighters and in particular female revolutionaries, 'it became my indomitable desire to follow in the footsteps of these great women [freedom fighters] and show the boys that it is not their exclusive privilege to fight for the freedom of their country.'[96] If elders told stories about Poles' heroic actions, juvenile fiction similarly indoctrinated youth: child citizens, both male and female, were waiting in the wings to become a patriotic combatant. Such lack of gender bias helps explain why, at school, 'we girls liked to play war'. When war broke out, just as in Western Europe, children were patriotically encouraged to write letters to soldiers, knit socks and raise money for war bonds – activities which were insufficient to satisfy Sofja's desire for personal involvement.

With hindsight, rebellious Sofja felt her position at the top of her class prevented her from being expelled from her convent school; when holidaying on the family estates in Romania and the Carpathians, she 'enjoyed the freedom of a tomboy'. Attempting to punish her unladylike ways, her aristocratic parents tried 'put[ting] pants [trousers] on me. The effect was rather exciting. My greatest heart's desire being fulfilled, now I could run round unhampered in the fields and woods with the village children, ride horseback and be independent'.[97] She would put these lessons in independence and mixing with people from different backgrounds to good use in the years ahead when, thanks to its geographical position much of what is now Poland became a scene of intensive (Eastern Front) operations. Immense human suffering, even by Great War standards, occurred. An estimated 'total of 2 million Polish troops fought with the armies of the three occupying powers, 450,000 died and close to one million were wounded', not to mention a million displaced persons.[98] Among those caught up in the early fighting were the Lipowicz family including 14-year-old Sofja.

As soon as war was declared, with her father who, 'bitterly resented the dire necessity to fight under a foreign banner', drafted as a major in the Austrian Army, the teenage tomboy, together with an eager young schoolmistress, Miss Szczesna, made an abortive attempt to run away and emulate the village lads who had joined Josef Pilsudski's Polish Legions.[99] Intercepted, she was returned to her family to help care for her pregnant mother and five younger sisters. During the clashes between Cossacks, Hungarians, Austrians and Germans, the Austrian Army retreated in disorder, 'mistreating the civilians', and her family joined thousands of refugees, caught in the crossfire; decimated by 'cannon fire', the civil population fled eastward behind the Russian lines. The Lipowicz temporarily lost their ravaged home and much of their property, including her little sister's 'doll [who] got broken'.[100] One of her sisters and her newborn brother, 'after having inhaled one deep breath of this infested air of misery', died.[101]

Between the winter of 1914 and 1916, Cossacks ransacked Sofja's home which was subsequently requisitioned by 'drink-crazed' Russian officers; her village changed hands three times between the Russians and the Germans, never knowing if they would see Russian or German uniforms the next morning; at one point shrapnel fell 'like hail into our little garden'.[102] 'Russian officers began to look wooingly' at Sofja who was, meanwhile, edging closer to her desire to become a soldier.[103] She began to serve the Polish Military Organisation as a courier smuggling letters, money and firearms.[104] After her wounded father's return, 'an old man with a grey beard in an Austrian uniform, on crutches' in the summer of 1918, she successfully ran away and enlisted in a volunteer Polish defence force.[105] By autumn 1918 Sofja was caught up in the Battle of Lemberg/Lwow (then part of eastern Galicia, now part of western Ukraine).

Having 'exchanged our coats for men's clothing in a Jewish store and joined the fighting ranks under the command of a Lieutenant Feldstajn, I already had a rifle and many cartridges.'[106] Having claimed she knew how to shoot, the sergeant watched her carefully. Unimpressed, he spat and addressed her as 'Girl citizen'. However, he conceded that he had also had to 'teach the other kids yesterday' how to handle a safety rifle. Nevertheless, she realised that if 'it were [widely] known I were a girl I would be subject to a great deal of unpleasantness'. Having been given a Polish national cap 'under which I hid my long braids, folded so tightly round my head that it began to ache', she got 'rid of my skirt at the first opportune moment.'[107] Although none of the young fighters had official uniforms,

> Great joy overcame [us] as soon as the Lieutenant announced that we would all receive the Polish eagles as emblems.[108]

> Freezing in [her] percale blouse, they gave me an Austrian uniform and a pair of very spacious boots, which caused blisters on my feet. It was in this disguise that an NCO questioned me: "What is your name?" "George Krawcyzk" I answered … why I had chosen that name I do not know.[109]

Drilling and being taught how to handle a rifle, Sofja became worried when one of the,

> officers looked at me wonderingly, and I, being afraid that he would realise that I was a girl, pushed my cap deeper over my ears and asked him for a cigarette. It did not help me much. He guessed my sex but he respected my secret.

Now famished and exhausted, 'for two days we marched constantly, without rest or sleep, without a roof over our heads, in rain and in mud.'[110] 'Marching mechanically … with a ringing in my ears', to Sofja's intense relief, they finally reached their quarters.

> I was assigned to a small corner in a peasant's hut. Asked "Why citizen do you not take off your cap in the house?", she took action against her long braids. I went outside [where] another soldier … without any ceremony cut off my long hair which, when spread out,

covered my uniform like an overcoat. I was generally taken for a 15-year-old boy.[111]

Teaming up with an even younger volunteer, 'a simple boy of humble descent [who] was very proud that such a young girl of refinement was fraternizing with him, he provided me with foot wraps when we had to return with our booty [captured canons] to Lwow.'[112]

'Young girl of refinement or not', soon she and her comrades were in the thick of the fighting, taking to heart their officers' advice that despite being ill-equipped, they should throw themselves into the fray, '"With sticks against rifles; with rifles against cannons", and direct ourselves accordingly.'[113] With the battle raging throughout the city, 'We had to drive out the enemy, conquering every single stair and every corner. I forgot I was a woman. I knew only that I had to fight hard to avenge the Polish losses. I did not feel the pain, though blood was pouring from my hands and forehead'. Evacuated to hospital, she noticed that many of the erstwhile child soldiers, members of what became known as the highly decorated Order of Eaglets, were contentedly playing with toys on their hospital beds.[114] Justifiably proud of the young fighters' record (in some instances, 'the rifle was bigger than the fighter'), she noted how 'at one time, sixty of us, mostly children had repulsed an attack of 700 Ukrainians'.[115] She won a number of decorations including two crosses for bravery and a silver Merit Cross.[116]

The Battle for Lwow was bloody and hard won. Children in their early teens, many of whom were killed, fought to repress the Ukrainians who were, 'mercilessly destroying the City.'[117] Polish artist Wojciech Kossak's painting of 'Lwow Eaglets' is a visual testimony to the fighters' youth; might the girl in the foreground represent Sofja? That there were so many youngsters is unsurprising, one of the initial pockets of resistance to the Ukrainian occupation of Lwow started in a school. The painting is however sanitised, the children clean and well-clothed. More realistically Sofja sees them as, 'little bums, soiled with mud, blackened with smoke … I am sure that my mother would not have recognised me now'.[118]

Private Tommy Ricketts VC: 'To drain the water out of him … we held him up by the legs'

On 14 October 1918, Private Tommy Ricketts of the Royal Newfoundland Regiment 'advanc[ed] under heavy fire from enemy machine guns'.

Having served on the Western Front for a year, this was far from his first brush with probable death. The first had occurred twelve years earlier when, aged 5, he had nearly drowned while playing near his home in the tiny settlement of Middle Arm, Newfoundland. Only the quick reactions of a visitor who, once he had dragged Tommy out of harm's way, held him up 'by the legs to drain the water out of him', saved his life. Born on 15 April 1901 to fisherman John Ricketts and his second wife Amelia, life was not kind to young Tommy. His mother died when he was still young, leaving his elder sister Rachel to raise him.

At some point between his wife's death and his younger son's enlistment, John Ricketts was sent to prison. Virtually illiterate, Tommy began working as a fisherman. When his brother George joined the Newfoundland Regiment in 1915, Tommy longed to follow and on 2 September 1916, aged 15 years and 4 months, standing 5ft 6in and with a chest of 37in, thus well inside the required measurement standards, he assured the recruiting sergeant that he was 18 years and 3 months old. Unable to sign his name, he duly marked an X on the attestation form. Waiting to go overseas, on 2 December he was on picket duty at the regimental depot when RSM George Paver found him drunk on duty. Let off with an admonishment as opposed to being charged, 3102 Private Ricketts' military career had got off to an inglorious start.[119]

Having completed his initial training seemingly without further incident, on 31 January 1917 Tommy left Newfoundland aboard SS *Florizel,* six months later he and 249 other soldiers were reinforcing the regiment in Belgium, forming working parties in the mud-soaked, rat-infested trenches around Passchendaele. Did the teenager stop and ask himself if this was really what he had lied about his age for? Maybe he felt things were looking up when he first went over the top on 16 August 1917. Against the odds, he survived the 9 October Battle of Poelcapelle unscathed, but six weeks later, he was hit in the right thigh during the Battle of Cambrai – when the Newfoundlanders so distinguished themselves that George V decreed that from henceforth they were the Royal Newfoundland Regiment (RNR). Although not life-threatening, Tommy's wound was serious enough to earn him a 'Blighty' ticket and he spent several weeks at No. 3 London General Hospital, Wandsworth, where he learnt that his beloved elder brother George was 'Missing'.[120]

Spared the bitter fighting at Masnières and Bailleul, in which his regiment was involved, Tommy returned to France on 30 April 1918. Soon, along with his comrades, he was providing the guard for Sir Douglas Haig's Headquarters at Montreuil.[121] His early brush with drunkenness and authority well behind him, he was noted as being 'a good soldier, smartly turned out, obedient, efficient'.[122] Now his father made a brief, perhaps unwelcome, comeback in Tommy's life. Released from jail, John Ricketts demanded to know why his daughter Rachel was receiving the allotment of 60c a day being deducted from Tommy's (and previously George's) army pay in favour of the sister who had helped raise them. Perhaps reluctantly, Tommy altered the beneficiary.

Soon Tommy would have more to occupy his thoughts than the man who told the authorities he was in 'a helpless and destitute state [without] the means of buying a mouthful of food', if his underage son did not chip in.[123] Now part of the 28th Brigade under General John 'Mad' Jack, and with the RNR consisting of mainly new recruits, 17-year-old Tommy was a hardened veteran.[124] 'B' Company Captain Sydney Frost MC was undoubtedly relieved that at least a few of those under his command, such as Tommy, had survived previous actions and might 'steady' the newcomers. Initially held in reserve, on 14 October 1918 the battalion was 'strung out along the railway bed north of the village of Ledeghem in anticipation of another advance.'[125] Captain Frost was ordered to use his own initiative for the taking of the company's objective: three German pillboxes 500–600 yards apart. Armed with machine guns, the pill-boxes covered a wide field of view with devastating results, the whole Brigade was under heavy fire.[126]

Captain Frost subsequently noted,

Pte. Ricketts at once volunteered to go forward with his section commander and a Lewis gun to attempt to outflank the battery. Advancing by short rushes under heavy fire from enemy machine guns ... their ammunition was exhausted when still 300 yards from the battery. The enemy, seeing an opportunity to get their field guns away, began to bring up their gun teams. Pte. Ricketts, at once realising the situation, doubled back 100 yards under the heaviest machine-gun fire, procured further ammunition, and dashed back again to the Lewis gun, and by very accurate fire drove the enemy and the gun teams into a farm ... Possibly single-handedly, [There is conflicting evidence] he captured the four field guns, four machine guns, and eight prisoners ... By his ... utter disregard

143

of personal safety, Pte. Ricketts secured the further supply of ammunition which directly resulted in these important captures and undoubtedly saved many lives.[127]

This brief summary of the day's actions tactfully omits to mention that 'Pte. Rickets' had run the risk of being felled by friendly fire. Brigadier-General 'Mad' Jack had 'set out from a ridge where he had been following the Brigade's advance and made an impromptu frenzied appearance in the Newfoundlanders' front line position inquiring why the advance was stalled.' Then, 'spying movement and wondering why men were not firing on what he mistook to be Germans retreating, Jack grabbed a Lewis gun and was about to fire when Captain Frost impetuously intervened, pointing out that the General was about to shoot his own troops'. [128] These troops were Tommy and men of his platoon.

When, two days later, Captain Frost sat down to write up the 14 October action and Tommy's heroic role therein, he may have been inwardly seething. The Brigadier, who did not appreciate a junior officer taking him to task for his actions in the field, had just hauled him over the coals. Now Frost faced a problem, the Victoria Cross can only be awarded when two officers substantiate the information and there was only one other surviving officer; as the author of the citation, Frost himself could not bear witness to Tommy's gallantry. Believing that Tommy's actions had spared countless lives, maybe even the whole battalion, but reluctant to ask 'Mad' Jack to corroborate the account, Frost sent it off anyway.[129] With no other possible signatory, it is likely that although Jack may have been furious with Frost, he too wished the teenager's valour to be rewarded. He had noted in his diary that, 'Private Ricketts ... was personally responsible for the capture of four field guns, 4 machine guns and eight prisoners...'.

Tommy himself almost certainly thought no more about these actions, which had taken place barely a month before the Armistice. Counting himself lucky to still be alive, he formed part of the British Army of the Rhine. On 23 December 1918, in a small German town, the regiment paraded in front of their commanding officer, Lieutenant Colonel Barnard. Frost takes up the story,

Ricketts, with his usual military bearing, marched to where the Commanding Officer was standing, saluted, and stood at attention.

Bernard ... shook his hand and congratulated him, whereupon Ricketts turned about and marched back to his place in the ranks. The commanding officer then ... gave the command – 'Remove Headdress' 'Three Cheers for Private Ricketts **VC**.'... Everyone gathered around the only VC in the Regiment, each man clamouring to grab him by the hand and ... from the depth of his heart offer him congratulations and best wishes.[130]

The Governor of Newfoundland sent a telegram offering his and all Newfoundland's 'heartfelt congratulations'. France had already honoured the 17-year-old private, bestowing on him the highest award open to a foreigner, the Croix de Guerre with gold star – the only Newfoundlander to be so decorated.

Still three months shy of his eighteenth birthday, the army's youngest living VC was slated for home. Now there was a potential problem. No investiture was planned before his departure. George V found the solution: a private investiture at York Cottage on the Sandringham Estate, held on 19 January 1919 in the presence of Queen Alexandra, Princess Mary, Prince George, Queen Maud and the Crown Prince of Norway, as well as General Dighton Probyn, the then second oldest living recipient of the Victoria Cross (decorated in India sixty-three years earlier). Having chatted with the nervous young private, a deeply impressed king presented 'the youngest VC in the British Army' to his family, subsequently writing in his diary, 'Yesterday I gave the VC to Private Ricketts, Newfoundland Regiment, who is only 17½ now, a splendid boy.'[131] General Probyn VC was less effusive about this 'splendid boy', commenting that rather than being a 'man of few words, Ricketts was a man of no words.' Perhaps the octogenarian general did not make allowances for the whirling emotions in the youthful, erstwhile fisherman's, breast.

On 31 January, still under-age but now sergeant, Tommy Ricketts VC, CdeG, was on his way home from Liverpool aboard SS *Corsican,* the very ship on which his brother George had made his one-way journey to Europe. Liverpool gave him and the remnants of the RNR which had borne such heavy casualties a rousing send-off. Interviewed about his plans, Tommy explained how in 1916, 'I was a fisherman and could hardly write'; now he wanted to study at Bishopsfield College, St John, 'embrace the chances open to me ... and make progress'.[132] His words preceded him. In Newfoundland, money poured in to enable him to pursue his dream.

On 8 February, rapturous crowds flocked onto Furness-Withy Pier to welcome home Newfoundland's hero. Despite his shunning the limelight as he would do for most of his life, 'An enthusiastic crowd hoisted Tommy into a horse drawn cab, unhooked the horses, and a few enterprising young men took over and pulled the cab with an adulating public cheering him on through the streets of St John's.'[133]

Demobilised in July 1919 aged 18 years and 3 months (still too young to serve legally overseas), in 1921, Sergeant Tommy Ricketts VC passed his First Year Preliminary Grade examinations. Having fulfilled his adolescent dream of becoming a soldier, he was now fulfilling his adult one of learning to read and write.

Conclusion

On Friday 3 July 1914, hundreds of Viennese children, demonstrating sympathy for three orphans travelling to bid a final farewell to their murdered parents, lined the railway route from Vienna's Belvedere Palace to Franz Joseph Station.[1] Could any child, either inside or outside the railway carriage, have foreseen the forces of evil that the assassination of these children's parents, Archduke Franz Ferdinand and Countess Sophie, would unleash and how, within a month, the world as they knew it would begin disintegrating forever?

Some of the children, inspired by the funeral's military pageantry (albeit low key due to the ambiguity of Franz Ferdinand's morganatic wife's position), may have returned home to play with the model soldiers and Red Cross nurses which filled millions of little Europeans' toy cupboards. At school with war declared, pupils across all combatant lands learnt that their country was involved in a righteous struggle. Picture books for pre-readers and exciting tales of derring-do and feminine assistance to war heroes for older pupils, enabled all age groups to enter vicariously into a war in which they were supposedly too young to participate. Nevertheless, all could guarantee themselves a place as young patriots by contributing their labour, their pocket money and pressurising adults into doing the same. They could further demonstrate patriotism and commitment to their nation's cause by adopting a soldier and striving to make his life less uncomfortable. Those with artistic talents could draw war as seen from the inside, others could hone writing skills by describing the war as they lived it.

If some children simply observed the war, others found themselves living cheek-by-jowl with the enemy. For some, he proved more evil than they had feared, others discovered my enemy could become my friend, irrespective of adults' opinions about such fraternisation. Before long, war in all its horrors was unleashed on these most innocent of civilians, sometimes they were 'collateral damage', other times victims of their own side's bigotry.

Courage is not an adult prerogative. Some youngsters demonstrated courage beyond their years. Teenage rebellion was not invented in the

Swinging Sixties; between 1914 and 1918, those wishing to kick against authority could run away and enlist. Many showed unimaginable fortitude when called upon to play a man's part in war.

Children's experiences of war were as varied as the children themselves. The theme that unites all the children you have met in this book, and the voiceless millions they represent, is that the shots fired at Sarajevo on 28 June 1914 changed not only their world, but children's exposure to war forever.

Endnotes

Chapter 1

1. http://www.bbc.co.uk/schools/0/ww1/25183931 See also Rosie Kennedy 'The Children's War: British Children's Experiences of the Great War' PhD thesis p. 197f
2. Henry Harris *Model Soldiers* pp. 23–4
3. Piete Kuhr *There we'll meet again* p. 127
4. https://gallica.bnf.fr/ark:/12148/bpt6k9679519t/f10.image
5. *At War!* pp. 12, 24, 30
6. *ibid.* p. 26
7. James Thirsk *A Beverley Child's Great War* p. 25
8. See http://fsu.digital.flvc.org/islandora/object/fsu%3A110774#page/Page+4/mode/2up
9. Susan Fisher *Girls and Boys in No–Man's–Land* p. 110
10. http://roadstothegreatwar–ww1.blogspot.com/2015/09/the–tsar–takes–his–son–to–work.html
11. Edith Hall *Canary Girls and Stockpots* p. 23
12. Manon Pignot *La Guerre des Crayons* pp. 118–19
13. *Toys and Games* October 1914
14. Nicholas Whittaker *Toys Were Us* p. 21
15. http://www.antiquetrader.com/2001web/
16. Exhibition 'Lucie, Paysanne en Guerre' April–October 2014, Villeneuve d'Asq, France
17. Muller, Sonja, 'Toys, Games and Juvenile Literature in Germany and Britain during the First World War. A Comparison' in H. Jones et al *Untold War: New Perspectives in First World War Studies,* pp. 233–57 p. 236
18. See *Wiener Zeitung*, supplement 'Programm Punkte', p. 7, 30 April 2014
19. Max Arthur *Forgotten Voices of the First World War* p. 15
20. Simone de Beauvoir *Mémoires d'une jeune fille rangée* p. 38 (throughout the text all French translations are my own unless otherwise specified)

21. Manon Pignot *La Guerre des Crayons* pp. 118–19
22. Françoise Dolto *Correspondances* pp. 74–5
23. Kuhr p. 87
24. Yves Congar *Mon Journal de Guerre* p. 111
25. Leonard Smith *A Tansley Boyhood* 1996 p. 45
26. Andrew Donson *Youth in the Fatherless Land* p. 170
27. Donson p. 170
28. Aaron Cohen 'Flowers of Evil' in ed. James Martin *Children and War A Historical Anthology* pp. 38–49 p. 44
29. Cohen p. 44
30. Cohen p. 43
31. Cohen p. 44
32. See Nazan Maksudyan "Agents or Pawns?: Nationalism and Ottoman Children during the Great War" http://www.jstor.org/stable/10.2979/jottturstuass.3.1.
33. See Rosie Kennedy *The Children's War* p. 208
34. Kuhr p. 34
35. Kuhr p. 151
36. Kuhr p. 223
37. Kuhr p. 202
38. Kuhr p. 313
39. David Parker *Hertfordshire Children in War and Peace* p. 104
40. [Hertfordshire] *Mercury* 1 May 1915
41. R. Selleck *English Primary Education and the Progressives* p. 8
42. Parker p. 120
43. Parker p. 33
44. Elsie Oman *Salford Stepping Stones* p. 23
45. Parker p. 43
46. Parker p. 43
47. https://www.rtbf.be/ww1/topics/detail_school–in–wartime?id=8355929
48. https://www.rtbf.be/ww1/topics/detail_school–in–wartime?id=8355929
49. https://www.rtbf.be/ww1/topics/detail_school–in–wartime?id=8355929
50. De Schraepdrijver and Proctor *An English Governess in the Great War* p. 189
51. Parker p. 34

ENDNOTES

52. See *Pall Mall Gazette* 1 Feb 1918
53. See http://www.bl.uk/manuscripts/Viewer.aspx?ref=add_ms_ 39258_fs001r
54. Frances Clamp *Southend during the Great War* p. 72
55. Parker p. 83
56. Hall p. 22
57. Hall p. 19
58. Oman p. 25
59. Oman p. 21
60. Parker p. 37
61. Kuhr p. 94
62. Parker p. 39
63. *The War Pictorial* August 1918 p. 34
64. Rosalie Triolo *Our Schools and the War* p. 221
65. Hall p. 23
66. Olivier Faron *Les Enfants du Deuil* p. 39
67. Faron p. 34
68. Kennedy p. 254
69. Cynthia Asquith *Diaries* p. 480
70. Parker p. 68
71. http://www.documentingdissent.org.uk/lancaster–girls–grammar
72. Pignot p. 30
73. Selleck p. 11
74. See ED11/14
75. MEPO2/1691
76. Donson p. 140
77. Tara Zahra 'Each nation only cares for its own': Empire, Nation, and Child Welfare Activism in the Bohemian Lands, 1900–1918 *American Historical Review* 2006 vol 111 p. 1378–1402 p. 1378 http://ahr.oxfordjournals.org/content/111/5/1378.short
78. de Beauvoir p. 40
79. Parker p. 83
80. Kuhr p. 16
81. Donson p. 110
82. Annie Droëge *Diary of Annie's War* p. 40; Donson p. 109, p.112
83. Donson p. 122
84. Donson p. 122
85. Donson p. 145

86. Fisher p. 42
87. Parker p. 92
88. Parker p. 92 ff
89. Fisher p. 49
90. Fisher pp. 43, 44, 56
91. Triolo p. 94
92. Triolo p. 100
93. Françoise Dolto *Correspondances 1913–1938* p. 30
94. Dolto p. 32
95. Dolto p. 34
96. Manon Pignot *La Guerre des Crayons* pp. 6–7
97. Pignot p. 10
98. Kuhr p. 53
99. Kuhr p. 77
100. *Moi Marie–Rocher Ecolière en Guerre* ed. Didier Guyvarc'h p. 11
101. *Marie–Rocher* p. 29
102. *Marie–Rocher* p. 20
103. Pignot p. 48
104. Pignot p. 70
105. Kuhr p. 51
106. Kuhr p. 73
107. See https://digital.library.illinois.edu/search?field=dls_subject&q=Posters+by+children
108. *Early Diary of Anaïs Nin 1914–1920* entry for 8 June 1916
109. Nin 11 May 1917
110. Yves Congar *Journal de Guerre* 1 October 1915
111. See www.jewsfww.london/the–first–world–war–through–the–eyes–of–londons–jewish–children
112. Triolo p. 179 (from Australian Lieutenant John Bourke)
113. www.jewsfww.london/the–first–world–war–through–the–eyes–of–londons–jewish–children
114. https://www.bl.uk/world–war–one/articles/recruitment–conscripts–and–volunteers

Chapter 2

1. Cicely Stewart–Smith in Rose Kerr *The Story of a Million Girls* p. 27

ENDNOTES

2. Mary Cadogan and Patricia Craig *You're a Brick, Angela* p. 141
3. Kerr p. 29 and https://lesliesguidinghistory.webs.com/guidesatwar.htm
4. Dorothy Scannell *Mother Knew Best* p. 90; Kerr p. 28
5. Janie Hampton *How the Girl Guides Won the War* p. 10
6. Scannell p. 90
7. Kerr p. 27
8. Hampton p. 11
9. See http://www.voicesofwarandpeace.org/portfolio/girl–guides
10. Hampton p. 11 (British Girl Guides Rifle Shot badge was withdrawn in 1932)
11. https://members.scouts.org.uk/supportresources/3230/awards–for–gallantry–and–meritorious–conduct
12. Tammy Proctor *A Centenary of Girl Guides and Girl Scouts* p. 32
13. Hampton p. 14
14. http://www.voicesofwarandpeace.org/portfolio/girl–guides
15. https://lesliesguidinghistory.webs.com/guidesatwar.htm
16. See /www.warmuseum.ca/firstworldwar/history/life–at–home–during–the–war/wartime–tragedies/the–halifax–explosion/
17. Proctor pp. 30–1
18. https://lesliesguidinghistory.webs.com/guidesatwar.htm
19. Hampton pp. 10–11
20. http://broqueville.be/?p=4388
21. Chris Northcott *MI5 at War 1909–1918: How MI5 Foiled the Spies of the Kaiser in the First World War* p. 115
22. All information about Girl Guides' employment at MI5 from http://www.scotlandswar.co.uk/guides_and_mi5.html
23. These Guides would have been drawn from the middle–classes who would have been able to afford a doctor.
24. http://www.scotlandswar.co.uk/guides_and_mi5.html
25. Hampton p. 13
26. Hampton p. 13
27. Hampton p. 16
28. See http://acsepagny.pagesperso–orange.fr/Journalgarcontreizeans 1914%201915.pdf
29. See Manon Pignot *Allons Enfants de la Patrie* p. 30
30. Pignot p. 28
31. Kuhr p. 11
32. See Pignot p. 28

33. de Beauvoir p. 43
34. Pignot p. 25
35. Thirsk p. 31 As an officer he would have had more frequent leaves than enlisted men
36. Richard van Emden and Steve Humphries *All Quiet on the Home Front* pp. 30–1
37. C. H. Rolph *London Particulars* p. 175
38. Pignot p. 33
39. Pignot pp. 34–5
40. Françoise Breuillaud–Sottas *Evian et le drame de la Grande Guerre: 500,000 civils rapatries* (bi-lingual) book, accompanying exhibition in Maison Gribaldi Evian April–November 2014 p. 45 Citations from English pagination. See also Henry Bordeaux *Le Retour des Innocents*
41. Breuillaud–Sottas p. 47
42. Quoted Breuillaud–Sottas p. 57
43. All information from www.14ansen1914.wordpress.com
44. A form of bank note issued in the occupied areas that were worthless outside these territories. Thus, rapatriates arrived all but penniless and had to be provided for by the French government who exchanged their billets de ville for the equivalent in French francs. As by late 1917, the German mark was increasingly worthless, the occupiers were keen to acquire as many French francs as possible.
45. Breuillaud–Sottas p. 59
46. Kuhr p. 1
47. See Pignot pp. 245, 244
48. Kuhr p. 37 – Piete grieved for the Russians who had died in the swamps around Tannenburg
49. Congar *Journal de la Guerre 1914–1918*
50. For complete run see http://archives.cd08.fr/article.php?laref= 398&titre=la–gazette–des–ardennes–disponible–en–ligne
51. Congar 2 April 1915
52. On these occasions the news she had read was broadly accurate
53. The best source for Henriette is Manon Pignot 'Avoir douze ans dans Ham, Picardie' in ed. Olivia Carpi et Philippe Nivet *La Picardie Occupée* pp. 137–46
54. Pignot p. 238
55. Pignot p. 238

56. For detailed information see editor's note 38 to Congar p. 32
57. Congar note 180 p. 161 Stephan Audoin–Rouzeau argues that due to ethnicity, Romanian, Serb, Russian and Italian prisoners fared far worse than French and British ones.
58. Pignot p. 246
59. Pignot p. 247
60. Pignot pp. 248–9
61. Pignot p. 178
62. Pignot p. 179
63. See also Emma Knuth *Als Fünfzehnjährige verschleppt, in Ostpreußen hinter Stacheldraht. Eine Sammlung ostpreussischer Kriegsgefangenen–Erlebnisse*
64. ed Karin Bork *Gefangen in Siberien Tagebuch eines ostpreußischen Mädchens 1914–1920* p. 33 See also Manon Pignot 'Déportée en Sibérie: Le Journal d'une Jeune Allemande pendant la Grande Guerre pp.131–166 in Phillippe Nivet et Olivier Forcade *Les Réfugiés en Europe*. See also Serena Tiepolato '...und nun waren wir auch Verbannte. Warum? Weshalb?' Deportate prussiane in Russia 1914–1918 DEP n.1/ 2004 pp. 59–85 http://www.unive.it/media/allegato/dep/Ricerche/5–Und_nun_waren_wir_auch_Verbannte.pdf
65. Bork p. 33
66. See Bork pp. 116–17
67. Bork p. 14

Chapter 3
1. www.uccla.ca/Plaque_Notice3b.pdf
2. Peeke, Jones, Walsh–Johnson *Lusitania Story* p. 56 (My emphasis)
3. Peeke p. 53
4. Peeke plates 39 and 40; statistics from inter alia http://www.rmslusitania.info and *Lusitania Story*
5. Diana Preston *Wilful Murder: The Sinking of the* Lusitania p. 124
6. Information from http://www.liverpoolmuseums.org.uk
7. http://www.rmslusitania.info also https://www.garemaritime.com/lest–forget–part–1/
8. Audrey, the last survivor, died in 2011. She had kept in touch with Alice throughout her life.
9. Matthew 19:14 (King James Version)

10. http://www.rmslusitania.info/people/second–cabin/barbara–anderson and https://www.garemaritime.com/lusitania–part–3–the–survivor

11. Interview with historian Michael Poirier quoted http://www.rmslusitania.info/people/second–cabin/barbara–anderson/

12. http://www.rmslusitania.info/people/second–cabin/barbara–anderson/

13. www.garemaritime.com/lusitania–part–3–the–survivor/

14. http://www.rmslusitania.info/people/second–cabin/helen–smith/

15. Peek, Walsh–Johnson, Jones, *The* Lusitania *Story: The Atrocity that Shocked the World* p. 72

16. http://www.rmslusitania.info/people/second–cabin/helen–smith

17. Preston p. 209

18. https://www.bbc.co.uk/news/uk–wales–south–west–wales–32622615

19. Hartford Courant 10 May 1915; http://www.rmslusitania.info/people/third–class/elsie–hook/

20. See https://www.encyclopedia–titanica.org/community/threads/thomas–quinn–senior–and–his–son.3897/ also http://www.liverpoolmuseums.org.uk and http://www.rmslusitania.info/people/deck/thomas–james–quinn

21. Information from Thomas' great niece https://www.encyclopedia–titanica.org/community/threads/thomas–quinn–senior–and–his–son.3897/

22. http://www.rmslusitania.info/people/deck/thomas–william–quinn/

23. http://www.rmslusitania.info and http://www.liverpoolmuseums.org.uk There is confusion on some *Lusitania* sites as to which is the elder of the Allan girls. The Canadian census states Anna was born in 1900 and Gwen in late 1898

24. http://smartpei.typepad.com/robert_patersons_weblog/2015/04/world–war–1–sailing–the–atlantic–part–1–martha–allan–makes–the–crossing.html

25. See *Retford, Gainsborough and Worksop Times*, *Newark and Mansfield Daily News* 11 June 1915

26. http://www.liverpoolmuseums.org.uk

27. http://smartpei.typepad.com/robert_patersons_weblog/2015/05/world–war–1–the–lusitania–part–3–the–sinking.html

ENDNOTES

28. http://smartpei.typepad.com/robert_patersons_weblog/2015/05/world–war–1–the–lusitania–part–5–the–aftermath.html
29. http://www.liverpoolmuseums.org.uk
30. On 15 April 1917 en route to Egypt *Cameronia* (now based in Marseille) was torpedoed and sank with the loss of 210 lives. For information on a German spy ring operating in Marseille see Vivien Newman *Régina Diana: Seductress, Singer, Spy*.
31. Preston p. 209
32. *Sunday Express* 10 February 1991
33. *Sunday Express* 10 February 1991
34. On 4 February, 1916, the German Government assumed liability for *Lusitania* losses sustained by American nationals see inter alia http://www.rmslusitania.info/primary–docs
35. *Boston Journal*, 10 May 1915 see also http://www.rmslusitania.info/people/second–cabin/kathleen–kaye/
36. *Huntington Press* 11 August 1915 see also *The Pantagraph* Illinois 17 July 1915; *Great War Illustrated* 2 p. 312
37. http://www.bbc.co.uk/guides/z2vj7ty
38. http://www.liverpoolmuseums.org.uk also http://www.rmslusitania.info/people/victualling/george–wynne/ (There is some divergence in the details in the two accounts of George Wynne) Additional information from Diana Preston *Lusitania: An Epic Tragedy*
39. http://smartpei.typepad.com/robert_patersons_weblog/2015/05/world–war–1–the–lusitania–part–5–the–aftermath.html
40. http://www.liverpoolmuseums.org.uk
41. Figure from http://www.rmslusitania.info/people/statistics/ which does not appear to include those above the age of 12 who paid 'full price' for their passage. see also Preston *Wilful Murder* p. 124
42. Winston Churchill *The Great War* (11) p. 680
43. *News of the World* 6 June 1937
44. *Woman's Dreadnought* 27 January 1917
45. *Woman's Dreadnought* 27 January 1917
46. Graham Hill and Howard Bloch *The Silvertown Explosion* p. 13
47. Dr F.A. Freeth *New Scientist* 30 July 1964. Additional information from http://www.newhamrecorder.co.uk/news/heritage/silvertown–explosion–remembered–100–years–on–1–4852489

48. J. J. Betts *I Was There* Volume 2 p. 1327 All information about the fire station is from this source
49. Betts p. 1328
50. *Birmingham Gazette* 23 January 1917
51. See also *Pall Mall Gazette* January 30 1917
52. *Birmingham Gazette* 23 January 1917
53. See Hill p. 118
54. Hill p. 167
55. *Stratford Express* 10 February 1917
56. Hill p. 164
57. *Lichfield Mercury* 9 February 1917
58. See Hill pp. 163, 164
59. *Stratford Express* 27 January 1917
60. *Stratford Express* 27 January 1917
61. *Stratford Express* 27 January 1917
62. Surnames given in newspaper but not identified here for privacy reasons
63. Hill pp. 131–2
64. See Hill p. 98
65. Hill p. 98
66. Hill p. 60
67. Hill p. 44
68. Hill p. 43
69. Hill p. 153 and http://www.childrenshomes.org.uk/TSArethusa/
70. http://www.newhamrecorder.co.uk/news/heritage/silvertown–explosion–remembered–100–years–on–1–4852489
71. *Stratford Express* 27 January 1917
72. Martin Easdown with Thomas Genth *A Glint in the Sky* p. 96
73. http://www.firstworldwar.com/airwar/bombers_gotha_giant.htm
74. https://www.dover.uk.com/forums/dover–forum/1878–shipping–accident
75. www.warrenpress.net
76. See www.warrenpress.net
77. http://sussexhistoryforum.co.uk
78. Easdown p. 44
79. www.warrenpress.net
80. Easdown p. 57
81. Easdown p. 90

ENDNOTES

82. Easdown p. 58
83. *Folkestone during the war [1914–1919] a record of the town's life and work* p. 106 available online See also *Folkestone, Hythe, Sandgate and Cheriton Chronicle* 2 June 1917
84. Easdown p. 76
85. *Folkestone during the war* p. 103 available at https//:www.archive. org/details/folkestoneduring00carliala/page/n103
86. https://www.a–n.co.uk/blogs/i–draw/post/52491834/
87. https://dancingledge.wordpress.com/2017/05/28/25th–may–1917–the–air–raid–that–blasted–folkestone–into–a–new–age–of–violence/ Easdown p. 99
88. Information from www.ancestry.co.uk
89. https://dancingledge.wordpress.com/2017/05/28/25th–may–1917–the–air–raid–that–blasted–folkestone–into–a–new–age–of–violence/
90. *The Scotsman* 30 May 1917
91. https://dancingledge.wordpress.com/2017/05/28/25th–may–1917–the–air–raid–that–blasted–folkestone–into–a–new–age–of–violence/
92. www.ancestry.co.uk Easdown p. 101
93. Easdown p. 104
94. Ukrainian Immigration Advertisement Library and Archives of Canada, c–6196
95. See Sarah Beaulieu 'Remembering the Forgotten: Archaeology at the WWI Internment Camp' MA Thesis
96. See Don McNair *Vernon Internment Camp 1914–1920* p. 4
97. *Vancouver Sun*, 4 September 1914
98. Jean Laflamme *Spirit Lake : un camp de concentration en Abitibi durant la Grande Guerre.* p. 9
99. Information from McNair p. 11
100. McNair p. 11
101. McNair p. 9
102. McNair p. 25
103. McNair p. 27
104. McNair p. 25
105. Beaulieu p. 36 see also 'Fernie at War: The Morrissey Internment Camp' www.internmentcanada.ca)
106. McNair p. 9
107. McNair p. 15
108. Laflamme 42

109. www.internmentcanada.ca
110. McNair p. 11
111. McNair p. 25
112. McNair p. 24
113. Beaulieu 97
114. Information from www.ancestry.com
115. Mark Forsythe and Greg Dickson *From the West Coast to the Western Front* p. 182
116. Forsythe p. 182 – she appears to have miraculously become English again!
117. Mc Nair p. 9 Victor seemingly died tragically young in 1927
118. Forsythe p. 182
119. bowjamesbow.ca/2007/11/22/prisoners–in–th.shtml
120. Lubomyr Luciuk *In Fear of the Barbed Wire Fence* p. 44
121. see Luciuk p. 6, p. 23, p. 33 see also p. 30 note 41
122. edited Kadriye Ercikan, Peter Seixas *New Directions in Assessing Historical Thinking* p. 108 and Bohdan S Kordan *Enemy Aliens, Prisoners of War: Internment in Canada During the Great War* p. 36
123. *The Globe and Mail* 11 October 1988 (my emphasis)
124. *The Globe* 3 August 1918
125. Laflamme p. 10, Luciuk p. 65
126. See 'Badly Treated in Every Way: The Internment of Ukrainians in Quebec during the First World War' Peter Melnycky http://www.infoukes.com
127. Melnycky
128. Luciuk p. 14
129. Melnycky; Laflamme p. 16
130. http://bowjamesbow.ca/2007/11/22/prisoners–in–th.shtm
131. Laflamme p. 38
132. [spelling taken from register of baptisms Laflamme 33]
133. Beaulieu p. 114
134. Interview with Mary's son, Jerry http://calgaryherald.com/news/internment–camps–a–dark–shadow–in–war–time–canada
135. Melnycky my emphasis; Laflamme p. 11
136. Melnycky
137. Laflamme p. 43
138. Melnycky
139. Melnycky

ENDNOTES

140. Laflamme p. 41
141. *Edmonton Journal* 6 August 2014
142. Luciuk p. 57
143. *Ukrainian Weekly* January 1994
144. Internment operations Government of Canada National Archives p. 3 section 16
145. http://www.pressreader.com/canada/national–post–national–edition/20111212/283781375717309
146. Luciuk p. 23
147. Luciuk p. 21
148. Luciuk p. 20
149. Dumont *Le pays du Domaine* pp. 37–41
150. http://bowjamesbow.ca/2007/11/22/prisoners–in–th.shtml

Chapter 4

1. www.poemhunter.com/poem/the–shadow–35/
2. E. Druart *Jusqu'à la mort: Nid de Patriotes* p. 112
3. de Schaepdrijver p. 230
4. Druart p. 113
5. Druart p. 114
6. Druart p. 118
7. *La Tragedie de marchienne* See http://www.europeanfilmgateway.eu/fr/detail/LA%20TRAGEDIE%20DE%20MARCHIENNE/crb::b67e616e7f1c27b43c69a0b3af5f54af
8. www.1914–1918.be/enfant_vieslet.php
9. See *International Women's Suffrage News* 5 June 1925
10. Joseph Morris *German Air Raids on Britain 1914–1918* p. 57
11. Morris p. 57
12. House of Harkness *A World War I Adventure: The Life and Times of RNAS Bomber Pilot Donald E. Harkness* p. 75
13. Harkness p. 75 See also https://www.cityoflondon.gov.uk/things–to–do/london–metropolitan–archives/the–collections/Pages/airborne–menace.aspx
14. *The Children's Story of the War (Volume 6)* pp. 191–2; also Thomas Fegan *The Baby Killers* p. 94
15. http://www.hellfirecorner.co.uk/pottersbar/pottersbar.htm.
16. Information about the Carnegie Hero Award from www.carnegiehero.org.uk/criteria and correspondence with Carnegie July 2018

17. See for example *Bendigo Advertiser* 19 January 1917
18. Eric Bush *Bless Our Ship (BOS)* p. 51
19. Eric Bush *Gallipoli* p. 21
20. *BOS* p. 44
21. *Gallipoli* p. 21
22. *BOS* 12
23. *BOS* pp. 22–3
24. *BOS* pp. 28–9
25. www.firstworldwarstudies.org/portraits.php?s=midhsipan–kit–wykeham–musgrave
26. www.firstworldwarstudies.org/portraits.php?s=midhsipan–kit–wykeham–musgrave
27. http://militaryhistorynow.com/2014/01/03/unsinkable–meet–military–historys–luckiest–mariner/
28. *BOS* 36
29. *Gallipoli* p. 82
30. *Gallipoli* pp. 95 and 99
31. *Gallipoli* p. 100
32. *Gallipoli* p. 104
33. *BOS* p. 48
34. *Gallipoli* p. 110
35. *Gallipoli* p. 110
36. *BOS* p. 51
37. *Gallipoli* p. 243
38. *Gallipoli* p. 267
39. *Gallipoli* p. 276
40. *BOS* pp. 56–7
41. *BOS* p. 59
42. *BOS* p. 60
43. *Gallipoli* p. 320
44. *BOS* p. 89
45. Mabel Lethbridge *Fortune Grass* pp. 16, 20
46. *Fortune* p. 32
47. *Fortune* p. 35
48. *Fortune* p. 41
49. *Fortune* pp. 39, 41
50. *Fortune* p. 41
51. *Fortune* p. 50

52. *Fortune* p. 54
53. *Fortune* p. 56
54. *Fortune* p. 61
55. *I Was There* Vol 2 p. 1345
56. *There* p. 1345
57. *Fortune* p. 64
58. *There* p. 1347
59. *There* p. 1347
60. *There* p. 1348
61. *Fortune* p. 81
62. *Sheffield Evening Telegraph* 1 September 1939
63. *There* p. 1348
64. *There* p. 1348
65. *There* p. 1348
66. *Fortune* p. 103
67. *Fortune* p. 104
68. *Fortune* p. 111
69. https://en.wikipedia.org/wiki/1918_New_Year_Honours#Civil_Division_8
70. *Fortune* p.105
71. *Fortune* p. 115
72. *Fortune* p. 115
73. *Lloyd's Weekly News* 12 December 1915
74. Emilienne Moreau *Guerre Buissonière* p. 32
75. *Buissonière* p. 32
76. Alison Fell *Women as Veterans in Britain and France after the First World War* p. 71
77. *Buissonière* p. 34
78. *Buissonière* p. 35
79. *Buissonière* p. 35
80. *Buissonière* p. 38
81. See *Illustrated Police News* 25 November 1915 and *Buissonière* p. 38
82. *Buissonière* p. 41–2
83. *Buissonière* p. 44f
84. Fell p. 72
85. *Birmingham Mail* 29 July 1916
86. Fell p. 72

87. *Buissonière* p. 49
88. *Buissonière* pp. 47–8
89. *Buissonière* p. 50
90. *Buissonière* p. 50

Chapter 5

1. Winifred Letts 'The Call to Arms in Our Street' in V. Newman (ed.) *Tumult and Tears* pp. 3–4
2. Marina Yurlova *Cossack Girl* p. 7
3. Yurlova pp. 8, 13
4. Yurlova p. 11
5. Yurlova pp. 3, 14
6. Yurlova p. 16
7. Yurlova p. 17
8. Yurlova p. 19
9. Yurlova p. 21
10. Yurlova p. 25
11. Yurlova p. 26
12. Yurlova p. 29
13. Yurlova p. 31
14. Yurlova p. 31
15. Yurlova p. 33
16. Yurlova pp. 34–5
17. Yurlova p. 36
18. Yurlova pp. 35–7
19. Yurlova p. 45
20. Yurlova p. 48
21. Yurlova p. 49
22. Yurlova p. 51
23. Yurlova p. 53
24. Yurlova p. 54
25. Yurlova pp. 59–60
26. Yurlova p. 64
27. Yurlova p. 68
28. Yurlova p. 86
29. Yurlova p. 87
30. Yurlova p. 89
31. Yurlova p. 91

32. Yurlova p. 96
33. Yurlova p. 104
34. Yurlova p. 105
35. Yurlova p.110
36. Yurlova p. 111
37. Yurlova p. 112
38. Yurlova p. 113
39. Yurlova p. 113
40. Yurlova p. 117
41. Yurlova p. 117
42. Yurlova p. 123
43. Yurlova p. 133
44. Yurlova p. 198
45. All quotations from this article unless otherwise stated
46. *Children and Armed Conflict* ed. Daniel Cook and John Wall 'Girl Soldiers in WW1: Marina Yurlova and Sofja Nowosielska' pp. 7–21 p. 14
47. Désiré's story is available at https://www.curieuseshistoires.net/desire–bianco–plus–jeune–13–ans–poilu–mort–durant–grande–guerre Additional infomration from *Var Matin*
48. The 58e RIC Regimental diary is available http://gallica.bnf.fr/ark:/12148/bpt6k6399806f/f6.image
49. In line with its constitution, the Légion was disbanded in 2003 on the death of its last surviving member
50. Anthony Hill *Soldier Boy* p. 36
51. www.awm.gov.au
52. Hill p. 132
53. http://www.france24.com/fr/20140501–premiere–guerre–mondiale–jean–corentin–carre–enfant–soldat–morbihan–bretagne–poilus
54. http://www.france24.com/fr/20140501–premiere–guerre–mondiale–jean–corentin–carre–enfant–soldat–morbihan–bretagne–poilus
55. All quotations are from this carnet unless otherwise stated
56. Manon Pignot *L'Enfant–Soldat XIX–XXIe siècle* pp. 77–8
57. *The Times* 10 March 1916
58. 31 May 1916

59. http://aufildesmotsetdelhistoire.unblog.fr/2009/09/02/adjudant–pilote–jean–corentin–carre/
60. Ernest Wrentmore *America's Youngest Soldier* p. 3
61. Wrentmore p. 4
62. Wrentmore p. 16
63. Wrentmore p. 18
64. Wrentmore p. 20
65. Wrentmore p. 27
66. Wrentmore, pp. 27–8
67. Wrentmore p. 30
68. Wrentmore p. 31
69. Wrentmore p. 31–2
70. Wrentmore p. 33
71. Wrentmore p. 34
72. Wrentmore pp. 35–6
73. Wrentmore p. 38
74. Wrentmore p. 39
75. Wrentmore pp. 39–40
76. Wrentmore p. 40
77. Wrentmore p. 41
78. Wrentmore p. 44
79. Wrentmore p. 46
80. Wrentmore p. 62
81. Wrentmore p. 73
82. Wrentmore p. 83
83. Wrentmore p. 105
84. Wrentmore p. 106
85. Wrentmore p. 107
86. Wrentmore p. 113
87. Wrentmore p. 135
88. Wrentmore p. 138
89. Wrentmore p. 149
90. Wrentmore p. 149
91. Wrentmore p. 151
92. Wrentmore p. 152
93. Wrentmore p. 154
94. Wrentmore p. 155
95. Sofja Nowosielski *In the Hurricane of War* p. 13

ENDNOTES

96. Nowosielski p. 22
97. Nowosielski p. 18
98. R. Bideleux, I. Jeffries. *A History of Eastern Europe: Crisis and Change* Routledge. 1998. p. 186
99. Nowosielski p. 24
100. Nowosielski pp. 25–8
101. Nowosielski p. 29
102. Nowosielski pp. 35, 37, 40
103. Nowosielski p. 37
104. Nowosielski p. 40
105. Nowosielski p. 44
106. Nowosielski p. 48
107. Nowosielski p. 48
108. Nowosielski p. 48
109. Nowosielski p. 50
110. Nowosielski p. 50
111. Nowosielski p. 53
112. Nowosielski p. 49
113. Nowosielski p. 53
114. Nowosielski p. 54
115. Nowosielski p. 55
116. Mararet Higonnet *Lines of Fire* p. 176
117. Nowosielski p. 55
118. Nowosielski p. 56
119. Information about all RNR troops available at http://www.rnr.therooms.ca/soldier_files/R
120. George is named on the magnificent Caribou Memorial to the men of the RNR Beaumont–Hamel, France
121. Black and Boileau *Old Enough to Fight* p. 353 ff
122. Black p. 355
123. See http://www.rnr.therooms.ca/soldier_files/Ricketts_Thomas_rnr–0425.pdf
124. Frank Gogos *Newfoundland's Reluctant War Hero* p. 9
125. Gogos p. 10
126. Gogos p. 10
127. Victoria Cross citation
128. Gogos p. 12
129. See Gogos p. 15

130. Sydney Frost *A Blue Puttee At War* pp. 424–25
131. Gogos p. 19
132. *Dundee Evening Telegraph* 31 January 1919
133. Gogos p. 20

Conclusion

1. Gordon Brook–Shepherd *The Romance and Tragedy of Franz Ferdinand and Sophie* p. 264. The children were prohibited from attending the funeral due to their undefined position in the Habsburg hierarchy.

Bibliography

Place of publication London unless stated otherwise

Arthur, M., 2003. *Forgotten Voices of the First World War.* Ebury.

Asquith, C., 1958. *Diaries 1915–1918.* Hutchinson.

Bideleux, R. & Jeffries, I., 1998. *A History of Eastern Europe: Crisis and Change.* Routledge.

Black, D. & Boileau, J., 2013. *Old Enough to Fight: Canada's Boy Soldiers in the First World War.* Toronto: James Lorimer.

Bloch, H. & Hill, G., 2003. *The Silvertown Explosion: London 1917.* Stroud: Tempus.

Bordeaux, H., 1918. *Le Retour des Innocents.* Paris: Nancy.

Bork, K. ed., 2001. *Gefangen in Siberien Tagebuch eines ostpreußischen Mädchens 1914–1920.* Osnabruck: Fibre Verlag.

Breuillaud–Sottas, F., 2014. *Evian et le Drame de la Grande Guerre.* Milan: Silvana.

Brook–Shepherd, G., 1984. *Victims at Sarajevo: the Romance and Tragedy of Franz Ferdinand and Sophie.* Harvill.

Bush, E., 1958. *Bless Our Ship.* George Allen & Unwin.

Bush, E., 1975. *Gallipoli.* George Allen & Unwin.

Cadogan, M. & Craig, P., 1976. *You're a brick, Angela!: a new look at girls' fiction from 1839 to 1975.* Gollancz.

Carpi, O. & Nivet, P., 2005. *La Picardie Occupée.* Paris: Encrage.

Churchill, W., 1933. *The Great War.* Home Library.

Clamp, F., 2014. *Southend–on–Sea during the Great War.* Barnsley: Pen & Sword.

Cohen, A., 2002. Flowers of Evil. in: M. J, ed. *Children and War A Historical Anthology.* New York University Press, pp. 38–49.

Congar, Y., 1997. *Journal de Guerre 1914–1918.* Paris: Cerf.

Cook, D. & Wall, J., 2011. *Children and Armed Conflict.* Macmillan.

de Beauvoir, S., 1958. *Mémoires d'une Jeune Fille Rangée.* Paris: Folio.

De Schraepdrijver, S. & Proctor, T., 2017. *An English Governess in the Great War.* Oxford: OUP.

Dolto, F., 1991. *Correspondances* Paris: Hatier.

Donson, A., 2010. *Youth in the Fatherless Land.* Harvard University Press.

Droëge, A., 2012. *Diary of Annie's War.* Guildford: Grosvenor House.

Druart, E., 1923. *Jusqu'à la mort: Nid de Patriotes.* Brussels: Éditions de la Revue des auteurs et des livres.

Dumont, J.-U., 1938. *Le Pays du Domaine.* Michigan: «L'Éclaireur»

Easdown, M. & Genth, T., 2004. *A Glint in the Sky.* Barnsley: Pen & Sword.

Faron, O., 2001. *Les Enfants du Deuil.* Paris: la Découverte.

Fegan, T., 2002. *The "baby killers": German air raids on Britain in the First World War.* Barnsley: Leo Cooper.

Fell, A., 2018. *Women as Veterans in Britain and France after the First World War.* Cambridge: CUP.

Fisher, S., 2011. *Girls and Boys in No–Man's–Land.* Toronto: Toronto University Press.

Forsythe, M. & Dickson, G., 2014. *From the West Coast to the Western Front.* Canada: Harbour Publishing.

Frost, S., 2002. *A Blue Puttee at War.* St Johns Newfoundland: DRC.

Guyvarc'h, D., 1993. *Moi Marie–Rocher Ecolière en Guerre.* Rennes: Apogée.

Hall, E., 1977. *Canary Girls and Stockpots.* Luton Branch WEA.

Hampton, J., 2011. *How the Girl Guides Won the War.* Oxford: ISIS.

Harris, H., 1972. *Model Soldiers.* Littlehampton.

Higonnet, M. (ed), 1999. *Lines of Fire: Women Writers of World War One.* New York: Plume.

Hill, A., 2001. *Soldier Boy.* Penguin.

House of Harkness, 2014. *A World War 1 Adventure.* Perfect Bound.

Humphries, S. & van Emden, R., 2003. *All Quiet on the Home Front.* Headline.

Muller, S., 2008. 'Toys, Games and Juvenile Literature in Germany and Britain during the First World War. A Comparison'. In: Jones, H., ed. *Untold War New Perspectives in First World War Studies.* Leiden: Brill, pp. 233–257.

Kadriye, E. & Seixas, P., 2015. *New Directions in Assessing Historical Thinking.* Routledge.

Kennedy, R., 2014. *The Children's War 1914–1918.* Palgrave.

Kerr, R., 1936. *The Story of a Million Girls. Guiding and Girl Scouting Round the World.* Girl Guide Association.

BIBLIOGRAPHY

Knuth, E., 1931. *Als Fünfzehnjährige verschleppt, in Ostpreußen hinter Stacheldraht. Eine Sammlung ostpreussischer Kriegsgefangenen–Erlebnisse.* Konigsberg: Hartung.

Kordan, B., 2002. *Enemy Aliens, Prisoners of War: Internment in Canada During the Great War.* McGill Queens University Press.

Kuhr, P. (Wright, W. trans) 1982. *There We'll Meet Again.* Walter Wright.

Laflamme, J., 1989. *Spirit Lake: un Camp de Concentration en Abitibi durant la Grand Guerre.* Montreal: Maxime.

Lethbridge, M., 1934. *Fortune Grass.* Geoffrey Bles.

Luciuk, L., 2001. *In fear of the barbed wire fence: Canada's first national internment operations and the Ukrainian Canadians, 1914–1920.* Canada: Kashtan Press.

McNair, D., 2017. *Vernon Internment Camp 1914–1920.* Vernon: Vernon Museum.

Moreau, E., 1970. *La Guerre Buissonnière.* Paris: Solar.

Morris, J., 1993. *German Air Raids on Britain 1914–1918.* Naval and Military Press.

Newman V., 2016. *Tumult and Tears: The Story of the Great War through the Eyes and Lives of its Women Poets* Barnsley: Pen & Sword.

Newman, V. & Semeararo, D., 2017. *Régina Diana: Seductress, Singer, Spy.* Barnsley: Pen & Sword.

Nin, A., 1980. *Linotte, Early Diary of Anaïs Nin.* Harvest.

Northcott, C., 2015. *MI5 at War 1909–1918: How MI5 Foiled the Spies of the Kaiser in the First World War.* Tattered Flag.

Nowosielska, S., 1929. *In the Hurricane of War.* privately published.

Oman, E., 1983. *Salford Stepping Stones.* Swinton: Neill Richardson.

Parker, D., 2007. *Hertfordshire Children in War and Peace.* Hatfield: Hatfield.

Parrott, E., n.d. *The Children's Story of the War vol. 6.* Thomas Nelson.

Peeke, M., Walsh–Johnson, K. & Jones, S., 2015. *The Lusitania Story: the atrocity that shocked the world.* Barnsley: Pen & Sword.

Pignot, M., 2004. *La Guerre des Crayons: Quand les petits parisiens dessinaient la Grande Guerre.* Paris: Parigramme.

Pignot, M., 2012. *Allons Enfants de la Patrie.* Paris: Seuil.

Pignot, M., 2012. *L'Enfant–Soldat XIX–XXIe siècle.* Paris: Armand Colin.

Preston, D., 2002. *Lusitania: An Epic Tragedy.* New York: Walker.

Preston, D., 2011. *Wilful Murder: The Sinking of the Lusitania.* Corgi.

171

Proctor, T., 2011. *Scouting for Girls: A Century of Girl Guides and Girl Scouts.* Santa Barbara: Praeger.

Rolph, C. H., 1980. *London Particulars.* Oxford: OUP.

Scannell, D., 1974. *Mother Knew Best.* Pan.

Schaller–Mouillot, C., 1914. *En Guerre.*Paris: Berger–Levrault.

Schaller–Mouillot, C., 1915 *L'Histoire d'un Brave Petit Soldat:* Berger–Levrault.

Selleck, R., 1972. *English Primary Education and the Progressives 1914–1939.* RKP.

Smith, L., 1966. *A Tansley Boyhood.* Loughborough: Loughborough.

Thirsk, J., 2000. *A Beverley Child's Great War.* Highgate.

Triolo, R., 2012. *Our Schools and the War.* Melbourne: Australian Scholarly.

Whittaker, N., 2001. *Toys Were Us.* Orion.

Wrentmore, E., 2014. *America's Youngest Soldier.* CreateSpace Independent Publishing Platform.

Yurlova, M., 2010. *Cossack Girl.* (reprinted from 1934 edition) Somerville MA: Heliograph.

WEBSITES Accessed January–August 2018

acsepagny.pagesperso–orange.fr/Journalgarcontreizeans1914%201915.pdf

archives.cd08.fr/article.php?laref=398&titre=la–gazette–des–ardennes–disponible–en–ligne

aufildesmotsetdelhistoire.unblog.fr/2009/09/02/adjudant–pilote–jean–corentin–carre/

bowjamesbow.ca/2007/11/22/prisoners–in–th.shtml

broqueville.be/?p=4388

calgaryherald.com/news/internment–camps–a–dark–shadow–in–war–time–canada

dancingledge.wordpress.com/2017/05/28/25th–may–1917–the–air–raid–that–blasted–folkestone–into–a–new–age–of–violence/

en.wikipedia.org/wiki/1918_New_Year_Honours#Civil_Division_8

fsu.digital.flvc.org/islandora/object/fsu%3A110774#page/Page+4/mode/2up

lesliesguidinghistory.webs.com/guidesatwar.htm

members.scouts.org.uk/supportresources/3230/awards–for–gallantry–and–meritorious–conduct

militaryhistorynow.com/2014/01/03/unsinkable–meet–military–historys–luckiest–mariner/

BIBLIOGRAPHY

smartpei.typepad.com/robert_patersons_weblog/2015/04/world–war–1–sailing–the–atlantic–part–1–martha–allan–makes–the–crossing.html

smartpei.typepad.com/robert_patersons_weblog/2015/05/world–war–1–the–lusitania–part–3–the–sinking.html

smartpei.typepad.com/robert_patersons_weblog/2015/05/world–war–1–the–lusitania–part–5–the–aftermath.html

sussexhistoryforum.co.uk

www.14ansen1914.wordpress.com

www.1914–1918.be/enfant_vieslet.php

www.a–n.co.uk/blogs/i–draw/post/52491834/

www.ancestry.co.uk

www.ancestry.com

www.antiquetrader.com/2001web/

www.awm.gov.au

www.bbc.co.uk/guides/z2vj7ty

www.bbc.co.uk/schools/0/ww1/25183931

www.bl.uk/manuscripts/Viewer.aspx?ref=add_ms_39258_fs001r

www.bl.uk/world–war–one/articles/recruitment–conscripts–and–volunteers

www.childrenshomes.org.uk/TSArethusa/

www.curieuseshistoires.net/desire–bianco–plus–jeune–13–ans–poilu–mort–durant–grande–guerre

www.digital.library.illinois.edu/search?field=dls_subject&q=Posters+by+children

www.documentingdissent.org.uk/lancaster–girls–grammar

www.dover.uk.com/forums/dover–forum/1878–shipping–accident

www.encyclopedia–titanica.org/community/threads/thomas–quinn–senior–and–his–son.3897/ also www.liverpoolmuseums.org.uk and http://www.rmslusitania.info/people/deck/thomas–james–quinn

www.europeanfilmgateway.eu/fr/detail/LA%20TRAGEDIE%20DE%20MARCHIENNE/crb::b67e616e7f1c27b43c69a0b3af5f54af

www.firstworldwar.com/airwar/bombers_gotha_giant.htm

www.firstworldwarstudies.org/portraits.php?s=midhsipan–kit–wykeham–musgrave

www.france24.com/fr/20140501–premiere–guerre–mondiale–jean–corentin–carre–enfant–soldat–morbihan–bretagne–poilus

www.garemaritime.com/lest–forget–part–1

www.garemaritime.com/lusitania–part–3–the–survivor

www.hellfirecorner.co.uk/pottersbar/pottersbar.htm.
www.infoukes.com
www.internmentcanada.ca
www.jewsfww.london/the–first–world–war–through–the–eyes–of–
londons–jewish–children
www.jstor.org/stable/10.2979/jottturstuass.3.1.
www.liverpoolmuseums.org.uk/
www.newhamrecorder.co.uk/news/heritage/silvertown–explosion–
remembered–100–years–on–1–4852489
www.pressreader.com/canada/national–post–national–
edition/20111212/283781375717309
www.rmslusitania.info/people/deck/thomas–william–quinn/
www.rmslusitania.info/people/second–cabin/barbara–anderson
www.rmslusitania.info/people/second–cabin/helen–smith
www.rmslusitania.info/people/second–cabin/kathleen–kaye/
www.rmslusitania.info/people/victualling/george–wynne/
www.rmslusitania.info/primary–docs
www.rnr.therooms.ca/soldier_files/Ricketts_Thomas_rnr–0425.pdf
www.rtbf.be/ww1/topics/detail_school–in–wartime?id=8355929
www.scotlandswar.co.uk/guides_and_mi5.html
www.uccla.ca
www.unive.it/media/allegato/dep/Ricerche/5–Und_nun_waren_wir_
auch_Verbannte.pdf
www.voicesofwarandpeace.org/portfolio/girl–guides
www.voicesofwarandpeace.org/portfolio/girl–guides
www.warmuseum.ca/firstworldwar/history/life–at–home–during–the–
war/wartime–tragedies/the–halifax–explosion/
www.warrenpress.net

Newspapers
Birmingham Gazette
Birmingham Mail
Boston Journal,
Dundee Evening Telegraph
Huntington Press
Illustrated Police News
Lichfield Mercury
Lloyd's Weekly News

BIBLIOGRAPHY

News of the World
Pall Mall Gazette
Sheffield Evening Telegraph
Stratford Express
Sunday Express
The Times
The War Pictorial
Ukrainian Weekly
Woman's Dreadnought

Index